Dedicated to Truth, Beauty, and Wisdom

Tribal Epistemologies

Essays in the Philosophy of Anthropology

Edited by
HELMUT WAUTISCHER
Department of Philosophy
Sonoma State University
California

Ashgate

Aldershot · Brookfield USA · Singapore · Sydney

Published by
Ashgate Publishing Ltd
Gower House
Croft Road
Aldershot
Hants GU11 3HR
England

Ashgate Publishing Company
Old Post Road
Brookfield
Vermont 05036
USA

Reprinted 1999

British Library Cataloguing in Publication Data
Tribal epistemologies : essays in the philosophy of
        anthropology. - (Avebury series in philosophy)
        1. Knowledge, Theory of 2. Anthropology - Philosophy
        I. Wautischer, Helmut
        301'.01

Library of Congress Catalog Card Number: 97-78420

ISBN 1 84014 128 X

Printed in Great Britain by
Antony Rowe Ltd, Chippenham, Wiltshire

Contents

Figures and Tables

List of Contributors

Hoyt L. Edge is the McKean Professor of Philosophy at Rollins College, Winter Park, Florida. He has studied Australian Aboriginal and Balinese cultures for a number of years, focusing particularly on their views of personhood. His latest book, *A Constructive Postmodern Perspective on Self and Community*, examines the Western atomistic view of personhood and juxtaposes it to a more relational concept of person.

Roberte N. Hamayon is Directeur d'etudes (Professor) at the Ecole Practique des Hautres Etudes, Section des Sciences Religieuses, at the Sorbonne in Paris. She is a member (and from 1988-1994 was the head) of the Laboratory of Ethnology and Comparative Sociology at the French National Center for Scientific Research and University of Paris-X-Nanterre. She has conducted intensive fieldwork in Mongolia and Siberia, specializing in shamanism, the topic of her Doctor's thesis, published as *La chasse a l'ame* in 1990.

Åke Hultkrantz is Professor Emeritus from the University of Stockholm, Sweden, where he has served as Professor and Director of the Institute of Comparative Relilgion for almost thirty years. He is a prolific writer on shamanism, North American Indians, and Saami (Lapp) religion and folklore. He is currently preparing his extensive field notes on the Shoshoni Indians for publication.

Douglass Price-Williams is Professor Emeritus from the University of California at Los Angeles and has been involved in cross-cultural psychology and psychological anthropology for nearly four decades. He has written numerous books, articles and chapters on these subjects. He is past President of the Society for Psychological Anthropology and past co-editor of *Ethos*.

Michael Ripinsky-Naxon is University Professor at the Pedagogical University in Kielce, Poland, Director of the Central American Institute of Prehistoric and Traditional Cultures at Belize, and Adjunct faculty at the California Institute for Human Science. He is a Fellow of the American Anthropological Association, Royal Asiatic Society; Member Elect of Sigma Xi – The Scientific Research Society, and the New York Academy of Sciences. His special interests include shamanism, ethnopsychopharmacology, tribal cosmologies, and consciousness studies. His recent books are *The Nature of Shamanism* and *Sexuality, Shamanism, and Transformation*.

Roma Mere Roberts is a New Zealander of Pakeha (European) and Maori (Tainui) descent. She lectures in the School of Environmental and Marine Sciences where her teaching responsibilities include the provision of bicultural perspective and understanding, particularly in conservation and ecological restoration and management. Her research interests include indigenous knowledge systems and the applications of Maori traditional ecological knowledge in modern resource management.

Nina Rosenstand received her terminal degree in philosophy from the University of Copenhagen, Denmark, and lectures extensively on issues of ethics at San Diego State University and San Diego Mesa College. She is author of *The Moral of the Story: An Introduction to Questions of Ethics, The Concept of Myth*, and several papers on ethics and philosophy of myth.

Rudolph C. Rÿser is Chair of the Center for World Indigenous Studies (CWIS) and a member of the CWIS Fourth World Institute faculty teaching graduate studies in Fourth World Geopolitics and traditional knowledge at the Institute's Learning Retreat in Mexico. He earned his doctorate at the Union Institute Graduate School in International Relations. He is the author of four books on Indian Affairs in the United States and more than fifty essays and articles on international law, environmental politics, government, and studies in modes of thought.

E Richard Sorenson began his long-term Study of Child Behavior and Human Development in Cultural Isolates as a graduate student in anthropology at Stanford University, where he received his Ph.D. He extended the study to a wide variety of cultural isolates of the world with generous support and sponsorship by Stanford University, the National Institutes of Health, the National Endowment for the Humanities, the Smithonian Institution (where he founded the National Human Studies Film Center), Gyudmed Tibetan University and the Library of Tibetan Works and Archives. During the course of this study, Dr. Sorenson authored approximately sixty professional publications, the most recent dealing with a preconquest type of mentality he observed across a broad spectrum of archaic cultures.

Robert M. Torrance is Professor of Comparative Literature and member of the Nature and Culture Program at the University of California, Davis. He is translator of Sophocles' *Philoctetes* and *The Women of Trachis*; author of *The Comic Hero*; *Ideal and Spleen: The Crisis of Transcendent Vision in Romantic, Symbolist, and Modern Poetry*; and *The Spiritual Quest: Transcendence in Myth, Religion, and Science*; and editor of *Encompassing Nature: A Sourcebook*.

Helmut Wautischer, Philosophy Lecturer at Sonoma State University in California, also teaches at the University of Klagenfurt in Austria. His primary research interests are in Philosophical Anthropology and Consciousness Studies. He is an executive board member of the Society for the Anthropology of Consciousness, author of several papers, and past guest editor for a special issue on dreaming in *Anthropology of Consciousness*.

Peter R. Wills is a theoretical biologist in the Department of Physics at the University of Auckland, New Zealand. He is currently working at the Santa Fe Institute in New Mexico, USA. His research interests include the molecular biological aetiology of spongiform encephalapothies, the thermodynamic basis of biochemical processes, and the physical origins of evolutionary self-organization. He has conducted extensive analysis of military applications of nuclear, biological, and chemical technology. He has also served as chairperson of Greenpeace, New Zealand.

Foreword

Douglass Price-Williams

Although the focus of this anthology draws primarily on research from folk cultures, it would be a mistake to limit its impact merely within the realm of philosophical anthropology. While crucially dependent on the kind of scholarship that only an anthropologist could offer, this collection of essays is nevertheless most properly framed as a contribution to the sociology of knowledge.

Participant observation has always been an influential tool for anthropologists. Yet, even this tool has been insufficient for understanding world views of different cultures. Such understanding requires what is now known as 'experiential anthropology,' which, though probably best exemplified in fields such as shamanism, is clearly extendible to other areas as well. Such research also requires a solid knowledge of a society's language, as well as an in-depth contextual analysis of key terms and symbols. These are all-consuming tasks that take not only many years of immersion in a culture, but much patience and insight to accomplish, and thus such an enterprise, as found through the chapters of this book, is rarely attempted and even more rarely completed. The requisite cultural immersion is well depicted by Dr. Sorenson in his chapter as he makes the critical point that it took him years to be able to perceive the subtle reactions of the New Guinea people he studied before he was able to understand their meaning and import in their Weltanschaung.

There are other reasons for this difficulty of understanding other epistemologies. One that tells us a great deal about ourselves is that we have tended to use our own culture as a standard against which we measure and assess others. In the beginning of anthropology this gave rise to such prejudicial extravagances as the idea of primitive mentality. Although this particular notion is no longer extant, we still have difficulty relating concepts of other cultures to our own. One subtle aspect of this unfortunate bias is the unconscious reliance the scholar places on written material, with the concomitant lack of exposure to oral traditions. Of course, this is inevitable for the scholar who is defined in terms of the written, and who needs to translate the oral to the written (something that many must do if they wish to survive in the scholarly world). Yet, by this very act of transforming from oral to written, so many modes of communication, like prosody and all the non-verbal skills, are lost. Here, again, the anthropologist has something to offer, but it involves tedious and expensive dependence on audiotape and film to preserve the original meaning.

We should also give thought to the screening process of the information we come to enjoy in Western culture and the rigorous selection of those who come to offer such knowledge. A person needs to go through a substantial ordeal of education and the gaining of degrees merely to reach the starting point for disseminating knowledge. Once successful in this endeavor, there is a strict filter of referees to be encountered. Perhaps not a trivial observation is that many professional journals have rigorous formats that must be adhered to, which further daunts all but the most professional scholar. This selective narrowing of the dissemination of knowledge unfortunately often results in a condition of insiders versus outsiders. Those inside the establishment of 'knowledge' dictate not only how a subject is to be discussed and analyzed, but more importantly, they determine what is discussed; while those on the outside, as a result, tend to create what might be called a 'second-class' body of knowledge. This can have the consequence of a bifurcation in presentable knowledge.

Another narrowing element is the tendency to contrast Western culture with folk culture. While at first approximation this may seem a valid endeavor, closer inspection reveals that it is too extreme a contrast, since there are both differences among epistemologies of folk cultures and similarities with our own world views. Dr. Edge, for example, shows that Bali and Australian aboriginal ideas of the self are not only different from our individualistic Western sense of self, but different from each other as well. At the same time, it would be correct to state that the world views described in this book are holistic, relational, and conjoined to the observer. As such, it is correct, but simplistic, to contrast them with our own detached, scientific, and analytic world view. Here again, closer inspection indicates a change in our own view. Holistic attitudes have emerged in systems theory, in chaos theory, and in the Gaia principle. The observer status in Western science has already been modified with relativity theory and in quantum mechanics. Some of these trends may be extreme and subject to change. We see here, though, a trend to a world view that is not too different from some of the philosophies considered in this book.

Another aspect of the theory of knowledge that these essays expose is the close relationship to nature. A person's relationship to his or her environment is usually not considered in depth within the development of our own corpus of knowledge. Text books may briefly allude to the difference between, say, nomadic groups in their accumulation of knowledge and people who live in stable environments. Nevertheless, these same text books do not consider the depth of the possible relationship to nature that is evident, for example, in the chapter on Maori metaphysics by Drs. Roberts and Wills. It is true that many gifted naturalistic observers in our Western scientific tradition have displayed an intimate relationship with insects and animals, such as white ants, wolves, and chimpanzees. However, here we are dealing with an entire community's connection with the animate – and often the inanimate – world that transcends naturalistic observation into a different metaphysic.

Several authors in this book have interjected histories of our own philosophy against which to compare their folk accounts. This is useful if only to accentuate what is usually missing from our chronicles, which largely devote their attention to the history of ideas. While this is undeniably necessary, it is not sufficient, as such ideas are embedded in a network of technology, social systems, and cultural factors. To take a contemporary example of cultural factors from anthropology: what we used to know of shamans and indigenous healers derived mainly from the male exemplars of the species. When women anthropologists became interested in these subjects, we came to know far more of female shamans and healers, who presumably had been there all along.

Yet another example, this time from psychology, was mentioned by Ernest Hilgard in a book on hypnotism. Hilgard stated (1986, pp. 2-3) that the stirrings of interest during the 1960s in psychedelic drugs, Eastern religions, and the occult prompted a reaction in the academic community that rekindled scholarly interest and research in these subjects. Hilgard reminded us that this has happened before in our history: the popular interest in spiritualism in the late 1840s eventually prompted a new science to be born, what is now called parapsychology. It is interesting to speculate that what is now called channeling, which is becoming more common in the United States, may prompt even further unexpected scholarly pursuits. What has hitherto caught only the attention of anthropologists – and perhaps a few religious specialists – interested in spirit mediumship, may soon expand to scholars in more diverse disciplines.

This volume of essays, which has been a long time coming, should be read with stereoscopic vision – one lens focusing on the rich ethnographic material of the folk societies, the other focusing on the wider awareness of how we come to know what we know.

Reference

Hilgard, Ernest R. (1986), *Divided Consciousness: Multiple Controls in Human Thought and Action*, Wiley: New York.

Acknowledgements

I wish to thank Marilyn Schlitz and the Institute of Noetic Sciences for their generous research grant. The following publishers cooperated in copyright matters (as indicated in the Notes of each chapter, if applicable): the American Anthropological Association, Molnar & Keleman Publishers, and Verlag für Wissenschaft und Bildung.

Special thanks to Anita Rosenfield for her skillful editing of style and coherence, a delicate and masterfully accomplished balancing act between the stylistic demands of each contributor and the convergent whole of the anthology. Of course, my thanks to the authors of the papers in this collection and for their support during the production period. I am also grateful to my colleagues at the Sonoma State University philosophy department for providing a supportive working environment, and I appreciate all the help that was generously offered by individuals of the campus community to solve problems, big and small, during the gestation of this work.

Finally, due respect to A., since magic is a state of mind.

Part One
Introduction

1   Pathways to Knowledge

Helmut Wautischer

> Viele sind hartnäckig in bezug auf
> den einmal eingeschlagenen Weg,
> wenige in bezug auf das Ziel.[1]
> Friedrich Nietzsche

The Modern Quandary

Knowledge is a serious business. Taking a view that consciousness is but a tool through which power symbols are recognized and managed, many postmodern thinkers place knowledge within the domain of politics. Such a view relegates truth claims to a shifting political landscape and denies to them a stability of their own. Individuals then become mere pawns in a game of wealth and power. Like commodities, they are stripped of heritage and place in history, and accept their newly defined individuality along with a belief in the finite nature of conscious life and their isolation from other humans.

This hypothetical situation emerges from postmodernist abstractions conceptually pursued perhaps a page too far; it does not represent the bulk of postmodern thought. Politics is scarcely the curse of humankind. Its paramount function is to hold most of humanity together. The educative function of politics reveals important insights into the human condition and allows one, for example, to see postmodernity in the context of historical events, such as the resourceful relationship between reason and capitalism, the transition from living law to positive law (cf. Northrop 1960), and the shaping of thought through liberalism and nihilism. An important feature of postmodern thought is its acceptance of multiplicities of viewpoints. By entertaining disparate claims for truth that originate in diverse methodological and historical origins, postmodernitsts learn to employ creative strategies to solve conceptual disjunctions much like anthropologists must learn to cope with the collapse of their worldviews when 'going native.' Such experiences, however, can be fertile ground wherein new scientific methodologies might have a chance to blossom.

Consider the following assertion from a classical type of thought:

3

The basic conflict in modern thought is one between diverse metaphysical approaches on the one hand, and anti-metaphysical tendencies on the other. Classical ontological thought attempted to view the phenomena of nature and life *sub specie aeternitatis*, whereas modern ontological thought tends to view cosmic reality *sub specie temporis* (Bidney 1958, p. 469).

By presenting a closed dichotomy, Bidney's reasoned statement demonstrates the chasm between irreconcilable worldviews that cannot give room to form interstices. He then presents Ernst Cassirer's philosophy of culture as a remedy to go between the horns of the dilemma by tolerating prelogical and mythological mentality as relevant constituent parts for a cultural unity and harmony in dissonance.

Much of what is touched on in the following chapters falls outside any perspective consistent with our age of reason. They purposefully present aspects of consciousness that escape demonstrability by what currently passes as scientific rigor. These philosophies of culture demonstrate a type of understanding that stands outside the methodological scope of naturalistic observation. In this context, philosophical discourse continues to fulfill a vital role in educating humanity. In spite of massive administrative efforts to change the role of higher learning, philosophy proper still allows for systematic exploration of mental states. In fact, we need look no further than within ourselves to perceive ineffability in some of our deeper sensibilities of life. Examine for a moment that human quality we all possess, yet it is not clear what it is or how it works: intention. It seems to pop up from murky realms that don't sit well with common reason. Sometimes it even ignores the syntactical separation between subject and object on which all systems of expressed reason depend. Nevertheless, despite its elusive nature, the occurrence of intention is undeniable. 'Introspection' is another of this ilk. It, too, escapes our rigor to locate clearly defined elements. Both intentionality and introspection seem to take place in an analogical environment where any attempt to objectify these epistemic phenomena will result in the traditional separation of subject and object. Such aspects of mentality are thorns in the side of our era's concepts of rationality. They engage experience non-linearly. As so elegantly pointed out by Rudolph Rÿser in chapter 2, 'the personal self is to the collective self as the upstream waters are to the full rivers below' (p. 15).

Ubiquitous though such analogical aspects of mentality may be, they show that our twentieth century sense of science is incomplete: objectifying methodologies cannot account for qualitative experiences, while introspective methodologies collapse under the scrutiny of noetic intrusion. If there is any relevance to multicultural, feminist, and even postmodern philosophies then it can only lie in the recognition of respect for a multiplicity of viewpoints. It is exactly this respect that requires the acceptance of many disparate claims

4

for truth as sincere results gained from a panoply of methodological origins. The problem is, however, how can we possibly assess the validity of claims for truth when these claims originate in incommensurate methodologies? While it may not be difficult to give a political answer to this question, it is certainly an arduous task to find a philosophically sound explication.

For example, I have reviewed for many years the various approaches to the study of human consciousness as it relates to knowledge. The selection of methodologies for this particular field of research yields significant consequences with reference to many aspects of private life, *viz.*, personal identity and continuity, freewill, and dignity, to mention only a few. Reductionist methodologies tend to explain consciousness with reference to mental states that originate in measurable neurophysiological events and fulfill causally identifiable functions. This interpretation of consciousness differs radically, for example, from phenomenological theories, and is still in its early stages of development.

The potential applications of this type of research are unsurpassed by any other areas of study with reference to its influence on future civilizations. Selective funding for this new era of consciousness research clearly demonstrates the guiding hand of political and economic forces in recruiting dutiful generations of scientists to set the conditions for linking neuroscience to qualitative states of awareness. This should come as no surprise, since the pragmatic use of human intelligence is a constituent part of population management. No matter how offensive an idea may first sound, given the right promotional rhetoric this idea will soon appeal to an increasing audience: once human intelligence is reduced to deterministic principles, its reasonable governance must take place in the context of neuropharmacology, reward, and punishment. It could be argued that sentient beings are then placed into a causal frame of reference where a person's disobedience to act in a predictable manner at last can be classified as a form of pathology.

Rhetoric is indeed a vital component in the justification of methodologies to verify vested interests; it is also a motivating psychological and emotional factor for winning an argument. This is one of many examples adding to a number of similar situations in the funding of research and the knowledge claims that result from it. Does this mean that truth claims are relative? For many postmodern thinkers the answer is clearly 'yes.' Also, historical records about the misappropriations of political or religious claims for absolute truth make it understandable why postmodernity is so successful in promoting relativistic accounts of knowledge, along with strategies to undermine established power structures. Take this statement by Foucault:

> Once knowledge can be analyzed in terms of region, domain, implantation, displacement, transposition, one is able to capture the process by which knowledge functions as a form of power and disseminates the effects of power (Foucault 1980, p. 69).

5

His position joins politics, history, and power in a perpetual war, one wherein knowledge becomes but a tool aimed to 'win' a never ending battle. To produce this view, he ignores a host of other human impulses, such as conviviality and love, conjoint inspiration, empathy and compassion, and the thirst for peace and justice. These qualities of humankind are not phantasms, they fill libraries across the world. His politics of knowledge has lost sight of them. Robert Torrance in chapter 10 gives a vivid demonstration of the affinities between Western philosophical and poetic traditions with those of tribal cultures in the ecstatic search for transcendental vision and shared humanity.

Political pressure can sometimes be used to control knowledge, but there is an overall philosophical assumption that truth will prevail. It is misleading to assume that philosophical inquiry is primarily a political enterprise. By way of contrast, consider this second example that signals a direction toward a different path to knowledge: an older, ever recurring perspective, *philosophia perennis*, has its origin in the belief that certain philosophical topics remain relevant for all societies, during all periods of history. The practice of perennial philosophy dates back to ancient Egypt, continued by Platonism, the Corpus Hermeticum, Scholasticism, contemporary Western philosophy, and Eastern thought as well,[2] while the concept of perennial philosophy can first be found in the sixteenth century, when the Papal librarian Agostino Steuco wrote a work devoted to it.[3] Principal themes of this perennial philosophy include reflections on pursuing truth, universal wisdom, and mystical unity. According to the philosopher Marsilio Ficino, founder of the Platonic Academy of Florence, it links into the occult wisdom of Pythagoras, the Orphic mysteries, Hermes Trismegistus, and Zoroaster – head of the *magi* (Schmitt 1966, pp. 508-9).

Even though the concept of *philosophia perennis* is recognized in and adopted by different – sometimes even contradictory – traditions, there is no overall consensus as to what constitutes an acceptable demonstration of a perennial theme. Following the tradition of Steuco, Schmitt had the following to say:

> the conception of perennial philosophy is an outgrowth of the Neoplatonic interest in the *prisca theologia* and of the attempt to produce harmony from discord, unity from multiplicity (op. cit., p. 532).

There is certainly no value in labeling the entire history of philosophy as an example of perennial philosophy; however, the practice of philosophy is the common thread that unites the craft guild, such as the celebration of philosophical discourse, the development of one's faculties of awareness through reason and transcendence, and the teaching of values that secures one's authentic existence, to mention only a few. This philosophical leitmotif must not be confused with the political demands of an era.

The Development of Philosophical Anthropology

The fundamental question in the development of philosophical anthropology is 'What is *ánthropos*?' Inherent in this question is a methodological presupposition: the separation of humanity from the rest of what exists. A person's ability to reflect upon one's death, gradually to distance himself or herself from land, animals, divinity, the other, and eventually oneself, challenges both reductionist methodologies as well as transcendental practice. The former becomes challenged in the solitude of ideational space where the noetic dimension of transcendence combined with a religious experience of *unio mystica* leads one to the realm of conscious participation in the co-creating universe. The latter is meaningless if we assume no purpose to the existence of organic and inorganic matter, where one is bereft of any hope to escape darkness. Many scholars have tried to give precise definitions for philosophical anthropology, but there is no overall consensus about the range of the subject matter. Michael Landmann places it in the context of 'a determining force on the self-realization of one's existence' (1974, p. 23), and he sees its origin in anthropomorphism and ethnocentricity.

In ancient Greece, philosophical anthropology is not spoken of as a distinct school of thought. It exists, however, in the context of *paideía* (as a system of education) and *pōliteia* (defining a system of social polity). Stoic and Roman philosophers addressed it in the context of humanity. Not until Immanuel Kant introduced philosophical anthropology as a legitimate field of study did it gain a clear status of its own. Placing his faith in the transcendental ego of rational human beings who prescribe the laws of reason *to* nature, Kant treated it primarily as philosophy of life (*Lebensphilosophie*) without offering any relevant cultural analysis related to ethnography. Upholding the Kantian tradition of placing anthropology into the realm of the phenomenal world, a shift in emphasis took place during the nineteenth century toward history (e.g., Dilthey's phenomenological historicism), and in the early twentieth century toward existential and biological philosophy, social criticism, and philosophy of culture. For a while, philosophical anthropology had become primarily a German affair, using knowledge from the natural sciences and advancing mathematical reasoning while at the same time striving to overcome the limitations of natural science by implementing the dialectic methods of existentialism, phenomenology, and hermeneutics. Leading scholars such as Ernst Cassirer, Max Scheler, Nicolai Hartmann, Helmut Plessner, and Arnold Gehlen each developed a distinctly different approach to find an answer to the question about the nature of *ánthropos*.

This unique blend of combining empirical research from a detached observer perspective together with a person's direct experience and awareness of the human condition – *viz.*, desire for authenticity, uniqueness, transcendence, and for a meaningful existence – allows for merging a traditionally ideational space with solid data. Most writings in philosophical anthropology during the early twentieth century did not utilize much of the ample ethnographic literature about other cultures and their relation to knowledge. Often these references are given as examples for earlier stages of mental development or in the context of ethnocentrism. As more ethnographic information became available, philosophy itself underwent an identity crisis. Consequently, the new ethnographic data were primarily utilized not only by anthropologists themselves, but also by psychologists, folklorists, sociologists, botanists, and so on; rarely, though, do we find a philosopher ready for unbiased assessment of ethnographies. The value of ethnographic data in contemporary philosophy is predominantly seen as providing evidence to attack the philosophical tradition in general, and Western thought in particular. It is generally overlooked that many themes relating to *philosophia perennis* can be found in tribal cosmologies as well, and awareness of the methodological bounty described in ethnography is generally met with opposition. One such example of rich ethnographic detail that lends itself to philosophical exploration is presented by Michael Ripinsky-Naxon in chapter 6 with reference to Maya cosmology and shamanistic acquisition of knowledge.

It is the responsibility of philosophers to consider ethnography seriously as a relevant narrative for breaking new ground in the advancement of philosophical theory. Altered states of consciousness, shamanic trance, insights gained through rigorous meditation, and so on, are generally excluded from philosophical discourse and disqualified as examples of religious experience, metaphysics, or mythology. Philosophers tend to contrast these examples of prelogical mentality with a presumably later state of cultural evolution, such as scientific mentality and rationality. For them, knowledge belongs to the realm of language and symbols, it requires objectivity, and it must be incorporated into a larger body of thought. Goethe gives a beautiful description of this situation:

> Truth, in its identity with the Divine can never be grasped directly; we perceive it only as reflection, in an example, a symbol, in single and related manifestations; we recognize it as incomprehensible life and yet we cannot disown the desire to comprehend it at last (1896, p. 74).[4]

The overwhelming evidence of ethnographic research suggests that humans may have the capacity to intuit the divine while at the same time giving descriptions through symbols and language that allow for developing methodologies to access this knowledge upon will. Åke Hultkrantz describes, in chapter 7, that a shaman's cognition of the mundane and supernatural world depends on his or her ecstatic contact with spirits: 'seen at its deepest, the communication with this other world is the source of health, harmony, and power ...' (p. 170). Since religious experience is rooted in symbols, the philosophical analysis of the epistemic potency of symbols remains a meaningful discipline. The schism between transcendentality and appearances is recognized in all cultures. Take, for example, concepts such as 'spirit realm' and 'a priori.' The phenomenal manifestations of these concepts and their noumenal descriptions are generally considered two separate ontological spheres – often viewed as being mutually exclusive. However, in ethnographic literature we find reports about liminal awareness in tribal people prior to their exposure to conquistadorial societies. A beautifully narrated example is E Richard Sorenson's contribution in chapter 5, when he brings to life how such liminal awareness obviates a separation of the mental and the divine.

In anthropological literature as well as in postmodern writings we can often find confusion over the differences between a 'way of knowing' (methodology) as opposed to a 'theory about knowledge' (epistemology). Both are valid and co-dependent criteria in the pursuit of knowledge. But both require distinctly different measures for their assessment of accuracy: 'ways of knowing' will allow for intuition, emotion, transcendence, body, and so on, while theorizing about such ways of knowing requires systematic analysis. Notwithstanding the various measures for the assessment of knowledge, their uniting element is found in the co-creating powers of a presumed consciousness that is not reducible to matter, but instead acts as the form giving principle for matter. Mere Roberts and Peter Wills have presented a lucid description of Maori epistemology in chapter 4, incorporating the presupposition that all things are related and of both divine and material substance. Philosophers might associate with this position a seventeenth century Spinozistic concept of 'God or Nature,' but the richness of Maori thought leaves no doubt that its epistemic value is rooted in a long-standing tradition that has maintained relevance for countless generations, past, present, and future.

Many Voices

After years of social-linguistic analysis, an ancient knowledge was rediscovered, namely, that language is utilized in different dimensions of communication. By linking language to breath, and breathing to sound, the vibrational intonation of sound patterns is practiced in all cultures as part of the ritual towards transcendence. While linguistic analysis ignores the knowledge related to vibrational sound, it does emphasize the social implications of structuring semantics. At the onset of this analysis we find feminist theories and their radical call for emotionality and body as a means for enhancement of communication; but soon it becomes clear that – without firm traits of character that reflect one's desire for wisdom – both body and emotion will be applied equally manipulatively, as we can see in sophistic rhetoric.

As more people have become the protagonists of their own lives and have

9

learned how to stage sadness, anger, or happiness, they have also learned how to direct their affect and use poses, mime, and emotions to get their way. In ethnographic literature we find this role often attributed, for example, to the Coyote, the Trickster, the Raven, and we find historical records about the function of masks, troupes, or jesters. Traditionally, these roles signal a state of reflection upon the meaning of life, in general, and society, in particular. Their function is recognized as mediator between the worlds – they are skillful reminders of one's mortality and are communicators of fearless death. For example, Roberte Hamayon discusses in chapter 8 how the shaman's role can be exhaustively described with reference to symbolic representations alone. She argues that ritual performances are collective affairs (p. 184), and that the psychological underpinnings of those who play such roles must not be confused with the roles themselves. Already Kant (1917) had suggested that civilization is directly linked to role play, when he claims that humans overall become better actors as civilization increases:

> The more civilized humans are, the more they become actors; they stage affection, respect for others, modesty, and selfless caring without deceiving anyone, since this deception is willingly accepted by everyone; besides, it is also laudable that this happens in the world (op. cit., p. 151, VII.i.1.14).[5]

Kant assumed that over time this staged kindness will eventually manifest itself as a learned and idealized character trait for humanity in general. We can find a deviation to Kant's thesis in modern service-oriented societies where the function of role play is exclusively linked to financial gain. Here, one's prosperity will often depend on an ability to stage loving or caring communication patterns. No longer is role play a means for moral guidance, let alone for transcendental awareness or visionary qualities. The guiding function of role play is still maintained in folklore, fairy tales, and mythology. However, the epistemological function of narratives is rarely appreciated in Western cultures as relevant device for human interaction. Nina Rosenstand draws a parallel in chapter 9 between tribal myths and Western theories of social ethics, and demonstrates how the concept of personhood in American Indian mythology allows for a holistic expansion in comprehending our role in the universe.

Any manipulative application of verbal and nonverbal linguistic devices affects both social realities as well as human interaction with nature and the physical world. The social adaptation of nature is supported by the methodologies derived from epistemological truths. Today we celebrate technology as providing us with the key to manipulate a meaningless universe. Surrender into this meaningless universe is made possible by accepting the paratelic goal of infinite games where rules keep changing during the play (cf. Carse 1986, p. 11). There is no exit from a strategic solipsistic universe;

the *bellum omnium contra omnes* has taken on dimensions to accommodate one's social and economic survival inconceivable even for Hobbes. In this context, the acquisition of knowledge is no longer a path toward eternity, instead it has become an existentialist theatre act, *viz.*, playing the roles of one's life for the mere joy of playing – and without vision to escape the finitude of *thánatos*.

> Where the finite player plays for immortality, the infinite player plays as a mortal. In infinite play one chooses to be mortal inasmuch as one always plays dramatically, that is, toward the open, toward the horizon, toward surprise, where nothing can be scripted. It is a kind of play that requires complete vulnerability. To the degree that one is protected against the future, one has established a boundary and no longer plays with but against others (Carse op. cit., p. 31).

 This notion of competitive play is a typical feature of ideologies that fail to recognize relational forms of coexistence. Only if an individual has accepted his or her solitude in the universe will a desire to overpower others temporarily compensate that individual for one's ultimate defeat of anticipating the cessation of consciousness. Hoyt Edge examines in chapter 3 so-called collectivist/relational views of personhood in the Australian Aboriginal and Balinese cultures emphasizing the concepts of relational selves that differ so radically from our Western perspective – although rooted in firm appreciation of individuality and autonomy, collectivist/relational views of personhood equally recognize a robust notion of community.

Ethnography in World Philosophy

Cultural anthropologists and ethnographers have written extensively about the challenges a person faces when going native. Just like the monolingual person may likely have difficulty understanding the linguistic abilities of persons who have acquired bilingual fluency, similarly it is also difficult for many scholars to accept the incompatibility of disparate methodologies.

It is the pragmatic use of knowledge that makes ethnography a highly political enterprise. Many tribal informants (or consultants, to use the politically correct term) have grown weary of seeing their sacred beliefs dissected, distorted, and dishonored, and as a consequence some have taken to selling deviant versions of their sacred knowledge, finding that the possibilities of the market place are many. In our modern times of 'global village' we have come to understand that allegiance for shared values is across cultures, across gender, across nations, and across corporate identities; it is a feature of authentic persons who assemble to manifest their shared visions.

In most cultures, knowledge is seen as belonging to a group of people rather than being the result of individual effort. Thus, claims for private ownership of knowledge leave out a culture's achievements over the course of history. Such genealogy of knowledge is most foreign to information age societies, where legal concerns about copyrights and private ownership constitute a revenue source of equal magnitude compared with the revenues obtained from the marketing of knowledge. Also, philosophical reflection owes a debt to the historical process in the formation of theories about the function and role of humans in the overall enigma of existence.

In all cultures, including the Western traditions, the importance of merging transcendental insights with subtle perceptions of reality is recognized as an undisputed fact. This knowledge stands in direct opposition to the use of reductionist methodologies for empirical testing of scientific hypotheses. I seriously doubt whether there is even one practicing philosopher who is not aware of the political consequences humankind will face once an unrestricted application of reductionist methodologies has provided the mechanisms for manipulating organic matter even to the extent of ideational surveillance. The mere fact that such applications may be possible does not guarantee the correctness of corresponding hypotheses purporting to explain the occurrence of consciousness A strict application of the Duhem-Quine thesis (cf. Duhem 1954, Quine 1953) should alert the scientifically minded philosopher that the nature of the currently dominant methodological approach in consciousness studies may need revision.[6] There are just too many so-called 'anomalous' phenomena surfacing through the channels of modern information highways. Suppressing the research about these phenomena by means of ridicule, patronizing methodologies, and denial for funding does, indeed, create an environment of censorship that is inhospitable to science proper.

The path to knowledge eventually leads one to explore the question of consciousness. There is no guarantee that by merely looking at this path one will come to understand consciousness. Perhaps it will help to walk this path and to experience one's own observations of it. Intercultural philosophy cannot take place within the confines of one dominant methodology. To consider subjective experience as an acceptable form of primary data in the acquisition of knowledge is certainly radically empirical in the sense of William James, and is also compatible with Bergson's vision that the union of science and metaphysics will lead the positive sciences to a level far higher than one can imagine.

The following chapters will explore areas of knowledge that are representative of different cultures and derived from different methodologies. They will touch on diverse approaches to cognition that have independently evolved outside Western culture, beyond the influence of its noetic sensibilities. Much like inquiries into intention and introspection, these explorations also dip into nonlinear areas of experience and reveal human attributes not easily dealt with by current science, e.g., sense of person, sense of others, continuity of being, freewill, dignity, the feeling of existence, etc. They illustrate unplumbed depths of human consciousness, reveal experiential understandings beyond linguistic thought, and stand aside from the view that behavior and intelligence can be understood by deterministic principles.

Notes

1. Nietzsche (1930, p. 314, I.494). 'Many people are determined to maintain the path once taken, few people have this regard for the destination' (trans. H. W.).
2. For a list of representative works see Schmitt (1966, pp. 505-6).
3. A ready available reprint is Steuco (1972).
4. 'Das Wahre, mit dem Göttlichen identisch, läßt sich niemals von uns direct erkennen; wir schauen es nur im Abglanz, im Beispiel, Symbol, in einzelnen und verwandten Erscheinungen; wir werden es gewahr als unbegreifliches Leben und können dem Wunsch nicht entsagen, es dennoch zu begreifen' (trans. H. W.).
5. 'Die Menschen sind insgesamt, je civilisirter, desto mehr Schauspieler; sie nehmen den Schein der Zuneigung, der Achtung vor Anderen, der Sittsamkeit, der Uneigennützigkeit an, ohne irgend jemand dadurch zu betrügen, weil ein jeder Andere, daß es hiemit eben nicht herzlich gemeint sei, dabei einverständigt ist, und es ist auch sehr gut, daß es so in der Welt zugeht' (trans. H. W.).
6. The scientific enterprise is based on a holistic web of beliefs to confirm or falsify hypotheses at different stages of scientific development. Every theory can be refuted in principle by the weight of newly gained evidence; consequently, one can argue that homogenous methodologies tend to create a false consensus about acceptable descriptions of reality. For a detailed analysis of the Duhem-Quine thesis see Harding (1976).

References

Bidney, David (1958), 'On the Philosophical Anthropology of Ernst Cassirer and its Relation to the History of Anthropological Thought,' in Paul A. Schilpp (ed.), *The Philosophy of Ernst Cassirer*, pp. 465-544, Tudor Publishing: New York.

Carse, James P. (1986), *Finite and Infinite Games*, Ballantine: New York.

Duhem, Pierre (1954), *The Aim and Structure of Physical Theory*, trans. Philip P. Wiener, Princeton University Press: Princeton.

Foucault, Michel (1980), *Power/Knowledge: Selected Interviews and Other Writings 1972 -1977*, Colin Gordon (ed.), Pantheon: New York.

Goethe, Johann W. (1896), 'Versuch einer Witterungslehre (1825); in Sophie von Sachsen (ed.), *Goethes Naturwissenschaftliche Schriften*, II. Abtheilung, 12. Band, pp. 74-96, Hermann Böhlaus Nachfolger: Weimar.

Harding, Sandra G., ed. (1976), *Can Theories be Refuted?*, D. Reidel Publishing Company: Dordrecht.

Kant, Immanuel (1917), 'Anthropologie in pragmatischer Hinsicht,' in Königlich Preußische Akademie der Wissenschaften (ed.), *Kant's Gesammelte Schriften*, Band VII, pp. 117-333, Georg Reimer Verlag: Berlin.

Landmann, Michael (1974), *Philosophical Anthropology*, trans. David J. Parent, Westminster Press: Philadephia.

Nietzsche, Friedrich (1930), *Menschliches, Allzumenschliches: Ein Buch für freie Geister*, Alfred Kröner Verlag: Stuttgart.

Northrop, F.S.C. (1960), Philosophical Anthropology and Practical Politics, Macmillan: New York.

Quine, Willard v. O. (1953), 'Two Dogmas of Empiricism,' in Willard v. O. Quine, *From a Logical Point of View*, pp. 20-46, Harvard University Press: Cambridge.

Schmitt, Charles B. (1966), 'Perennial Philosophy: From Agostino Steuco to Leibniz,' *Journal of the History of Ideas*, Vol. 27, No. 4, Oct. - Dec., pp. 505-32.

Steuco, Agostino (1972), *De Perenni Philosophia*, Johnson Reprint Corporation: New York.

Part Two
Methodological Conundrums

2   Observations On 'Self' and 'Knowing'

Rudolph C. Rÿser

Cowlitz is a consciousness of people, place, and cosmos that embraces the notion of eternal changeability. Cowlitz is a mixture of many parts that evolved from generations of contact with neighbors and visitors from distant places. It is a single consciousness born of countless generations of interaction among individuals, their extended families (which includes other animals, plants, water sources, stones, mountains, the Moon, the Sun, the stars, and prairies), and revered ancestors.

Shaped like the head of a deer (*mowich*), Cowlitz territory begins at the mouth of the Cowlitz River in the south, where the Splutlamilx live, then goes north, following the river's path, and then heads east, up the river to the mountains where the Taidnapum live; the left check of *mowich* is Mount St. Helen's and on the right cheek are the Black Hills. The southern base of Tahoma, or what is now called Mt. Rainier, forms the crown of *mowich*, and Cowlitz Prairie forms the flat space on the snout. All of this is Cowlitz territory. The Cowlitz people – the Taidnapum of the northern upper head of *mowich* and the Splutlamilx of its southern mouth – are a smoke-house people bounded by the river. We Cowlitz remain in the place that was first peopled by our ancestors.

The great river flowing from the mountains defines, nourishes, and sustains the people; it informs them and holds the promise of bounty or the threat of disaster for their future. Living is made up of good and not-so-good choices taken by the people. While virtually all things change and recycle, certainty in the people's mind comes from experiencing daily differences and repeated reminders of what has already occurred.

Individual personality is only distinguishable from the collective self by virtue of its physical separateness – and that is only illusion itself. <u>The personal self is to the collective self as the upstream waters are to the full rivers below.</u>

No part of the river is truly indistinguishable from any other part. One cup of river water is the same as the water passing by. The distinguishing quality of the cup of river water is the 'cup.' The water takes the form of the cup, an elastic attribute that permits adjustment to change. The Cowlitz who lives rightly knows that the superficial differences among the people give meaning only to relational concepts. No significant meaning can be attached to a fractional quantity of water except that it is a part of the whole. It is the totality of water that has meaning.

I use the river's water as a metaphor for the collective self and the fractional quantity of water as a representation for the 'personal self.' It is the relationship, the interdependence, and the simultaneous capacity for independence of the self that must be emphasized. These seemingly contradictory capacities are the source of knowing. Without this simultaneity, life could not exist. It is, therefore, essential that one recognize the relationship between 'self' and 'knowing.' This observation has greatest significance for comprehending 'knowing' as a consequence of relationships discerned by the self.

Fluid Simultaneity and the Sense of Singleness

When one is standing in the middle of a prairie, a person may experience a sense of being alone, vulnerable, and disconnected. Yet, when one is surrounded by trees and other people,[1] like *mowich*, the bear, and flying things, there is a sense of being a part of or joined with all other things. This can be quite the opposite experience if one is born in a place that is open, like the rolling lands of western Yupic territory (Alaska) – there one can be alone and vulnerable in the forest. The point remains the same. Yet it is equally possible to be in the open prairie and 'lose oneself' in the immensity of things. What accounts for both the singular sense and the sense of unified submersion? It can be an illusion or some other trick of the mind, or it can be the spirit seeing the instance of singleness when there is a separation. Humans are not the only people who sense this singleness and contrast it with the unified submersion. *Mowich*[2] always travel collectively, even when they can't see each other. They can look like trees and bushes. They can even pretend to be a stone. In these ways *mowich* is at once itself and also all other things. Still, owing to a trick, *mowich* can be single, a distinct self – vulnerable, at risk. At such times, when making a trick *mowich* can give itself to a good hunter whose hunger is surpassed only by a wish to ask *mowich* for its life.

Mowich chooses a time when it will give up its life – exposing its single self. However, when it remains a part of the whole, *mowich* is not exposed. No harm can come to it. Like other people, *mowich* exists simultaneously within the 'collective self' even as it exposes the single self. When choosing to express the personal self, *mowich* is exposed and can offer itself.

18

The natural condition of things is for people to experience simultaneity; and it is a trick or exercise of will to choose singleness. As a part of the collective self, one is not aware of singleness or its possibility. There is only an awareness of the tensions and inclinations that give rise to change. This awareness is shared among all people. It is a common knowing – a common consciousness. *Mowich* experiences a calm serenity and demonstrates this when its tail is not nervous – its ears do not turn every which way, and it feeds quietly on grass or blackberry leaves.

These same ways can be observed in the salmon as well. Throughout its life, salmon exhibits a thorough serenity as it travels from its birth place, down the river, finally to the ocean. For most of its life, salmon lives in the ocean – a part of the fluid great self – satisfied. Not until it returns to its mother river to gather in cool dimples in the river bottom, and then to rush upstream to its birthplace, does salmon finally expose its singleness. Each individual salmon must challenge the swift stream by jumping and swimming against the down flowing water. Only those with the courage, strength, and power of *tamonowith* will meet the great challenge. Reaching the place of their birth, each salmon then spawns new life – giving up its body and rejoining its spirit with the great consciousness.

Singleness of consciousness is always temporary and fleeting while the collective consciousness is the permanent and perpetual condition of things. All the beings, all the people experience these things just the same.

Braided Rivers to Knowing

Time, space, and place animate the great consciousness filling the universe. At different periods in the brief history of human beings at least five different, but related, modes of thought have led to knowing, achieving the ultimate expression of consciousness: apprehending the living universe. To comprehend the great consciousness one might reflect on these modes of thinking that characterize different kinds of human attempts at knowing. While contemporary thinkers consider most of these different modes of thought as expressions of 'more primitive ways of thinking,' I suggest that they are all coincident with each other. They are merely streams originating at different places – all leading to a common river fed by the same rain. They are different strands eventually braided into a single cord. Certain strands in the braid are more significant at some times and less significant at other times.

Consider, if you will, the different streams of thought that flow, not necessarily comfortably, into a single river of thought that offers ways of knowing. These are Cyclicism (typically a synthesis of Persian, Greek, Nubian, and other influences rooted in the eastern Mediterranean and Africa), Cuarto Spiralism (rooted in the Americas), Fatalism (rooted in Asia), Providentialism (transformed from the eastern Mediterranean and Africa into Europe), and

Progressivism (formed in Europe as a synthesis of influences resulting from the modern interaction among Europe, the Americas, and the Pacific Islands). A brief discussion of each stream reflects the diversity of human cultures over time, and their similarities too, thus presenting a range of ways of knowing.

Cyclicism

The Greek/Persian/Nubian reality of three thousand years ago comprehended a past and a present formed in a great circle. At any time before the present there is a point of the circle that is the past – usually the remembered past. As time proceeds around the circle, one encounters the past and repeats the transactions and events as the present. This mode of thought provided a closed, reassuring, and satisfying existence. One could predict the future merely by remembering the past. This cyclical reality proved quite adequate for the social, economic, and political life that grew and flourished across the Mediterranean and throughout Africa.

Aristotle reflected the *cyclical reality* in his thinking when he engaged in observations that served as the basis for his scientific, ethical, and political commentaries. It was with the certainty of a well-practiced marksman that Aristotle asserted in his *Politics* that some people are 'born slaves' while others are born to rule and direct slaves. Those who were born slaves, Aristotle reasoned, will always be slaves and will produce new slaves because they had always been slaves before. While Aristotle's claim was propounded as an absolute certainty, and his assertion remained a key element in Christian liturgy throughout the ages, his claim is clearly wrong – even though many people still believe what is a patently absurd idea. Still, Aristotle's idea of 'born slave' survives as an example of cyclical reality despite its absurdity.

Limiting as cyclical thinking is, it remains a potent part of the human intellectual tool – set for comprehending and engaging consciousness. Though not a dominant influence in contemporary thought, cyclicism remains a fundamental stream feeding the contemporary river of thought.

So powerful was cyclical thinking and so weak were those competing ways of thinking three thousand years ago, it continued to dominate and shape the thinking of all peoples within the reach of eastern Mediterranean influence through to the eighteenth century of the common era.

In the fifth century of the common era the Roman Catholic Church began to build its fortunes upon the intellectual foundations of the Greeks and their successors, the Romans. Though the Persians and Nubians had a profound influence on the development of Greek intellectualism, the Church's historical bias in favor of 'classical Greek superiority' ensured a dominant role for Greek ideas in Christian Church liturgy. As the emerging successor to the collapsed Roman Empire and the primary political body with administrative capabilities throughout Europe, the eastern Mediterranean, and northern Africa the

Roman Catholic Church proceeded to define a conceptual era that still echoes in Providentialism.

Cuarto Spiralism

Students of Maya literature commonly view the calendar of these ancient people – the 5,125-year 'Great Cycle' – as evidence of a mode of thought fundamental to the original Central-American and South American cultures. Associating the Maya mode of thought with cycles, where time and space repeat in infinite circles – as the Maya and Aztec calendars appear to suggest – is so common among scholars that few have stopped to consider how they may actually be projecting their own cultural templates onto the evidence of Maya and other western hemispheric ways of thinking. Though satisfied with a match for their templates, by imposing cyclicism into the context of the western hemisphere Maya scholars conceal the reality of a mode of thought unique in the world.

In an attempt to reveal the underlying character of this distinct mode of thinking, I shift the symbolism slightly from a circle to a spiral. With this change, I believe it is easier to apprehend a mode of thought I have labeled 'Cuarto Spiralism,' or more simply, 'Spiralism.' More than any iconographic image, the *Hunab Ku*, translated as 'One Giver of Movement and Measure' (Argüelles 1987, p. 52), affirms Cuarto Spiralism. This mode of thought takes its name from the infinite repetition of four spiraling arcs, four 'cycles' in the Maya conception of time.

Figure 2.1 Hunab Ku.

The *Hunab Ku* symbolizes the ideas: 'Movement corresponds to energy, the principle of life and all-pervading consciousness immanent in all phenomena' (*ibid.*). Though similar to the Yin and Yang of the Tao, *Hunab Ku* is much more. As the symbol of Spiralism, the *Hunab Ku* illustrates the interconnectiveness of all life, the four cardinal directions, the four arcs of time, and perpetual movement in all directions through space. The past, the present, and the future are all represented in the spiralist mode of thought. A spiral in space moves outward, inward, forward, and backward, occupying space and not occupying space all at the same time. Life and death are, therefore, two aspects of the same thing. Wholeness and particularity are manifestations of one and the same quality of existence. These are the central attributes of Cuarto Spiralism.

21

Cuarto Spiralism predominates as the underlying mode of thought among the many cultures in the western hemisphere: it is recorded in their literature, stories, songs, dances, and symbols. Peoples as remote from one another as those living in the Arctic North to those living in Patagonia and the Micmac, Cowlitz, Hopi, and Kiowa, as well as the Mapuché, Yanomami, Aymara, Sumo, Pipil, and Zapotec all share a common, underlying mode of thought that infuses a wide diversity of cultures.

Cuarto Spiralism permits apprehension of the universe as a whole while giving respect to particularities. Mutuality of respect is the essential glue that both connects and separately identifies all parts of the whole, living universe. It is necessarily the case that all aspects of the universe are alive and possessing of the capacity to choose. It is this capacity of the living universe to choose that leaves the future unpredictable and open to surprise. Describing this concept from the Lakota perspective, Vine Deloria, Jr. writes:

> The willingness of entities to allow others to fulfill themselves, and the refusal of any entity to intrude thoughtlessly on another, must be the operative principle of this universe (1996, p. 41).

The discipline demanded of each entity to fulfill the obligations of mutual respect establishes yet another level of unpredictability for the future. Failure to achieve perfect discipline would most surely introduce variability and thus alter the quality of choice and the mutuality of respect. It is just this condition of the living universe that drives each entity to learn, to acquire knowledge, or as Pamela Colorado says, 'to find [a] knowledge system in the west that would be capable of "carrying the weight of God"' (1996, p. 6).

Cuarto Spiralism shapes systems of tribal thought throughout the western hemisphere as a structure that permits aspects of experience that come before to combine with aspects of the present to provide the basis for interpreting the future. Modern Maya Day Keepers demonstrated their reliance on this structure, on the mode of thought, when they stepped from a cave (1 January 1994) in the highlands of Chiapas to announce the coming of the end of the fourth cycle and the impending arrival of the 'Sixth Sun.'[3] By their interpretation of the sacred texts, the Day Keepers set in motion a series of events that began to transform the Mexican and Guatemalan states and the peoples of the entire western hemisphere and beyond. Such a simple act and the events that followed demonstrate the powerful influence of the spiralist mode of thought.[4]

Fatalism

The overwhelming power of nature and its determinate control over all matters of existence is the central view of fatalism, a mode of thought predominant among peoples throughout Asia – particularly those who embrace the influence of Confucianism, Taoism, and Buddhism. Human beings can aspire to and achieve the attribute of 'superior man' and perform acts of piety that conform to the 'will of heaven.' Acting 'rightly' is the goal of fatalism, but it is recognition of the 'order of things' that ensures achievement of the 'superior man.' Confucius (551-479 B.C.E.) is commonly considered the primary and most influential exponent of the philosophies that form the underlying structure of fatalism. *Li*, the term used by Confucius when discussing human conduct in relation to nature, suggests the requirement that humans observe true piety and thus make it possible to interpret the 'will of heaven' as acts on earth. By virtue of the preeminent order in heaven, a fatalist is obliged to 'act rightly' to conform to this order, or to discover the path on which to travel to become 'superior man.'

Confucius always encouraged caution and deliberate care in the pursuit of becoming 'superior man.' When surrounded by disorder, Confucius urges a person to 'be still,' to take guidance from the orderly nature of things. In his words, quoted by Wilhelm, we can readily see that it is the person who must recognize limitations and await order:

> Where disorder develops, words are the first steps. If the prince is not discreet, he loses his servant. If the servant is not discreet, he loses his life. If germinating things are not handled with discretion, the perfecting of them is impeded. Therefore the superior man is careful to maintain silence and does not go forth (Wilhelm 1977, p. 232).

Fatalism gives human beings an active role in choosing a course of action, but the greater powers of the 'will of heaven' ultimately hold sway.

Providentialism

Augustine, the powerful and influential fifth century North African Bishop of Hippo, modified the emphasis of classical Greek cyclical thinking to support the liturgical, economic, and political needs of the Church even as he affirmed 'original sin' and described the place of virtue in the afterlife. Bishop Augustine (354-430 A.D.) bridged what some called the classical era with the beginning of the Christian era and was the father of Christian philosophy and theology. He was also the originator of the idea of Divine Providence.

Through Incarnation, God has given assurance that an elect group will receive salvation. Augustine insists that God is just in condemning the majority for Adam's sin. However, a few men such as Saul (who became Paul) will be saved 'on the road to Damascus.' A small minority will be chosen along with the good angels for eternal salvation. They will constitute the City of God, and will live forever in heaven in perfect peace and happiness (Bury 1932, p. 46).

As he incorporated Aristotle's cyclical reasoning into his own, Augustine proceeded to affirm the essential element of Providentialism – that salvation would only come at the end of time, which he conceived as being virtually the end of his own life. Creating dichotomy as the basis for his analysis,[5] Augustine advanced the

> concepts of self-love and love of God, first, to criticize the pagan political order and especially the Roman Empire and, second, to sketch in the broad outlines of a Christian political order. The two cities are commingled on earth, and mankind will not actually be separated into the elect and the unredeemed until the end of time (op. cit., p. 47).

By the twelfth century of the present era, Providentialism claimed center stage of the Christian world, which by then had a wide reach over the world known to Christians. And by the sixteenth century, it could be said, Providentialism claimed predominance. Louis Le Roy, a French translator of Greek classical works, began the process of de-emphasizing cyclicism as he claimed the preeminence of Divine Providence:

> If the memory of the past is the instruction of the present and the premonition of the future, it is to be feared that having reached so great excellence, power, wisdom, studies, books, industries will decline, as has happened in the past, and disappear – confusion succeeding to the order and perfection of to-day, rudeness to civilisation, ignorance to knowledge. I already foresee in imagination nations, strange in form, complexion, and costume, overwhelming Europe – like the Goths, Huns, Vandals, Lombards, Saracens of old – destroying our cities and palaces, burning our libraries, devastating all that is beautiful. I foresee in all countries wars, domestic and foreign, factions and heresies which will profane all things human and divine; famines, plagues, and floods; the universe approaching an end, world-wide confusion, and the return of things to their original chaos (quoted in Bury 1932, pp. 46-7).

Foreseeing the conceptual trap he created, Le Roy quickly affirmed Divine Providence:

> However much these things proceed according to the fatal law of the world, and have their natural causes, yet events depend principally on divine Providence which is superior to nature and alone knows the predetermined times of events (op. cit., p. 47).

While Providentialism accepted repeating history as a mark of truth, and, indeed, claimed for all of Christendom deep roots in 'classical Greek culture,' a slightly different wrinkle was introduced: the purpose of all this human activity is to attain 'grace' and eternal goodness in heaven. The wealthy, the chosen few, were guaranteed a good place in heaven if they led a 'good life.' The poor and the enslaved were guaranteed only that they would always be poor and enslaved, but the privileged need only think good thoughts and occasionally extend a helping hand to those unfortunates to get a seat next to Saint Peter. Like Cyclicism before it (and alongside it, to be more precise), Providentialism has continued to wield a strong influence in the daily lives of people all over the world despite the absurdity of its major thesis. While Providentialism reached its peak in the late nineteenth century, a competing way of knowing was already in full bloom: Progressivism.

Progressivism

The predominant mode of thought in the modern era is Progressivism. Though it cannot be said that Progressivism began on a specific date, scholars agree that French Historian Jean Bodin's (1566) rejection of sixteenth century theory of the degeneration of man and the popular notion of classical Greek virtue and felicity marked a major departure from the views of his contemporaries (cf. Bury, op. cit., p. 37). Commenting on Bodin's departure, and laying out the principle tenets of Progressivism, Bury notes:

> For history largely depends on the will of men, which is always changing; every day new laws, new customs, new institutions, both secular and religious, come into being, and new errors.[6] But in this changing scene we can observe a certain regularity, a law of oscillation. Rise is followed by fall, and fall by rise; it is a mistake to think that the human race is always deteriorating. If that were so, we should long ago have reached the lowest stage of vice and iniquity. On the contrary, there has been, through the series of oscillations, a gradual ascent. In the ages which have been foolishly designated as gold and silver men lived like the wild beasts; and from that state they have slowly reached the humanity of manners and the social order which prevail to-day (op. cit., p. 39).

Avoiding Fatalism and pushing aside Providentialism, Bodin attempts to bring human history into close synchrony with the divine universe while affirming the power of man's will over events (cf. Bury op. cit., p. 43). This conceptual view placed the human being in the dominant role as controller of destiny on earth. As progressive thinking matured with popular adoption of its basic premises it became the foundation of what is widely understood to be 'western' thinking due to its association with western Europe – the successor to the 'western Holy Roman Empire.' Bodin provided the stimulus for Descartes to formulate his nascent Progressivism, which, in turn, provided the foundation for Pascal's thinking and the development of the French Jansenist movement (similar to the Puritan movement in England) in the seventeenth century of the common era (op. cit., p. 69). The Cartesian formulation of the supremacy of reason and the invariability of natural law struck directly at the foundations of Providentialism and established the 'supremacy of man' as a major pillar supporting the progressive mode of thought.

With human beings in the seat of power, profound changes became possible in the natural environment, in relations among human beings, and in conceptions of history, intellectual development, and in religion. Bury attributes to Turgot the rather modern understanding of

> universal history as the progress of the human race advancing as an immense whole steadily, though slowly, through alternating periods of calm and disturbance towards greater perfection (op. cit., p. 155).

Progressivism launched potent human movements from the eighteenth century to the present that spread from western Europe to touch nearly every corner of the earth, virtually every society. The 'inevitability' of progress became for peoples in the industrial world a proven reality as guns, commerce, politics, and disease overwhelmed non-industrial peoples throughout the world. The preeminent modes of thought that were influential among non-industrial peoples became subordinate to the forces of Progressivism.

Weaving the Braided River

In the short span of six thousand years, human beings conceived of numerous modes of thought that reflected their relationship with their natural environment and their interpretation of the cosmos. I have mentioned just five of these different modes, and noted that each was comprehended as an infallible way of demonstrating consciousness. No doubt each mode of thought contains infallible truths about ultimate consciousness, but it is apparent from even the brief survey given above that there are aspects of absurdity as well.

Among the modes of thought suggested above, it might be noted that a major difference has to do with the perception of what position humans occupy within the broad scheme of things. Where humans are perceived to be the dominant, and therefore primary, determinant of reality, consciousness is presented as a one-dimensional concept – wholly dependent on human beings. Consciousness is apparently conceived as a much more multi-dimensional concept where humans are perceived as a part of a greater reality.

26

When one takes all five modes of thought together and weaves them into a single braid, the potential for a more thorough comprehension of consciousness in the universe becomes possible.

Tribal diversity reflects the evolved relationship between people, their geography and natural environment, and their interpretations of the cosmos. Considered separately, interpretations seem at odds, and may, indeed, conflict. But when one sets aside the apparent conflicts it appears that humans and other peoples – including plants, minerals, fire, water, winds, and other animals – share a common consciousness within the living universe. Where there are differences in modes of tribal thought one only need recognize 'local influences,' or cultural particularities as the explanation. Such cultural particularities are important and cannot be dismissed, but they must be understood to have their unique importance in the specific context in which they arise. Differing cultural contexts help to ensure opportunities for diverse discovery, a constant source of renewal and replenishment. Yet, it is apparent, all modes of thought recognize the common consciousness in the universe.

Relativity of Self and Knowing

For all peoples, no less for Cowlitz, the particular cultural context inspires a sense of existing at the vortex of all consciousness. This is mainly due to the rather limited capacity of humans to comprehend the fullness of the living universe. It is due to the relatively recent arrival of humans on the earthly plane that humans have this limited capacity, and must, as a consequence, learn from other peoples. The eagle has the ability to travel over vast distances and see events from the sky; and so it is that the eagle can teach humans. The mountain is old and has seen many things over vast amounts of time; and so it is that the mountains can teach humans. The sun, the moon, and the stars play a part in the creation of all things; and so it is that the sun, the moon, and the stars can teach humans.

Through the cultural practices of each distinct people, individual human beings come to know their personal identities and learn to know truth through distinct modes of thought. The diversity of human experience serves as a vast library for ways of comprehending and thus serves human beings in their effort to survive. The diversity of human cultures reflects the diversity of other peoples and shows how humans have learned. It is this immense diversity that creates the relativity of self and knowing and the appearance of particularity. Cultural relativity merely demonstrates the wholeness of consciousness, of self and knowing, when taken together - just as a unified mode of thought is conceivable when many modes of thought are entwined into one braid.

Living as a Part of the Universe

In such a short time given to live, each human being seeks to find a proper place in relation to all things. Achieving such a place ensures balance, alignment, and happiness. When one balances relations with the river, the mountains, the flying people, the four-legged people, and with the cosmos one becomes properly aligned in relation to the living universe. Such alignment produces balance when one gives respect to the nature and character of all things encountered. When one fails to comprehend the nature and character of things, it is necessary to make an effort to learn from other people. Like all people, humans have the capacity to learn; but humans have a greater need to learn owing to their relative youth, inexperience, and lack of knowledge. It is because of this serious limitation that humans have needed a brain that allows them to learn more things.

Other peoples, like the fish, the eagle, and the mountain, have great knowledge that permits them to comprehend the nature of other peoples. They achieve balance in relation to other peoples because of this greater knowledge. Human beings are the 'little brothers and sisters,' and so they must take special measures to learn to live in proper respect and relation to all things. The ultimate goal appears to be that humans will live as a part of the universe as do all living things. Humans will come to comprehend their part in the consciousness of the living universe and its eternal changeability.

Notes

1. All beings are thought of as people in different forms in the way of thinking among nations in the Pacific Northwest. Each 'people' has a name and an age, and virtually all 'people' are older and more experienced than human beings.
2. This is the word for 'deer people' used here respectfully recognizing the proper name.
3. Maya spiritual leaders commonly refer to 'Day Keepers' (or 'keepers of the days') when they discuss interpretations and interpreters of the Maya calendar.
4. *The New York Times, Boston Globe, Los Angeles Times*, and other leading papers all gave front page coverage to the mobilization of so-called guerilla activities. The Mexican government moved thousands of troops and military armor into the Southern State of Chiapas, beginning a military confrontation that continues to the present. The Mexican economy collapsed and the entire political system faultered. These events affect the economies of other States as well and raise important questions about the future stability of the Mexican State.

5. The dichotomy often advanced pits 'feminine paganism' against 'masculine' Christianity resulting in an assertion of masculine dominance.
6. Bodin (1566), cap. VII. p. 353.

References

Argüelles, José (1987), *The Mayan Factor*, Bear & Company: Santa Fe.

Bodin, Jean (1566), *Methodus ad facilem historiarum cognitionem*, Apud Martinum Iuuenem: Parisijs.

Bury, John B. (1932), The Idea *of Progress*, Dover Publications: New York.

Colorado, Pamela (1996), 'Indigenous Science,' *Revision*, Vol. 18, No. 3, Winter, pp. 6-10.

Deloria Jr., Vine (1996), 'If You Think About It, You Will See that It Is True,' *Revision*, Vol. 18, No. 3, Winter, pp. 37-44.

Le Roy, Louis (1577), *De la vicissitvde ov variété des choses en l'univers*, Pierre L'Huillier: Paris.

Wilhelm, Richard (1977), *The I Ching*, trans. Cary F. Baynes, Bollingen Series XIX, Princeton University Press: Princeton.

References

3 Individuality in a Relational Culture

A Comparative Study

Hoyt L. Edge

The 'modern' notion of a unitary, individual self has been heavily criticized by Western philosophers over the past few decades. While those criticisms have provided useful insight, it would be even more constructive to expand our philosophical approach by examining non-Western conceptions of self. In this paper, I will offer a comparative analysis of the traditional Western view of the self, with two more relational views of self found in the Balinese and the Australian Aboriginal cultures.

This approach is appropriate for two reasons. First, it offers a clearer picture of the classical Western understanding of self. While it is possible to make progress in this task by examining the empirical data, through conceptual analysis, and from studying the historical development of concepts of self and personhood (and I will use those terms interchangeably in this paper), a more productive perspective on our view of self can be achieved by juxtaposing it against other such concepts. The second reason to compare notions of a unitary self with those of a relational self is to broaden and expand our limited notion of self, and to develop other possible concepts of the self and other terminology by exploring non-Western cultures.

The main thesis of this paper is that the Australian Aboriginal concept of self, as opposed to the atomistic Western notions of self, is a profoundly relational view. This point should come as no surprise to anyone; however, careful analysis will yield some surprising conclusions. Perhaps counter-intuitively to our own view of – and fear of – collectivist cultures, I will show that the Australian Aboriginal values autonomy, and, at least conceptually, values individuality in a deeper sense than do Western individualists. In my argument, I will point out that there are different kinds of collectivisms, and our Western view of collectivist cultures tends not only to be monochromatic,

31

but also takes such an extreme position as to become paradigmatic. Indeed, it is probably inappropriate to call the Aboriginal culture collectivist.

Let me begin, however, by outlining what I take to be two basic concepts in the Western view of personhood: atomism and an essential human nature.

Modern Western Notion of Self

The modern Western notion of self is complex, with many nuances, and that complexity lends itself to numerous analyses. This paper, however, will be limited to a discussion of atomism and an essential human nature, two concepts that have combined to give the Western notion of self its unique flavor.

Atomism in one form or another was adopted in 'the new science' as a reaction to Aristotelian teleology, and it became a general approach to explanation in areas far beyond the physical sciences, including our Western concept of self. There are three aspects to the version of atomism that has become the dominant interpretation.[1] The first asserts that reality is ultimately composed of independent, indivisible, self-sufficient units; therefore, whatever aspect of reality is being described should be broken down and analyzed in terms of these basic building blocks.

The second aspect of atomism asserts that these atoms are in 'space,' or a void. The function of this notion is to reinforce the independence and self-sufficiency of these atoms. Space essentially separates the atoms, and since there is no action at a distance, the only connection or relationship that can exist becomes a combining of atoms to build up larger units, or the agency of one atom 'bumping' into another. Since no connection is thus inherent, each atom is sufficient in itself and has no essential relationship to another atom. Connections and relationships are only external and contingent.

The third aspect of atomism indicates that the job of scientific explanation is to develop the laws governing these connections. Since the world consists of complex units built out of the connection among atoms – molecules being collections of atoms – the job of science is to explain their association or relationship. Thus the job of chemistry in an atomistic framework is to explain how one atom affects the others, and to develop the laws of how they associate or combine to build larger units.

The Cartesian concept of substance is, of course, a prime example of this view applied to an understanding of the self (with less stress on the second aspect, the void, than English versions, following Newtonian atomism). Descartes' idea of the mind as a simple substance, as an indivisible, self-sufficient unit, is an exact description of an atom. This atomistic standpoint gives rise to such philosophical problems as the connection between mind and body, as well as knowledge of other minds – or whether other minds even exist. In Locke and Hume's associationist description of mind, where mind

32

is a blank tablet or void, ideas become the atomic units. Just as in Skinnerian behaviorism (which is simply seventeenth century associationism applied to behavior), the job of Empiricist associationism is to describe how these simple units combine and arrange themselves into larger units in memory, in thinking, or in behavior.

Atomism applied to the social and political realm results in a social contract that views, quite clearly in the Lockean version, the individual as the primary political unit. Locke asserts that in the state of nature (the 'void') these units are without association. The function of the social contract is to give an explanation of how contingent, nonessential relationships develop between these independent, self-sufficient atoms.

The second key component of the modern Western notion of self, an essential human nature, has been a fundamental part of the philosophical arsenal since Plato. It is important, and worth mentioning in this context, that one could theoretically have an atomistic perspective that views each atom as fundamentally unique and different; however, until recently, the thrust of modern philosophy has been to assume essentialism, and the urge has been to understand 'human nature.' Different descriptions of human nature have been advanced, but the view that reason defines our unique humanness has, by far, been the most philosophically influential. However one analyzes reason, the important point remains the same: atoms are not unique units, but rather, they share a common essence; all atoms are fundamentally alike in their essential nature. Reason is universal and describes the fundamental nature of each atom; sameness, not diversity, characterizes our essential nature as human beings.

One implication of defining human nature as rational is that individual autonomy is given a central place in this system. Each atomic unit is autonomous, making free, rational decisions, although, as I will describe later, given the universality of reason, all rational creatures would be expected to come to basically the same conclusions.

This modern Western notion of self has had an extraordinarily positive influence in the West, as well as in other cultures. The American Revolution and, in fact, virtually all liberation movements in our culture, have assumed this view of self that, since we are all independent due to atomism, and since we have ultimate value due to our universal human nature, ultimate respect is due each individual, and the equality of these atomic persons is fundamental. The respect that accrues to every person is typically folded into our notion of autonomy, and since Westerners are profoundly suspicious that organic views of social arrangements undercut autonomy, it is assumed that such respect is lost in collectivist cultures. I will argue that this is not the case, at least in some relational cultures, although I would agree that any adequate notion of personhood should emphasize respect for all persons.

33

Relational Views of the Self

Anthropologists and cross-cultural psychologists often make the distinction between individualistic and collectivist cultures (Hui & Triandis 1986, Triandis et al. 1985). Rather than employing their terminology, I will use the terms 'relational culture' or 'holistic culture' (Shweder & Bourne 1991) in place of 'collectivism.' The term 'collectivist,' to me, at least, implies a unit, with the emphasis on the whole into which the individual parts are radically subsumed. Indeed, Triandis defines collectivism in just this way. Such a definition does not fit Australian Aboriginal cultures, however, although it does seem to describe the two modern attempts at more relational social arrangements in Europe: communism and fascism. These approaches envelop the individual within the greater whole in a radical way, with political power vested in the whole and flowing from the top down; the individual loses autonomy and fundamental freedoms. Such an organic view implies that the whole supersedes the individual in a way that readily permits sacrificing the individual for the good of the whole: e.g., the finger being chopped off for the good of the hand.

Across the broad spectrum of relational views, such an organicism lies at one extreme. It may well be that the Central Desert Aboriginal view lies at the other conceptual extreme, but the Aboriginal view probably better exemplifies relational cultures in general than these examples of modern Western organicism.

The Balinese relational culture lies conceptually between these two positions. Let me now turn to a short description of the Balinese notion of self. A relatively extensive literature exists on the Balinese conception of self (Geertz 1973, Hobart 1983), but for our quick overview, Stephen Lansing's (1974) focus is most useful. In his *Evil in the Morning of the World*, Lansing explains Balinese culture in term of *kaikêt*, which literally means 'to be tied.' Although Lansing's interests are more social, economic, and religious, we can extend *kaikêt* to the idea that the person is defined in terms of the ways in which he or she is 'tied' to social, religious, and political organizations, understanding that organizational structure is highly developed in Bali. It is these relationships, rather than any common human nature, that define who the individual is.

Geertz (1973, pp. 388-9) makes a similar point when he suggests that the Balinese concept of person is best understood by looking at the concept of their gods. These entities come to the annual three-day religious ceremony, where they achieve individuality and specificity by descending to a particular temple in a particular location; otherwise, they are perceived as amorphous and in an important sense not completely formed. In other words, it is only by assuming a particular locus in the social network at a particular time in Balinese society that the divinities are formed. In an analogous fashion, it is only through relationships defined by membership in the village political unit, in specific temples, in clubs or craft organizations, and through kinship relationships, that the individual becomes formed and assumes a particular identity. The person is defined by the particular relationships that the individual has assumed, and since individuals tend to be differently tied, being members of different but overlapping organizational units, each person is defined individually by that person's unique set of relationships. I will return to this idea later.

What is important in our discussion of the Balinese are two points: that individuals are defined and assume their identity through relationships, and that these relationships are primarily to organizations – political, religious, social.

Australian Aboriginal Concept of Self

Let me re-emphasize the complexity of dealing with any culture's concept of self. This is true whether we take the Australian Aboriginal view or any other. But let us approach the issue from the context of the previous discussion, *viz.*, that the Aboriginal view rejects atomism and de-emphasizes the notion of an essential human nature. Let us examine first the anti-atomistic, relational view of the Aborigines.

As befits a great mythic tradition, the creation story of the Australian Aboriginals is profound. If we distill general features of various myths, the story begins with Australia as a featureless plane. The ancestral spirits began to awaken and ascend from out of the ground, or descend out of the sky, or rise up out of the ocean, depending on the particular story, and in their wanderings across Australia, as they hunted and gathered (and sometimes fought), their actions formed the geographical features of the land, e.g., the great serpent slithered across the land to form the bed of the Murray River, or the great emu laid an egg, which became a mountain. In this way, virtually every geographical feature in Australia has a story about its creation.

As they appeared in various locations, the ancestors left part of their essence in the form of spirit children. Then, at the end of their journeys, the ancestor spirits returned to the ground, or the ocean, or the sky. Today, as women go about their daily tasks, they may walk near one of these special sites where the animal spirit enters into her body, completing impregnation; thus, the child who is born has the essence of the ancestor spirit – the emu, the crocodile, the mosquito, etc. This conception totem, as anthropologists have called it, not only connects the person in an essential way to the spiritual world, but also to the land itself, since the land, too, is an instantiation of the spiritual essence.

For our purposes, however, it is even more important to note that conception totems connect people, since other members of the linguistic group will share the same conception totem. While it is, perhaps, easiest to explain how one acquires a conception totem, we must note that there are a number of ways to become associated with an ancestral being, and any individual may have half a dozen or more totemic connections. Given that these totemic relationships define the person, one's identity is tied up with one's particular set of totemic relationships. A person is not an isolated unit, an independent, self-sufficient atom. Practically speaking, such self-sufficiency is inappropriate in a traditional hunter-gatherer society, but more basically, one's self-concept is tied to and by these relationships.

The rejection of atomism is further illustrated by the fact that the idea of an accidental relationship, or an event happening by chance, makes little sense to the Aborigines. The notion of such contingent relationships, of events randomly occurring, is a Western concept. There are no blind forces of nature for the Aborigines, and any connection is rife with meaning. Therefore, the connections and relationships that one has are fundamental and impart important information about the self; they are definitional, not contingent. I will return to questions of relationship, but let me proceed to the second component of the Western notion of self, the essential human nature that defines who we are.

The Aborigines de-emphasize any notion of human nature. Deborah Rose (1992, pp. 64-5), in her study of the Yarralin from the Central Desert, points out that they distinguish between aspects of the person that are common – denoted by blood – and aspects that are particularizing – denoted by skin and milk. In doing so, they de-emphasize any essentialist notion of human nature. In the Yarralin conception, skin and milk relate to mother. Skin places the person in a particular sub-section, or totemic relationship. The body is grown from the mother's milk, which is synonymous with her country or totem; therefore, the mother gives a particular life in nursing the child. Since mother's milk is common with the kin in the same totemic relationship, the child partakes of the essence of the mother and her brothers and their ancestry back to the Dreamtime. This relationship is specific and relates the individual to a particular totem, to having specific relationships.

On the other hand, blood is more diffuse. All humans have blood and therefore it is not usually an identifier with any specificity; rather, it is used to emphasize that there is something common about humanity. This concept differs from our traditional Western notion of human nature in two respects. First, while it brings together all humanity under one category, the category seems to be virtually empty. There is little specificity.[2] All people share blood, which makes them all human, but unlike the Western notion of human nature, there is no essential quality attached to it. Therefore, and this is the second point, while they have a notion of human commonness, there is no essentialism. Further, as befits such a contentless category, the notion of commonness is de-emphasized in favor of particularity and relationship. Thus, what defines us is not our commonness, but our uniqueness.

Fred Myers (1986) studied the Pintupi, another Central Desert group.

Myers' analysis implies that the Lockean question of the relationship between the individual and the 'state' is not what one might be led to expect in a relational society. A collectivist society is normally described as one where the individual is subsumed within the group – where the group has priority over the individual, as Aristotle (1987, p. 509) described it, deriving from the self-sufficiency of the community. Such is not the case among the Pintupi. For them, relationships are more fundamentally dyadic.[3] In other words, the Pintupi do not identify in any strong sense with a community or organization, as do the Balinese, but relationships take place on an individual level through negotiation.

In light of the crucial focus on mediational relationships, the mobility of traditional Aboriginal society is fundamental. If an individual finds that group consensus is going in the direction opposed to his own views, he can leave. Therefore, there is no real sense of the collective; hence the idea of collectivism, or even of a community 'unit,' is foreign to them. Collectivism is only one type of relational society, and may not be representative of the majority of relational cultures. At least Australian Aboriginal groups, who never had a chief or a boss (at best a group of elders may be viewed as having special knowledge) cannot be viewed as a collective. In fact, the emphasis on individual relationships is so strong that fostering community presents a problem for them (Myers 1986, pp. 258-61); ritual tries to ameliorate this problem, but that subject is not within the scope of this paper.

I asserted earlier that individuality is valued more in relational societies than in Western individualism. Having offered the appropriate background, I can now offer support for that argument. As I pointed out previously, Western individualism is based on atomism combined with the notion of an essential human nature, and thus the Western notion of self de-emphasizes the individual in favor of a common essential nature. Each of us, as an atom, has a particular personality, but what is valuable about us – and what is definitive about us – is not our individuality, but our commonness, the essential nature that all of us share and which, in turn, must be respected by all people. Rationality has often been thought to define this nature, and rationality is universal; hence, what is most special about us as humans, and what is most valuable about us as human, is a universal capacity. It is ironic that Western individualism values most something that is completely universal and common, and any behavior that deviates from what might be expected of essential nature is often highly suspect.

By contrast, in a relational culture, at least in the Aboriginal culture, where persons are defined by their relationships – and each individual even in the same family might be expected to have a unique set of relationships – each person will be viewed as unique. Since it is expected that one's view of the world will be formed by these defining relationships, each person will be expected not only to be different, but to take a different perspective on the world. Difference is expected and approved; that's 'his own business,' the

37

Pintupi say (op. cit., p. 124). Hence, individuality is expected and valued more in such relational societies, at least theoretically, than in Western individualism.

This analysis gives a new twist to the notion of autonomy. As in the West, autonomy among the Aborigines is a fundamental trait of humans and therefore is valued absolutely; however, the Aboriginal form of autonomy does not result from a universal capacity of reason and atomism, but from one's individuality and relationships. A person does not have autonomy as a part of basic human nature, but grows into autonomy by developing the uniqueness and particularity found in a set of totemic relationships. Autonomy is not a capacity, but rather a project that one achieves through growth, which is basically spiritual.

Conclusion

While it is no surprise that I should argue that certain non-Western views of self are different from the modern Western notion of self, I have tried to deepen that discussion by suggesting that there are different versions of relational societies, and consequently there are differing concepts of a relational self. The Balinese and Australian Aboriginal concepts of self are both relational, yet they are fundamentally different; indeed, the value of autonomy among the Balinese is questionable. Further, the Australian Aboriginal concept of self is radically particular, and depends on one's relationships. Thus, given the emphasis on the uniqueness of the individual and on the value of autonomy, individual differences – even aberrations – are more acceptable in Aboriginal society than in Western individualism.

This conclusion is particularly important for reconsidering our Western understanding of community. Since a detailed discussion of this problem requires more space than I have, let me add a small 'coda,' as it were, to this paper. Traditionally, Westerners have conceived of community as being formed out of sameness, not difference. We search for common experiences (as in a small town), or common enemies (as in a war), or common allegiances (as in a church or club) to eplain the sense of community. The idea of a common human nature even suggests the possibility of a grand community, of our being citizens of the world. Likewise, it is difference – of language, of customs, of beliefs, of race – that seems to bring the sense of community into question. However, an analysis of the relational self suggests that we can form a robust notion of community based on difference and individuality. In a postmodern world in which we have come to question foundations, essences, and absolutes, and one that is increasingly becoming more multicultural at the local level, we have the chance to reconceive the idea of a community, basing it on relational selves in which individuality and difference are the norm rather than the notion of atomistic selves that share a common human nature.

Notes

An earlier version of this essay under the title 'Individuality in a Relational Culture: A Study of the Australian Aboriginal View of Self' was presented at the 70th Annual Meeting of the American Philosophical Association (Pacific Division) in Seattle, Washington, 3-6 April 1996. Copyright © 1997, Dr. Hoyt L. Edge.

1. For a more detailed discussion of atomism, see Edge (1994, pp. 9-13, 19-25).
2. If anything, shape separates humans from other animals, not rationality or speech.
3. 'There is no self-conscious collective representation of the "common welfare." What is interesting for the Pintupi is that sociality is constituted largely out of dyadic relations' (Myers 1986, p. 124).

References

Aristotle (1987), 'Politics,' in John L. Ackrill (ed.), *A New Aristotle Reader*, pp. 507-39, Princeton University Press: Princeton.

Edge, Hoyt L. (1994), *A Postmodern Perspective on Self and Community*, Edwin Mellen Press: Lewiston.

Geertz, Clifford (1973), 'Person, Time, and Conduct in Bali,' in Clifford Geertz (ed.), *The Interpretation of Cultures*, pp. 360-411, Basic Books: New York.

Hobart, Mark (1983), 'Through Western Eyes, or How My Balinese Neighbour Became a Duck,' *Indonesia Circle*, Vol. 30, March, pp. 33-47.

Hui, C. Harry and Triandis, Harry C. (1986), 'Individualism – Collectivism: A Study of Cross-Cultural Researchers,' *Journal of Cross-Cultural Psychology*, Vol. 17, No. 2, June, pp. 225-48.

Lansing, J. Stephen (1974), *Evil in the Morning of the World*, Michigan Papers on South and Southeast Asia, No. 6, The University of Michigan: Ann Arbor.

Myers, Fred R. (1986), *Pintupi Country, Pintupi Self*, Smithsonian Institution Press: Washington.

Rose, Deborah B. (1992), *Dingo Makes us Human*, Cambridge University Press: New York.

Shweder, Richard A. and Bourne, Edmund J. (1991), 'Does the Concept of the Person Vary Cross-Culturally?' in Richard A. Shweder (ed.), *Thinking Through Cultures*, pp. 113-55, Harvard University Press: Cambridge.

Triandis, Harry C.; Leung, Kwok; Villareal, Marcelo J.; and Clack, Felicia L. (1985), 'Allocentric versus Idiocentric Tendencies: Convergent and Discriminant Validation,' *Journal of Research in Personality*, Vol. 19, No. 4, December, pp. 395-415.

Part Three
Ethnographic Assessment of Knowledge

4 Understanding Maori Epistemology
A Scientific Perspective

Roma Mere Roberts and Peter R. Wills

Introduction

In his study of the Maori, Schwimmer (1966) opined that 'among the peoples of the world, Maori mythologists have the distinction of peering most deeply into the infinite darkness that existed before life began.' This statement provides us with a challenge: to represent the nature and function of the indigenous knowledge of Aotearoa/New Zealand on an equal footing with academic inquiry into the epistemology of science. Convincing others of the truth of Schwimmer's statement is a difficult task, because in today's globally dominant Western culture, science is assumed to be not simply *a* way of seeing but *the* way of seeing reality. As a consequence, many of the efforts of indigenous peoples to achieve equality are denied by the lack of recognition given to their own knowledge system. Within Aotearoa/New Zealand there are some signs of a reversal of this trend. In line with a raft of internationally recognized legislation (IUCN 1996) that acknowledges the rights of indigenous peoples, the Resource Management Act (1991: Part II; S6e) requires recognition of and provision for 'the relationship of Maori and their culture and traditions with their ancestral lands, water, sites, *wahi tapu* and other *taonga*' (sacred sites and other treasures). However, in spite of increasing evidence of a bicultural approach in New Zealand's health and education systems, the partnership between Maori and Pakeha (non-Maori) established by the Treaty of Waitangi in 1840 has not yet bridged the cultural divide that separates Western science from other worldviews, especially that of the first people of Aotearoa/New Zealand.

To represent the different knowledge systems or worldviews that coexist in Aotearoa/New Zealand is an inescapably political task, for there are not only concerns about the potential disclosure of knowledge belonging to indigenous cultures, but also competing claims as to what should count as knowledge in the first place. Our situation in respect of Maori knowledge is problematic. In the first place, any attempt by us to claim ownership of this knowledge would amount to usurpation. The very authenticity and integrity of what is called *matauranga* and *wananga* would be lost in the process of our exposition. Therefore, all we can hope for is to bring to light those aspects of this knowledge that have been publicly disclosed and discussed in academic circles within the broad context of comparing epistemologies.

Because frequent use will be made in this essay of the term 'knowledge system,' some definitions are appropriate. One of Maoridom's foremost thinkers puts it this way:

> Cultures pattern perceptions of reality into conceptualisations of what they perceive reality to be: of what is to be regarded as actual, probable, possible or impossible. These conceptualisations form what is termed the 'worldview' of a culture ... to which members of a culture assent and from which stems their value system. The worldview lies at the very heart of the culture, touching, interacting with and strongly influencing every aspect of the culture (Marsden & Henare 1972, p. 3).

Another explanation defines a knowledge system as possessing four major attributes: a theory of knowledge that explicates what counts as knowledge and how that knowledge can be known; how knowledge can be transmitted, and learned; how knowledge is distributed internally and externally to a community (knowledge relationships and power); and knowledge innovation – to what extent and how knowledge can be changed or modified (cf. Whitt 1995, p. 231).

Our own contribution to this area of comparative epistemology has been the development of a course entitled 'Indigenous Knowledge and Western Science: Perspectives from the Pacific' for the Centre for Pacific Studies at the University of Auckland (Morrison et al. 1994, Roberts 1994). In this, we attempt to analyze and present the epistemology of science in a way that makes it comparable with other knowledge traditions of the peoples of the Pacific; a task made difficult by the claim of science to universal, context-free knowledge. Our approach does not hold up Western science as the prime exemplar of knowledge against which other traditions should be measured. Instead we seek to understand the epistemological framework underlying each system of thought, and to search for an intellectual common ground on which other worldviews can be accommodated alongside that of science. We then explore some of the consequences that the coexistence of these distinct epistemologies engenders in contemporary society. Development of this course has also provided us with a personal challenge to obtain a deeper understanding of some of the more accessible characteristics of the knowledge system of the Maori of Aotearoa/New Zealand, as well as of the intellectual history that has led to modern science. Within this context, our essay represents 'work in progress,' and our perspective as natural scientists will be seen to differ from that of philosophers and anthropologists. What we share with those from other disciplines is the desire to make a positive contribution toward cross-cultural discourse and understanding.

Towards an Understanding of Maori Epistemology

E kore au e ngaro	I will never be lost
He kakano i ruia mai i Rangiatea	I am the seed that was sown in Rangiatea

To Maori, 'to know' something is to locate it in space and in time. This applies to individual persons, tribes, all other animate and inanimate things, and even to knowledge itself. For example, the *whakatauaki* (proverb or aphorism) quoted above locates all persons of Maori descent relative to an origin within the ancestral homeland, referred to in the traditions as Hawaiiki, and today considered to be the island of Raiatea (Rangiatea) in the Society group, French Polynesia. Introductory speeches often contain aphorisms of this sort that give additional information about a person's tribal identity and ancestry. The words

Ko Tainui te waka	Tainui is the ancestral canoe
Ko Taupiri te maunga	Taupiri is the mountain
Ko Waikato te awa	Waikato is the river

enable the listener immediately 'to know' the speaker, in terms of origins, ancestry, and place. The name Tainui, one of several voyaging canoes that brought the colonizing ancestors of the Maori to Aotearoa/New Zealand about 1000 years ago, establishes tribal origin and ancestry. Reference to place: to one's mountain and river (or lake or harbor) further establishes one's tribal and personal identity.

Whakapapa

Fundamental to this ability to locate a thing in time and space is knowledge of its *whakapapa* – its genealogy or lines of descent. To 'know' oneself is to know one's *whakapapa*. To 'know' about a tree, a rock, the wind, or the fishes in the sea – is to know their *whakapapa*. In its literal translation, the word *whakapapa* means 'to place in layers, one upon another.' In its genealogical sense, it provides a framework for an understanding of historical descent, pattern, and linkages, whereby everything, animate and inanimate, is connected together into a single 'family tree' or 'taxonomy of the universe.'

45

In the Maori worldview all things have a *whakapapa* and, as these reveal, all things are related (cf. appendices). Of significance is the fact that there is no distinction or break between the cosmogonic and anthropogonic *whakapapa*, so that everything living and nonliving shares descent from the same ancestral, and ultimately divine, primal origin. *Whakapapa* thus encapsulates the Maori worldview. It acts as a cognitive template for the ordering and understanding of the visible and invisible worlds, as a paradigm of reality; 'of what is to be regarded as actual, probable, possible, or impossible' (Marsden & Henare 1992, p. 3).

Expressed in Maori terms, *whakapapa* provides the 'metaphysical *kaupapa*' (ground plan; first principles) whereby Maori order, locate, and 'know' the phenomenal world. Moreover, by transcending this world and connecting all things on earth to the gods in the heavens, to the universe, and ultimately to the Creator, it provides the framework for an all-encompassing, universal knowledge system.

By locating things in time and place, *whakapapa* also functions as a 'mental map,' analogous to but in contrast with the 'knowledge as landscape' metaphor commonly used in creating cognitive spatial metaphors in Western discourse about knowledge (Salmond 1982, Turnbull 1994). As Turnbull has described, perhaps the most outstanding demonstration of this cognitive ability to 'map the world in the mind' is the star maps of the Polynesian ancestors of the Maori, who in the process of peopling the Pacific carried out some of the most daring long distance sea voyages of discovery in human history (Lewis 1975, Turnbull 1991). In his compilation of the astronomical knowledge of the Maori, Best (1922) records 206 star names. He also notes that this extensive, empirically-based knowledge was combined with allegorical knowledge (astrology) that included the *whakapapa* and narratives relating to each of the heavenly bodies.

As revealed by tradition, even knowledge itself has an origin and a *whakapapa*. Tribal accounts vary in detail, but in all there is an essential order expressed not only in *whakapapa* but also in *karakia* (chants; prayers) such as that of Te Kohuora (recorded in 1854 by Taylor; taken from Salmond 1985, pp. 244-5).[1]

Na te kune te pupuke	From the source (conception)[2] of growth the rising (swelling)
Na te pupuke te hihiri	From rising the thought
Na te hihiri te mahara	From rising thought the memory
Na te mahara te hinengaro	From memory the mind
Na te hinengaro te manako	From the mind (spleen), desire
Ka hua te wananga	Knowledge became conscious (was named, became fruitful)
Ka noho i a rikoriko	It dwelt (mated with) in dim light
Ka puta ki waho ko te po	And darkness emerged (was born)

46

Ko te po i tuturi, te po i pepeke	The dark for kneeling, the dark for leaping
Te po uriuri, te po tangotango	The intense dark, to be felt
Te po wawa, te po te kitea	The dark to be touched, unseen
Te po i oti atu ki te mate	The dark that ends in death
Na te kore i ai	From nothingness (primal void) came the first cause (begetting)
Te kore te whiwhia	Unpossessed nothingness
Te kore te rawea	Unbound nothingness
Ko hau tupu, ko hau ora	The wind of growth, the wind of life
Ka noho i te atea	Stayed in (mated with) empty space
Ka puta ki waho te rangi e tuu nei	And the atmosphere emerged (was born)
Te rangi e teretere nei	The atmosphere which floats
I runga o te whenua	Above the earth
Ka noho te rangi nui e tu nei	The great atmosphere above us
Ka noho i a ata tuhi	Stayed in red light
Ka puta ki waho te marama	And the moon emerged (was born)
Ka noho te rangi e tu nei	The atmosphere above us
Ka noho i a te werowero	Stayed in shooting light
Ka puta ki waho ko te ra	And the sun emerged (was born)
Kokiritia ana ki runga	Flashing up
Hei pukanohi mo te rangi	To light the atmosphere
Te ata rapa, te ata ka mahina	The early dawn, the early day, the midday
Ka mahina te ata i hikurangi !	The blaze of day from the sky!

Salmond comments

consider, for instance, the relationship between mind and matter described in the chant quoted above. A primal energy produces thought, memory, the mind, and then desire. From desire *wananga* (ancestral knowledge) generates darkness, and then the Kore – 'primal power of the cosmos, the void or negation, yet containing the potentiality of all things afterwards to come' (Best 1924: 60). From Kore, space emerges, and then light, land, the gods, and men. Thought and mind constitute phenomenal intelligibility in this account; they have efficacy in the phenomenal world (1985, p. 246).

In their account of Creation, Marsden and Henare (1992, p. 16) describe the existence of three 'worlds' and identify each with one of the 'baskets of knowledge' obtained by the demigod Tane (see later). What could be approximated by the idea of 'Being' in Western metaphysics, is called *Te Ao Tua-Atea*, the world beyond space and time. In some tribal accounts this is the abode of Io, who represents the Supreme Being. Whereas science might identify 'Being' with the ultimate principle of material reality (the grand unified field, perhaps), Maori take the infinite, transcendent, eternal world of the spirit, *Tua-Atea*, as the ultimate reality. *Tua-Atea* precedes the other realms but is also regarded as that to which cosmic processes are tending. The second realm, *Tua Uri*, is likewise immaterial, but it is a world where *whakapapa* begins. *Tua Uri* means 'beyond the world of darkness' and represents the actual reality behind what we experience in the phenomenal world of everyday experience. *Tua Uri* has been characterized as the 'fabric of the universe,' but what distinguishes it primarily from the Western scientific conception is not that it is immaterial, but rather that its *whakapapa* begins with *mauri*, divine power or agency, instead of being derived from some inherent principle of mechanics or a random event. *Mauri* precedes *hihiri*, pure energy, in the cosmological genealogy and *hihiri* is further refined to give rise to *Mauri-ora*, the life principle, and thence *Hau-ora*, which represents the spiritual breath of animate life. These precede shape, form, space, and time. The *whakapapa* of *Tua-Uri* ends with the birth of heaven and earth – the sky-father, Ranginui, and the earth-mother, Papatuanuku. The third world is the phenomenal world, *Te Aro-Nui*, which translates as 'that before us' (cf. Marsden & Henare 1992, p. 10). *Te Aro-Nui* came into being when Tane led a revolt of his sibling gods against their parents, Ranginui and Papatuanuku, and forced them apart to let light into the world. Until then Tane and his brothers had lived in darkness between the conjoined heaven and earth.

Other cosmogonical accounts such as that of the Tainui people (cf. Appendix 1) talk of three stages of creation beginning with *Te Kore* (The Vast Nothingness), followed by *Te Po* (The Great Darkness). During these two timeless eons the 'seeds of the universe' came together to form earth and sky. This was a period of awakening in which thought emerged, in turn producing the desire in the mind that led to knowledge becoming conscious. Then came *Te Ao Marama* (The World of Light) in which anthropogenic creation occurred culminating in the appearance of humans. Variations occur in the divisions of each of these epochs. Common to all however, is the use of ontogenetic (developmental) analogies with plant growth or human sexual procreation (for example, the third and fourth strands in Appendix 1, and the *karakia* quoted above.)

Once created, knowledge had to be obtained from the abode of the gods and brought back to earth for use by humankind. Tradition has it that Tane ascended to the uppermost (twelfth) heaven to obtain knowledge (*wananga*) from Io. Best (1924, p. 103) records that this knowledge was contained in three baskets (*kete*): *te kete aronui* (knowledge pertaining to peaceful acts and endeavor), *te kete tuauri* (knowledge of ceremonial and rituals for communicating with the gods and for conduct of all earthly activities), and *te kete tuatea* (knowledge of all things evil including warfare). As described above by Marsden and Henare (1992, pp. 8-11), the knowledge contained in

48

these three baskets relates to, is located in, and representative of the three-world concept of the Maori. The return journey was beset with difficulties before Tane was able to place the baskets, along with two sacred stones, in the specially constructed *Whare Kura* (house of learning). Thus, just as light entered the world and allowed humankind to flourish, so did knowledge enter the world and provide enlightenment for the mind (Walker 1993).

Maori lore then recounts how Tane, in many different guises, engaged in numerous procreation events, as did each of his siblings (cf. Appendix 2). For example, when personified as Tane Mahuta, god of the forest, he cohabited with different wives each of whom produced as offspring the native plants and insect fauna of Aotearoa/New Zealand.

Attributes of Knowledge in Maori Society

Maori have at least three words that translate into the English 'knowledge': *matauranga*, which essentially means 'reliable knowledge' and which is almost synonymous with *mohiotanga*, knowledge acquired by familiarity and the exercise of intelligence; and *wananga*, knowledge for activating ancestral power. Salmond (1985) has provided an explanation of how some understanding of Maori knowledge may be achieved within the Western intellectual tradition. She points out that *matauranga* and *wananga* are regarded as exhaustible and destructible resources that must be carefully conserved by a group and only given or shared under the correct circumstances. Knowledge is a sacred power that belongs to a group rather than the particular individual who may hold it for a time, and can only be passed on to chosen members of the group. As a sacred power knowledge can be 'talked into' physical objects as in the blessing of a building or a ceremonial ornament. Likewise, stories are told of how ancestors, in claiming territory, named landmarks, rocks, trees, waterfalls, and so on, and thereby locked together tribal understanding with the entities themselves so that a place and its knowledge could not be separated.

In this way, the tribe's heritage and the local environment come to share in a single *whakapapa*, and the world is not separated into a hierarchy of ontological categories corresponding to things of physical, biological, and cultural origin. The cosmic generative power, the common dynamic process in which all things unfold (*tipu*), already contained the form of every possible being. Consequently, all things in the phenomenal world alike unfold their nature (*tipu*), live (*ora*), and have form (*ahua*) and so come to possess a body (*tinana*), an immaterial self (*wairua*), an abiding place of divine power (*mauri*), and characteristic vitality (*hau*). Hence Salmond (1982) comments

it is difficult to imagine a philosophy based on a distinction between an

49

"internal" subjectivity and an "external" objectivity being elaborated in such a system of thought (op. cit., p. 85).

In Maori metaphysics, this Cartesian dichotomy between an observing, thinking self and the outside world cannot and does not exist. As Marsden (1981, p. 143) says, any understanding of the Maori worldview must come from a subjective approach; 'the route ... through abstract interpretation is a deadend.' Ultimately however, it is the nature of the relationship between knowledge (as *wananga* or *matauranga*) and *whakapapa* that provides the 'flesh' on the epistemological 'bones.' One is not complete without the other. *Whakapapa* provides the information that enables knowledge to be situated; on this, in ever developing layers of meaning, is applied *matauranga* (in the sense of 'everyday knowledge') and/or *wananga* (esoteric knowledge). Collectively, these layers of meaning and understanding form an 'epistemological *whakapapa*' or knowledge paradigm. It is the understanding of, and explication of the relationship between them that leads to wisdom (Hohepa, personal communication).[3]

In ordinary discourse (or 'talk,' *korero*) various forms of expression are given to *matauranga*, especially that which occurs during ceremonial meetings between kin groups on *marae*. Such meetings are characterised by vigorous debate in which contests of prestige (*mana*) take place between male orators when making formal speeches. Precise judgments are made concerning the truth of different accounts that may range from *korero tuturu* ('permanent talk,' reliably attested) through *korero purakau* (legend, myth) as far as *korero tito* (fabrication). Competing accounts, particularly of tribal history, are judged according to whether they are *tika*, that is, validated by reason, precedent, and experience. *Tika* means 'just' and 'customary' as well as 'true' or 'correct,' reflecting a judgment of propriety that goes beyond what is valid and true (*pono*) through belief or ritual ratification. An early European record of dealings with Maori states that the most certain method of prevailing in discourse is to appeal to reason and obtain assent that one's account is *tika*. Correspondingly, at the other end of the scale of truth is *he* which means 'dead' as well as 'wrong' and 'false' and to judge an account to be *he* has dire connotations. Between these two extremes lies *tito* which has a range of meanings from 'invention' to 'lying.' In such ways knowledge was explicated, put to the test, refuted, revised, or validated according to principles recognized by Maori law (cf. Salmond 1985, p. 250).

Transmission of Knowledge

In traditional tribal Maori societies, *wananga*, knowledge for activating ancestral power, was generally taught to selected high-born boys in special houses of learning (*Whare Wananga*) which, by way of certain rituals, had been made *tapu* (sanctified). Strict observance of ritual and custom (*tikanga*) in both teaching and learning was also necessary to ensure that there were no mistakes or deviations from that which was handed down as *nga taonga tuku iho o nga tupuna* (a priceless gift from the ancestors). Thus the accumulated knowledge held by a tribe, even as it pertained to the natural world, was not freely available to be held by all in common. Knowledge was imparted to specially chosen individuals within particular contexts designed to constrain and sanction the receiver so that its application would serve the tribe as a whole. Metaphorical representation of knowledge as food or sustenance for the mind is clearly expressed in the symbolism of the three baskets. Extension of this metaphor occurs in the practice (in some tribal

Figure 4.1   Tane-nui-a-Rangi, the carved meeting house at the University of Auckland.

Whare Wananga) of the *tohunga* (priestly expert) spitting into the mouth of the initiate and so symbolizing the transmission of knowledge that was to follow. Another ritual of induction involved a candidate placing a white stone in his mouth, symbolically swallowing it and then replacing it. Known as *Hukatai*, which means 'sea foam,' this stone was one of two given to Tane by Io when he received the three baskets of knowledge. Upon graduation, the student repeated the ritual with the second red-colored stone, *Rehutai*, which means 'sea spray.' The act of swallowing symbolizes the transition from knowledge to wisdom through a process of ingestion, while the names of the stones convey the metaphor of a canoe journey. White sea foam generated in the wake of a canoe represents the accumulation of knowledge as facts picked up along the way. At the end of the journey, the rays of sunrise piercing the spray at the bow of the canoe represent the spiritual experience of illumination when the knowledge is integrated into the center of one's being (Marsden & Henare 1992).

Further elaboration of this metaphor (cf. Best 1923, p. 12) was provided by the tradition, in some schools of learning, of dividing the curriculum into

Figure 4.2   Interior of Tane-nui-a-Rangi showing some of the carved ancestors.

two primary classes: *kauwae runga* (i.e. 'upper jaw' knowledge of the superior mythologies, cosmogonies, and esoteric knowledge for communicating with the gods) and *kauwae raro* (i.e. 'lower jaw' knowledge that is 'everyday' knowledge of the natural world, of tribal law, and mythology). Schools, especially those in which 'higher' forms of teaching and learning took place, were *tapu* as were the *tohunga* and the students who were selected for receiving the sacred lore. According to tradition the first *Whare Wananga* was located in the twelfth heaven. On earth, Rua-te-pupuke (a personifcation of knowledge) created the first school of learning, known as a *Whare Kura* (Best 1923, p. 7). Each tribe then set up its own schools for teaching specialised aspects of the knowledge contained in the three baskets. For example, advanced or esoteric teachings were taught in *Whare Wananga*, tribal lore in *Whare Kura* or *Whare kau po*, and magic arts and rituals in *Whare Maire* (op. cit., pp. 10, 12). Organization of these schools of thought varied considerably from tribe to tribe, as did what was taught; indeed each tribe had different versions of parts of their common history as well as of cosmological history. Acceptance of these variations amounted to a style of epistemological relativism in which affirmation of one's own version of the truth constituted a statement of tribal identity.

Numerous mnemonic devices were employed to assist both teaching and learning of tribal lore; these included not only oral (e.g., poetry, proverbs, place names, song, oratory, and recitation) but also visual cues. Maori excel at carving (*whakairo*). This word is derived from the proto-Polynesian root *iro*, which means 'knowledge.' Thus *whaka iro* means 'to make knowledge visible' by the act of carving. By this means knowledge of the ancestors and the narratives was recorded in the carvings, as well as into the symbolic patterns on the rafters (*kowhaiwhai*) and woven into decorative patterns lining the walls (*tukutuku*). For many tribes these carved houses represent the equivalent of libraries, art galleries, and museums. Knowledge was also incorporated into the patterns of cloaks (*taniko*), in facial decorations (*moko*), and in string games (*whai*) in which each pattern re-enacts a part of the narrative. In such ways the creation or performance of Maori art, craft, and games all involved story telling and thus helped to keep the knowledge alive (Haami in prep.).

In common with most knowledge systems including Western science, Maori make extensive use of personification, of metaphor, and of narrative to facilitate understanding. Much of Maori discourse is metaphorical, in the cosmogonies, the allegories, in oratory (*whaikorero*) as well as in 'everyday talk' (*korero*). Further elaboration of these metaphors is created by the multiple interpretations of many words, so that their true meaning is dependent not only on context but also on the knowledge status of the listener. In Maori metaphysics then, metaphor along with language creates a '*whakapapa* of the mind,' revealing and concealing the many layers of meaning of *matauranga* and of *wananga*.

Extended metaphors in the form of linked 'narrative cycles' are of central importance to Maori knowledge. Indeed, narrative, along with the propensity for classification, appears to be an inherent property of all knowledge systems in their attempt to make sense of the world.

Two major cycles involve the demi-gods Maui and Tawhaki, who acted as intermediaries to fetch knowledge from the gods and transmit it to their human descendants. Collectively, they provide the 'moral *kaupapa*' or basic tenets for Maori society as well as causal explanations for the origin and occurrence of important natural phenomena. Among his more famous deeds, Maui (who is also a trickster) harnesses the sun, procures fire, fishes up Aotearoa/New Zealand from beneath the sea, creates its major landforms, and (finally) brings mortality into the world through his failure to reverse the birth process. Tawhaki's deeds provide a rationale for brother-in-law conflicts, filial responsibilities, revenge, and the need for an environmental ethic involving respect and reciprocity toward Papatuanuku and her other children. In this way the narratives provide causal explanations for the philosophical questions 'why?' and 'how?' Just as importantly narratives provide an authoritative (supernatural) precedent and sanction for cultural mores and customs, and thus bring order into the world.

All of these pedagogical tools were enhanced by the highly developed abilities of Maori to memorize oral information. Best (1923, p. 5) recounts how Tamarau Waiari, in an appearance before the nineteenth century Land Commission at Ruatoki, spent three days establishing his tribe's claim to a piece of land by recounting their *whakapapa*, which, including all extra-tribal histories, linkages, and relationships, contained over fourteen hundred names back to an ancestor 34 generations distant. Additional pedagogical devices included the extensive use of organic analogies in both *whakapapa* and the narratives (referred to earlier). In some the analogy is human while in others it relates more closely to plant growth and development. Given that Maori *whakapapa* make explicit the relationship of all things to each other based on common descent from the parental ancestors Ranginui and Papatuanuku, it is not surprising that Maori have articulated the phylogenetic unity of diverse phenomena by way of organic analogy. Thus the combined use by Maori of *whakapapa* and *wananga* to 'make sense of the world,' and its expression in narrative and *whakairo* creates a 'metaphysical Gestalt' for communicating knowledge in an oral culture (Hohepa, personal communication).

Whenua

A second aspect fundamental to Maori epistemology is the notion of 'place' or *whenua*. This word means both 'Earth' and 'placenta,' and as such it metaphorically represents the connection of people and individuals to their origins: material, historical, and spiritual. Eloquent expression of this relationship is provided in the *whakatauaki*:

Ko Papatuanuku to tatou whaea	The land is our mother
Ko ia te matua atawhai	She is the loving parent
He oranga mo tatou	She nourishes and sustains us
I roto i te moengaroa	When we die
Ka hoki tatou ki te kopu o te whenua	She enfolds us in her arms

Marsden and Henare elaborate upon this metaphor by explaining that

> just as the fetus is nurtured in the mother's womb and after the baby's birth upon her breast, so all life forms are nurtured in the womb of Papatuanuku and upon her breast. Man is thus an integral part of the natural order and recipient of her bounty. He is her son and therefore as every son has social obligations to fulfill towards his parents, siblings and other members of the *whanau* (family), so has man an obligation to mother earth and her *whanau* to promote their welfare and good (1992, p. 16).

54

Thus,

> it is the spiritual significance of land which is most dear to Maori. Whenua (land) also means placenta; hapu (extended family or sub-tribe) also means pregnant. The expression 'te u kai po' refers to the area where you were brought up, but it also means to be breast fed. The land's significance derives from Papatuanuku, hence the dual meaning of these words whereby the land is identified as the source of human creation, from which we were born, by which we are nurtured, and to which we return. This relationship is expressed symbolically in such customs as the burial of the pito (umbilical cord) and by appropriate karakia acknowledging the mana (authority; power) derived by Maori from Papatuanuku (Roberts et al. 1995, p. 10).

Maori share such concepts of connectedness to land with most, if not all, other peoples who have long resided in a particular place and have been directly dependent upon the earth and its resources for their survival. Place names express this reciprocal relationship by locating tribal knowledge in place and in time – the latter by virtue of the fact that names may change to reflect changing histories, and hence place names, too, have a *whakapapa* (Hohepa, personal communication). To indigenous peoples place and place names act as constant reminders not only of where one is, but of who one is; without one, the other does not exist. The land thus serves as a living encyclopedia in which names act as mnemonic devices whereby the narrative related to that particular place, and its meaning, can be recalled. Recounting the narrative at that very location enables the knowledge associated with the name to be experienced; to be felt as well as heard. In this way, as Norman explains (1988, pp. 5-8), place names and their narratives 'marked the land and domesticated it,' forming the 'emotional landscape' of a particular tribal area by representing and describing the spiritual as well as the physical typography of the area. Place names and their meanings are thus local knowledge, embedded within and specific to a particular place.

Different cultures have different ways of activating and accessing such knowledge rooted in place. For Maori, this is done by way of *whakapapa*, *waiata* (song), and *whakatauaki* (aphorisms or proverbs) such as those quoted at the beginning of this section. Expressed in this form, place names not only record and express important mythological and historical aspects of that particular tribe, but by virtue of the knowledge contained in the names, they, and the landscape they represent, are the physical manifestation of the tribe. Thus a great chief may speak of himself as the mountain or the river; these cannot be objectified or externalized. They are not 'out there,' but 'in here.' For this reason, Maori, along with many other indigenous cultures, cannot conceptualize an entity called 'Nature' as something separate from oneself and one's tribal identity.

The Character of Scientific Knowledge

In stark contrast to most aspects of Maori knowledge and that of other traditional cultures, Western science is based on the premise that the ordered reality that exists independent of perception is universal and purely material, and that knowledge of this reality can be achieved only through systematic observation. Thus scientific conclusions are depicted as independent of any arbitrary biases, prejudices, or other subjective choices that may be made as a result of one's own cultural heritage, gender, ethnicity, or other factors. Scientists argue that their theories ultimately stand or fall according to the sole criterion of consistency with the observable facts. On the other hand, many philosophers of science and sociologists of knowledge have argued that all observation is theory-laden and that every statement of fact requires the use of language whose contextual meaning cannot be exhaustively defined (Kuhn 1962). From such a standpoint, science, like *matauranga Maori* in Aotearoa/ New Zealand, is just one of many equally valid 'ways of seeing' or knowing about the world (Feyerabend 1993). By tracing science back to its historical roots, one comes to appreciate why it is that science has become the dominant knowledge system to the point that all others have been either assimilated in a process of epistemological imperialism, or ignored. As Atran (1990) puts it

> before some rigidly minded Greeks arbitrarily decided their world was the one and only right one, there were presumably no absolute hierarchies, no underlying natures, no natural distinctions between the artifactual and the living, no facts of the matter to separate the natural and the supernatural (op. cit., p. 215).

Many scientists dismiss the constructivism of sociological thinking as arrant nonsense in which 'science-as-practice' is confused with 'science-as-knowledge.' In response, the sociologists argue that Kuhnian paradigm shifts that lead to the reinterpretation of bodies of data are influenced by value judgments and other sociological factors and do not depend solely on the outcome of definitive, decisive experiments.

In our view, both claim and counterclaim can be substantiated. Science provides an operational prescription for what is, in principle, perfect observation. Since the time of Newton this has meant that the only valid terms of description are those expressible as algebraic composites of the basic dimensions of length, time and mass. And only those composites whose relationships are consistent with Newton's laws of motion and gravitation are acceptable. From time to time, extra irreducible abstractions like that of electric charge and the indivisible atomic (or molecular) granularity of distinguishable substances have been added to the list of core, irreducible, physical dimensions, some to be later eliminated as separate distinct theories have been unified. But the character of scientific knowledge has not changed

56

significantly in the process. This holds true through the development of Einstein's theory of relativity, quantum mechanics, the theory of elementary particles (more latterly 'strings') and modern cosmology. A statement cannot be scientific in the modern sense unless it is expressed in terms of elementary concepts that can be related to the experimental observation or manipulation of the world through observer-independent operations and procedures. But this is precisely why the counterclaim, essentially against the completeness of science, is also valid. Scientific observation is not laden with the prejudice of one theory as opposed to another, it is laden with the limitations and restrictions that accompany its prescription of abstractions concerning which there is absolutely no choice, so long as one wants to remain scientific, or unless one expects to initiate another scientific revolution. From the multitudinous possibilities open to consciousness, only those that can be compressed into the mold of a small number of abstractions can be specified accurately in scientific terms.

The basic terms of scientific discourse do not have any exact specification that is given in experience as self-evident and concrete. They are terms that have been carefully constructed, and sometimes reconstructed, through a long, arduous, and, to the extent possible, exhaustive historical process. As happened with the inception of relativity theory, even the abstractions corresponding to physical length, time, and mass have had to be reconstructed on a different mathematical foundation in order to maintain consistent and coherent knowledge. And in quantum mechanics, the construction taken to be the most basic 'reality' is a wave function that can never be observed or measured directly but whose manifest effect in the realm of events open to experience comes about only through some reduced aspects which correspond to a contraction of the potential interactions among its parts. The elementary fallacy of scientific fundamentalism is the claim that we know with absolute certainty that the whole of reality is somehow comprised of what these wave functions (or some grand unified quantum mechanical field) describe because all appropriate observations can be more accurately and consistently interpreted using quantum mechanics than any other theory.

From its inception in ancient Greece, Western science has conceived of 'the nature of things' in terms of quantitatively expressible, universal, abstract principles – that of an underlying material substance, and those corresponding to formal numerical relationships and symmetries. With the advent of Galileo and Newton's inertial physics the practically unattainable limit of some procedural progression (the exact balancing of opposing forces) was elevated to the level of 'the natural state of things.' Later, during the twentieth century, entities whose constitution is purely mathematical have supplanted those which, until then, could be conceived as bearing some relation to tactile and visual experience: real, solid, and space-filling. But in relation to the comparison of modern science with *matauranga Maori* the

57

most important feature of the transition to modern science was not the beginning of a rapid increase in the level of abstraction required for scientific thinking but rather the abolition of any conception of causative agency. By separating events in the world of matter and mechanism from the rest of experience, Descartes and Newton left no room for causative agents: intelligent, conscious, or otherwise. The autonomous expression of intentionality is not something that can be 'known' in any way that relates to science.

Agency and Mechanism in Western Science

Science is often said to have begun with the Ionian idea that a single, unchanging, material substance underlies all natural phenomena. However, the material 'nature of things,' *physis*, was not yet distinguished from the divine power, *mauri* perhaps, that was thought to pervade it (Cornford 1912, Heidegger 1975). The modern view of matter as a lifeless substance governed by mechanical rules was an invention of the Atomists who sought an explanation of change in what Aristotle later called 'efficient causation' – the temporal relationship between the occurrence of a particular event, action, or creation and the antecedent, contingent circumstances. Aristotle was not satisfied that such explanations could be complete. His grand synthesis of Greek natural philosophy incorporated Plato's emphasis on the rational and purposive character of human action in an organic conception of the whole of 'Nature.' For Aristotle, all natural phenomena found their ultimate explanation in the goal or ends to which they aim, the reason for which events happen and things exist. Thus, natural vertical motion in the terrestrial sphere reflected the drive of the four elements (earth, water, air, and fire) to find their proper places relative to one another. In physics, this teleological conception of 'Nature' was brought to an abrupt end by Galileo and Newton's law of inertia: natural motion has nothing to do with goals, purposes, or 'final causes.' It is indistinguishable from a state of rest. Similarly a force can be described in purely mechanical terms, and its 'origin' or 'cause' is irrelevant in any scientific sense. Indeed the exact symmetry between action and reaction expressed in Newton's third law disallows the production of any effectively isolated force which might intervene in mechanical processes as a 'final cause' in the Aristotelian sense.

Aristotle's two most basic principles, the division of the cosmos into the terrestrial and celestial spheres, and his principle of teleology, were both thoroughly repudiated in the revolution that gave rise to modern science. With his laws of motion and gravitation, Newton was able to reduce the Aristotelian 'natural' motions of both terrestrial and celestial bodies to a single mechanical form. However, this unification of the description of the Cosmos in terms of universal principles had a cost. The 'real' material world described by the natural sciences was now severed from the 'subjective' world of appearances and could only be apprehended in terms of externally imposed rational principles. By way of contrast, tribal cultures like the Maori of Aotearoa feel no need of unifying the plurality of experience through the formal exercise of logical argument. All the particulars of differentiated experience are taken to be anchored to physical reality by virtue of their momentary temporal instantiation, rather than through the manifestation of mathematical relationships between quantities that must be forced into consciousness by application of abstract reasoning. In Maori epistemology, the anchoring of experience in the unity of physical reality is guaranteed by the successive layers of *whakapapa*.

With the advent of Darwin's theory of evolution, the last bastion of purposeful, teleological agency outside the reach of science was assigned to mechanical causes. Biological structure and function themselves came to be viewed as results of natural selection – the process of reproductive competition among genetic variants within interacting populations. Evolutionary theory appears to provide an epistemological bridge between *matauranga* and science by enabling a comparison to be made between the concept of phylogenetic descent and that of *whakapapa*. On closer inspection, however, one perceives the superficial nature of this resemblance, beneath which lies an impassable chasm created by the exclusion from evolutionary theory of any explanation in any terms other than material and contingent. For Maori, life cannot be reduced to some material mechanism. It is the expression of an immaterial principle of agency that is ultimately divine: *mauri*. Hence *whakapapa* cannot be viewed as an incidental historical succession derived from independent, randomly occurring events.

In the twentieth century the investigation of organisms, their parts, products, and processes, based on physical principles alone, has deepened this intellectual rift between science and other systems of knowledge. By reducing all analysis to empirical questions of material constituents and interactions, and the relative frequency of different categories of events, molecular biology has precluded any critical discussion of its metaphysical foundations or completeness. In its most extreme form (Dawkins 1976, 1982), genetic reductionism defines an organism as nothing but a material vehicle which happens, in its historically imposed milieu, to optimize the rate of reproduction of the DNA it carries. Whole organisms exist not for their own ends, or for that of the social group they are part of, but merely to out-compete other organisms and so maximize the spread of their own genes. In this view, at every level whether it be molecules, organisms, or ecosystems, the biological characteristics of entities can be explained in only two ways: either they are the direct expression of genetic information encoded in extant DNA or they are incidental contingencies that have no relevant cause.

To end this account of scientific epistemology here would be to suggest that there is no hope of rapprochement between it and other knowledge traditions. Quite recently, however, and starting from premises quite independent of those behind the successes of molecular biology, there has been a serious challenge to the assumption that all scientific explanation must be in terms of elementary material mechanisms, especially explanations pertaining to systems as complex as those studied in biology. It has been demonstrated theoretically and experimentally that systems comprised of large numbers of components with very simple properties can display dynamic behavior of enormous complexity that often appears to be virtually independent of any of the fine details of the mechanics of their material constituents (Kauffman 1993). These studies of 'complex systems' have led to the realization that the concept of autonomous agents is foreign to science as we know it and that a different approach to the study of biological systems is required if some common intuitions about organisms are ever to be formalized in a scientifically satisfactory manner (Kauffman 1996, Kay & Schneider 1994, Lovelock 1979). Such ideas reveal much in common with those of more traditional knowledge systems.

At this point biology is confronted with the mind-body problem posed by Descartes' separation of the objective world of 'Nature' and the subjective world of experience. Although this question has generally been left to the domain of computational theory and the field of 'artificial intelligence,' recent work on complexity in formal systems in which the definition of an entity as an object or an action is purely arbitrary (cf. Fontana & Buss 1996) has shown that there is no necessary inconsistency between the existence of material mechanism and autonomous causal agency.

Discussion

In one of the few comparative studies of traditional knowledge systems and Western science, Horton (1967) cautions that anyone embarking on this quest should not be blinded by differences of idiom. Beyond and beneath the subjective:objective, natural:supernatural, holistic:reductionist dichotomies so frequently used to differentiate science from traditional knowledge systems, lie fundamental cognitive properties common to the worldviews of all human societies, but expressed and communicated in culturally different ways. Horton selected a number of general attributes he considered to be fundamental to all epistemologies. The first of these was that

(1) the quest for explanatory theory is basically the quest for unity underlying apparent diversity; for simplicity underlying apparent complexity; for order underlying apparent disorder; for regularity underlying apparent anomaly (op. cit., pp. 50-1).

One manifestation of this common attribute of diverse epistemologies is revealed in the universally shared property of biological classification, or 'folk taxonomies' (Atran 1990). Maori philosophers extend this property from living things to the entire universe, conceiving of it as a vast genealogy or *whakapapa* incorporating and transcending space as well as time. In this way *whakapapa* provides a grand, unifying framework for understanding the origin and appearance of regularity in the entire universe, one that in the process unites biological with social and cultural order. Knowledge (as *wananga* and *matauranga*) associated with this order requires understandings derived from all sources open to human perception: subjective as well as objective. Hence, Maori epistemology is based on a view of the world in which the unifying ontological principle is *whakapapa* (manifesting *mauri* and *wairua*) rather than matter (driven by mechanism). Manifestations of *mauri* and *wairua* arise as a result of influences and 'laws' whose meaning cannot be expressed in terms of pure mechanism or contingency. It is tempting to make a comparison with the Western concept of teleology, but any 'purpose' apparent in the unraveling of Maori *whakapapa* is driven by knowledge of the past, rather than being directed towards some future goal. For this reason it is sometimes said that Maori are a people who walk backwards into the future, meaning that it is the deeds of the ancestors (real and mythical) that control and guide the present generation and help determine the fate of future generations.

It is interesting to speculate why *whakapapa* should provide the basis for the Maori worldview. The utilization of genealogy as the repository of knowledge and dominant mode of epistemological discourse might be explained by the comparatively recent history of the peoples of the Pacific. Polynesian ancestors of the Maori arrived in the central Pacific (Fiji, Tonga, Samoa) around 3000 years ago, while Aotearoa/New Zealand was reached only about 1000 years ago – the last major land mass in the world to be settled by humans (Roberts 1991). As the appendices demonstrate, it is well within the capabilities of living descendants to memorize genealogies of this comparatively short duration, back to the founding *waka* (canoes) that brought the ancestors to the islands of Aotearoa. The importance placed on the maintenance of this orally

Figure 4.3 Two *taniwha* (sea or freshwater monsters) who act as *kaitiaki* (guardians) of their domain, appropriately protecting or punishing those who enter it.

recorded and transmitted history may have resulted in *whakapapa* providing the cognitive framework for ordering and classifying the entire phenomenal world, and also for developing theories about knowledge. Place appears to play a secondary role in the cognitive processes underlying Maori knowledge and becomes significant in matters specific to a particular tribe, hence its knowledge is more local in content.

This suggestion is consistent with the absence of genealogy as a primary epistemological template among more ancient peoples (e.g. Aboriginal Australians and Native North Americans). Instead, in these cultures, place more often constitutes an original repository of knowledge, with names and rituals associated with place acting as powerful mnemonics for the recalling and transmission of knowledge. As Whitt (1996, p. 1) explains, when a Cherokee medicine man dies and is buried, his knowledge too is returned to the land. There it resides for others to experience. Among the Dineh, so symbiotic is this relationship between knowledge and place that to relocate is unthinkable, and so their language contains no such word. Hence, 'to move away means to disappear, never to be seen again' (ibid.). Similar associations with the land are also fundamental to the worldview of Australian aboriginals. Entire features of the landscape were brought into being through the activities of mythological ancestors during the creative period known as the 'dreaming' (Berndt & Berndt 1977). Natural as well as supernatural linkages between these places continue to form physical and cultural networks across a particular tribe's country. Through the enactment of particular rituals such as song cycles, these networks are 'sung into being' and so the past becomes one with the present; the mythical with the actual.

Whakapapa as a theoretical construct also satisfies Horton's second and third propositions, i.e., that

theory places things in a causal context wider than that provided by common sense, [and that] common sense and theory have complementary roles in everyday life (Horton 1967, pp. 53, 58).

His fourth criterion (the ability of theory to vary with context) was clearly understood by Maori, both in the division of knowledge into 'everyday' and more esoteric categories, as well as in the use of metaphor to create many layers of meaning appropriate to the situation and to the person. This should not lead to the conclusion that the information conveyed in each context varied; the causal relationship between *whakapapa* and *wananga*, derived from the gods, must always be consistent and non-contradictory, and hence *tika* (Hohepa, personal communication).

Whakapapa also provides the vehicle whereby the criterion for Horton's fifth proposition is met, i.e., the ability of theory to abstract, examine, and then re-integrate. The widespread use of personification and of organic analogies by Maori, including their selective application to objects of particular relevance satisfies his propositions six and seven, and in the process amply fulfills Horton's claim that

> all theories take their departure from the world of things and people, and ultimately return us to it. In this context, to say that a good theory reduces something to something else is misleading. Ideally, a process of deduction from the premises of a theory should lead us back to statements which portray the common sense world in its full richness. In so far as this richness is not restored, by so much does theory fail (ibid., p. 155).

Concurring with Horton's analysis, we find that for all seven aspects considered, Maori knowledge, as well as the African traditional religious belief systems he studied, contain theoretical models that have much in common with modern science for understanding and explaining all manner of phenomena. However, in Part II of his study Horton focuses on what he calls the 'closed' and 'open' predicaments, i.e., that

> in traditional cultures there is no developed awareness of alternatives to the established body of theoretical tenets; whereas in scientifically orientated cultures, such an awareness is highly developed (op. cit., p. 155).

Put another way, traditional knowledge systems are said to be opposed to alternative views, challenge, and change, and they actively punish error or deviation from the established doctrine. Science, on the other hand, it is claimed, actively solicits challenge (tests) of established theories and constantly seeks their improvement or replacement by alternatives if they are shown to be in error. In reality this 'openness' often falls short of the ideal (cf. Collins & Pinch 1993). There are subtle systems of authority that operate in the scientific community to suppress challenge and to bolster a particular theory by determining the 'correct' interpretation of large bodies of experimental data for long periods of time. The distinction between 'open' science and 'closed' traditional knowledge systems is thus blurred on both sides of the supposed boundary. Both are vulnerable to the active repression of contrary ideas and to the proliferation of alternative hypotheses to explain anomalous results. For example, explication of Maori knowledge may involve different categories of discourse including *te pae-a-waha* in which information is freely available; *te pare-a-waha*, in which information is partially concealed, and *tautohetohe*. In the last mentioned, knowledge is subjected to the test of debate and argument, and by this means is verified or corrected (Haami, in prep.). Encouragement of such debate concerning differences in interpretation provides for the expression by orators (and through them each tribe) of their own individuality and *mana* (prestige). This relativism of tribal knowledge assisted Maori to respond positively to the challenge of colonization and literacy whereby selected aspects of an alternative worldview were woven into the fabric of their own cultural

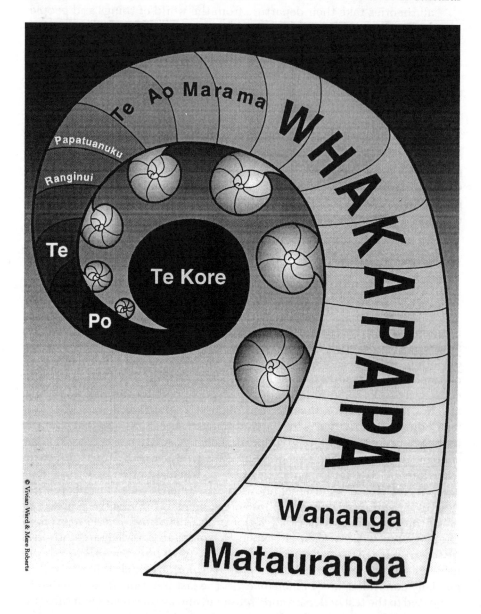

© Vivian Ward & Mere Roberts

Figure 4.4 Maori epistemology conceptualized ontologically as a spiral or coil (*koru*) analogous to the unfolding frond of a tree fern (*ponga*), e.g. the mamaku *Cyathea medullaris*.[4]

paradigm without destroying the underlying pattern and process. Thus, the Maori worldview has always been characteristically dynamic and open to challenge and to change, all without relinquishing its unique epistemological foundation. In this, and yet another way – that of *whakapapa* conceived as a 'phylogeny of the universe' – Maori knowledge qualifies as an 'open' system in that it has the potential to incorporate completely new and previously undefined categories of phenomena. Only when *whakapapa* descends to the particular, to the tribal, and hence to place, does it become local and, apparently, 'closed.'

There are, however, some other aspects of Maori knowledge (especially *wananga*) in which, by virtue of its traditional restriction to a chosen few, it can be classified as 'closed.' But in this sense a great deal of science is also 'closed.' Blanket restrictions are frequently placed on the availability of scientific information by commercial enterprises or military institutions. Moreover, these restrictions, upheld by legal processes at both national and international levels, are used by different sectors of society as a means of gaining and maintaining advantage over others. Ziman (1996) traces the problem to the heart of the scientific endeavor in its departure from traditional academic values, recognizing that what counts as scientific knowledge at any given moment is obviously influenced by the way in which research is organised:

> Research results that an academic scientist would have published immediately are being identified as 'intellectual property' which may be kept secret for commercial reasons. In other words post-academic science may no longer be so committed to the principle of 'public knowledge' – traditionally the linchpin of academic science (op. cit., p. 752).

In the process, science itself has become primarily a method – 'a way of doing' rather than 'a way of seeing' – and no longer a field of philosophical inquiry. This leads back to the blurred distinction between 'open' and 'closed' knowledge systems in relation to their tolerance of alternatives. In clarification of this aspect, Roberts (1997) has suggested that the major disjunction between indigenous knowledge systems and Western science lies in the different functions they serve. Whitt (1995) expresses it this way:

> Central to the beliefs of many cultures of indigenous North America is the conviction that knowing and valuing are interdependent; they are implicated or embedded in one another. As processes that mutually inform, and are informed by, each other, they constitute a single, integrated system (op. cit., p. 240).

Likewise, the Maori worldview is overtly value-laden: its purpose is not simply to provide 'neutral' or unbiased information that individuals are then free to

65

interpret and use as they see fit. Instead it seeks to impart those values that provide the moral and ethical guidelines for the entire society, and thereby keep the world intact. Knowledge is not the sole property of humans: other animals, plants and inanimate things are also repositories of knowledge, to which access may be gained only through appropriate ritual, dreams, or visions. Respect is inherent in this belief, and it extends to learning: knowledge is not a right but a reward for respectful behavior. Hence

> the integration of the processes of knowing and valuing leads to ... knowledge that is transformative rather than acquisitive. To know is not to increase one's holdings of true facts about external reality, but to enhance one's relations with the natural world by learning about how to live well within it, in a manner that acknowledges and respects the essential interdependence of human and non-human. Such knowledge is experientially based in the fullest sense – integrating and involving all that one is (op. cit., p. 249).

Traditional thought then has concerned itself not with establishing rules of logic and the norms governing reasoning and knowing, but instead with the development of contextually relevant explanatory theories (expounded as narratives), and by means of these, the inculcation of culturally defined values and rules of conduct. In contrast, science proudly proclaims to be value-free, and to provide strictly objective knowledge, unbiased by culture, gender, geographical, political, or other influences. Paradoxically, this epistemological prescription of science is probably the most restrictive that has ever formed the kernel of a functional corpus of knowledge in any society. Most scientists would say that these restrictions give the only 'correct' or 'true' representation of 'Nature.' But what proves by observation, a posteriori, to be 'correct' is guaranteed as much by the a priori choice of the manner in which features of the world are observed and manipulated as by some absolutely immutable quality of 'Nature.'

One consequence of this worldview which, as laid down in ancient Greece, has never required processes of social or political sanction, is that modern techniques in molecular biology can be used to manipulate and modify organisms and genes in purely material terms, according to individual whim and for commercial gain (Wills 1994). In practice, however, the epistemological claims of science have been readily challenged on each of the above grounds. Despite these differences, it is possible, as we have explained, to find much in common between Western science and the knowledge systems of other cultures. Concepts such as *whakapapa*, which acts at different levels to provide a taxonomic framework, a source of logic, and the rules for knowing provide support for Horton's (1967) claim that

> the goals of explanation and prediction are as powerfully present in

traditional ... cultures as they are in cultures where science has become institutionalised (op. cit., p. 162).

Conclusion

Our major aim in this chapter was to present an understanding of Maori epistemology from the perspective of scientists engaged in teaching indigenous worldviews (namely, that of the peoples of the Pacific) alongside that of Western science. In so doing, we hope to have highlighted what seems to us to be the unique contribution of Maori knowledge to human understandings of the natural world and beyond, i.e., the concept of *whakapapa* as a template for knowledge. This conception of the whole of reality as a continuous unfolding of vital generative processes, rather than as mechanical occurrences within inert material substance, is irreconcilable with most of modern science. However, the Maori worldview contains the seeds of a more sustainable relationship between humanity and the world that science studies. Assimilation of conceptions like *whakapapa* and *mauri* into science would make it no longer possible, especially in biology, to separate questions of science and ethics. The continuity of relationships and processes that constitute *whakapapa* carry intrinsic obligations, manifest not only in tribal society as mores of kinship, but in the responsibilities of humans to all other living and non-living descendants of Papatuanuku.

The rift in Western science that separates the concepts of mechanism and causal agency precludes any meaningful incorporation of a vast body of traditional knowledge that might otherwise have a significance comparable with that of mainstream science. We accept that a single chapter in an anthology will hardly serve to initiate a revolution in Western thought that can facilitate a rapprochement of worldviews whose fundamental differences span a 2,500 year history. However, if the rigorous reduction of all experience to descriptions in terms of events within the material world were regarded as a limitation of science, rather than as a necessary precondition for reliable knowledge, we believe science would have much to gain. Only if a proper bridge can be built within Western thought to reconnect mechanistic explanations with subjective interpretations of experience will there be any opportunity for the epistemologies of Maori, or of other indigenous peoples, to be afforded their rightful place in the modern world. In Aotearoa/New Zealand, reasoning motivated by considerations in which *whakapapa* and *mauri* are central has recently been afforded legal recognition in the area of resource management and environmental sustainability. It would not be inappropriate that by such means Maori and other traditional worldviews achieve acceptance by, and accommodation within, the Western scientific paradigm.

Notes

Roma Mere Roberts would like to acknowledge the debt owed to her late mother, Roma Melvern, who taught her the importance and the implications of *whakapapa*. She also thanks the Association of Commonwealth Universities for a Development Fellowship in 1995. Peter Wills wishes to acknowledge his late father, Norman, and the work he did (Wills 1992) to record the genealogy and history of his migrant Pakeha family and their peaceful partnership with *tangata whenua* in Taranaki. Both authors would like to acknowledge the Centre for Pacific Studies at the University of Auckland which provided them with an opportunity to extend their academic and personal horizons to knowledge systems beyond Western science.

1.   Salmond uses an abbreviated and edited version of the original Taylor (1855) manuscript, with her own translation in preference to that of Taylor.
2.   Meanings additional to the literal English translations are indicated in parentheses.
3.   Patu Hohepa is Professor of Maori Studies at Te Whare Wananga o Tamaki Makaurau (University of Auckland).
4.   As each frond unfolds it 're-enacts' the creation of the universe, i.e., commencing with nothingness (*Te Kore*), thought comes first, then spirit and last of all, matter (Best 1924, pp. 61, 71). In the Paki o Matariki (the coat of arms of the Maori King Movement), a double spiral is used to represent the creation (Hurinui 1960, pp. 231-2). Used in carving, the spiral symbolises 'latent and potential energy, the life principle, light and enlightment' (Department of Maori Studies 1988, p. 19), a notion equally applicable to knowledge.

Bibliography

Atran, Scott (1990), *Cognitive Foundations of Natural History: Towards an Anthropology of Science*, Cambridge University Press: New York.

Berndt, Ronald M. and Berndt, Catherine H. (1977), *The World of the First Australians*, Ure Smith: Sydney.

Best, Elsdon (1982), 'Maori Religion and Mythology, Being An Account of the Cosmogony, Anthropogeny, Religious Beliefs and Rites, Magic and Folk Lore of the Maori Folk of New Zealand,' Part 2, *Dominion Museum Bulletin*, No. 11, P. D. Hasselberg: Wellington.

— (1924), 'Maori Religion and Mythology, Being An Account of the Cosmogony, Anthropogeny, Religious Beliefs and Rites, Magic and Folk Lore of the Maori Folk of New Zealand,' Part 1, *Dominion Museum Bulletin*, No. 10, W. A. G. Skinner: Wellington.

— (1923), 'The Maori School of Learning: Its Objects, Methods, and

Ceremonial,' *Dominion Museum Monograph*, No. 6, W. A. G. Skinner: Wellington.

— (1922), 'The Astronomical Knowledge of the Maori, Genuine and Empirical: Including Data Concerning their Systems of Astrogeny, Astrolatry, and Natural Astrology, with Notes on Certain other Natural Phenomena' *Dominion Museum Monograph*, No. 3, W. A. G. Skinner: Wellington.

Collins, Harry M. and Pinch, Trevor (1993), *The Golem: What Everyone Should Know about Science*, Cambridge University Press: New York.

Cornford, Francis M. (1912), *From Religion to Philosophy: A Study in the Origins of Western Speculation*, Edward Arnold Ltd.: London.

Dawkins, Richard (1982), *The Extended Phenotype: The Gene as the Unit of Selection*, W. H. Freman: San Francisco.

— (1976), *The Selfish Gene*, Oxford University Press: New York.

Department of Maori Studies, eds (1988), *Tane-nui-a-Rangi*, University Printing Services: Auckland.

Feyerabend, Paul (1993), *Against Method*, Verso: London.

Fontana, Walter and Buss, Leo W. (1996), 'The Barrier of Objects: From Dynamical Systems to Bounded Organizations,' in John L. Casti and Anders Karlqvist (eds), *Boundaries and Barriers: On the Limits to Scientific Knowledge*, pp. 56-116, Addison-Wesley: Reading.

Haami, Bradford Teapatuoterangi (n.d.), Putea Whakairo, manuscript, 86 pages.

Heidegger, Martin (1975), *Early Greek Thinking*, trans David F. Krell and Frank A. Capuzzi, Harper & Row: New York.

Horton, Robin (1967), African Traditional Thought and Western Science Parts I and II, Africa Vol. 37, No.1, pp. 50-71, 155-87.

Howe, Gwen P. and Howe George (1983), *From Kent to Kawhia: The Cowell Story*, W. J. Deed Printing Ltd.: Waiuku.

Hurinui, Pei Te (1960), *King Potatau: An Account of the Life of Potatau Te Wherowhero, the First Maori King*, The Polynesian Society: Auckland.

Jones, Pei Te Hurinui and Biggs, Bruce (1995), *Nga Iwi o Tainui: The Traditional History of the Tainui People*, Auckland University Press: Auckland.

Kuhn, Thomas (1962), *The Structure of Scientific Revolutions*, University of Chicago Press: Chicago.

Kauffman, Stuart A. (1996), 'Investigations: The Nature of Autonomous Agents and theWorlds They Mutually Create,' Working Paper 96-08-072, http://www.santafe.edu/sfi/People/kauffman/Investigations.html, 13 September, The Santa Fe Institute: Santa Fe.

— (1993), *The Origins of Order: Self-Organization and Selection in Evolution*, Oxford University Press: New York.

Kay, James J. and Schneider, Eric (1994), 'Embracing Complexity: The Challenge of the Ecosystem Approach,' *Alternatives*, Vol. 20, No. 3, pp. 32-9.

Lewis, David (1975), *We, the Navigators: The Ancient Art of Landfinding in the Pacific*, Australian National University Press: Canberra.

Lovelock, James E. (1979), *Gaia: A New Look at Life on Earth*, Oxford University Press: New York.

Marsden, Maori (1981), 'God, Man and Universe: A Maori View,' in Michael King (ed.), *Te Ao Hurihuri: The World Moves On*, pp. 142-63, Longman Paul: Auckland.

Marsden, Maori and Henare, Te Aroha (1992), *Kaitiakitanga: A Definitive Introduction to the Holistic World View of the Maori*, unpublished manuscript, 26 pages, Department of Maori Studies Library, University of Auckland: Auckland.

Morrison, John; Geraghty, Paul and Crowl, Linda (1994), *Science of the Pacific Island Peoples*, Vols 1-4, Institute of Pacific Studies, University of the South Pacific: Suva.

Norman, Waerete (1988), *Evidence of Waerete Violet Beatrice Norman Ma in Respect of Claim to Wharo Oneroa A Toke (Ninety-Mile Beach)*, unpublished document presented as evidence to The Waitangi Tribunal hearing in the matter of the Treaty of Waitangi Act 1975, File # Wai 45.

Roberts, M. (1997), 'Indigenous Knowledge and Western Science: Perspectives from the Pacific,' in Derek Hodson (ed.), *Science and Technology Education and Ethnicity: An Aotearoa/New Zealand Perspective*, pp. 59-75, The Royal Society of New Zealand: Wellington.

— (1994), 'Can and How Should Disparate Knowledge Systems be Worked Together?' in David Turnbull and Helen Watson-Verran (eds), *Working Disparate Knowledge Systems Together*, Sciences in Society Working Papers, Second Series No. 15, pp. 45-55, Deakin University: Victoria.

— (1991), 'Origin, Dispersal Routes, and Geographic Distribution of *Rattus exulans*, with Special Reference to New Zealand,' *Pacific Science*, Vol. 45, No. 2, April, pp. 123-30.

Roberts, Mere; Norman, Waerete; Minhinnick, Nganeko; Wihongi, Del and Kirkwood, Carmen (1995), 'Kaitiakitanga: Maori Perspectives on Conservation,' *Pacific Conservation Biology*, Vol. 2, No. 1, August, pp. 7-20.

Salmond, Anne (1985), 'Maori Epistemologies,' in Joanna Overing (ed.), *Reason and Morality*, pp. 240-63, Tavistock: London.

— (1982), 'Theoretical Lanscapes: On Cross-Cultural Conceptions of Knowledge,' in David Parkin (ed.), *Semantic Anthropology*, A. S. A. Monograph 22, pp. 65-87, Academic Press: New York.

Schwimmer, Eric (1966), The World of the Maori, A.H. & A. W. Reed, Wellington.

Shortland, Edward (1856), *Traditions and Superstitions of the New Zealanders*, Longman, Brown, Green, Longmans & Roberts: London.

Sutton, Douglas G. (1994), *The Origins of the First New Zealanders*, Auckland University Press: Auckland.

Taylor, Rev. Richard (1855), *Te Ika a Maui, Or New Zealand and Its Inhabitants*, Wertheim and Macintosh: London.

Turnbull, David (1994), *Cartography and Science: Mapping the Construction of Knowledge Spaces*, Sciences in Society Working Papers, Second Series, No. 4, Deakin University Press, Victoria, Australia.

— (1991), *Mapping the World in the Mind: An Investigation of the Unwritten Knowledge of the Micronesian Navigators*, Deakin University Press: Victoria.

Walker, Ranginui J. (1993), *A Paradigm of the Maori View of Reality*, unpublished paper presented at the David Nichol Seminar IX: Voyages and Beaches: Discovery and the Pacific 1700-1840, Auckland, 24 August 1993, 19 pages, 10 appendices.

Whitt, Laurie A. (1996), *Metaphor and Power in Indigenous and Western Knowledge Systems*, Paper presented at the Conference on Narrative and Metaphor Across the Disciplines, University of Auckland, Auckland, New Zealand July 1996, 19 pages.

— (1995), 'Indigenous Peoples and the Cultural Politics of Knowledge,' in Michael K. Green (ed.), *Issues in Native American Cultural Identity*, pp. 223-71, Peter Lang: New York.

Wills, Norman W. (1992), *A Good West Country Name: James and Betsy Wills's Family in New Zealand*, Priority Press Limited: Hamilton.

Wills, Peter R. (1994), 'Correcting Evolution: Biotechnology's Unfortunate Agenda,' *Revue Internationale de Systémique*, Vol. 8, No. 4-5, pp. 455-68.

Ziman, John (1996), 'Is Science Losing its Objectivity?' *Nature*, Vol. 382, No. 6594, August, pp. 751-4.

Appendix 1

The genealogies (*whakapapa*) shown in this appendix include both metaphysical lineages [(a), (b), (c), and part of (d) adopted from Hurinui (1960, pp. 257-64)] and physical lineages [remainder of (d) from Hurinui (ibid.), and (e) adopted from Howe & Howe (1983, p. 27)]. Taken together, they serve to demonstrate that all Maori are directly descended from the Creator; as are all other things animate and inanimate. Hence all things are related, and of both divine and material substance.

A Deistic, Cosmogonic, and Anthropogonic Whakapapa of the Cosmos

(a) Te Aho Tuatahi (The First Strand): The Genealogy of Io

Te Kore	The Formless Void
Kotahi Te Ki	The One Unspoken Thought
Kotahi Te Korero	The One Spoken Word
Kotahi Te Wananga	The One Sacred Assembly
Te Kore Whiwhia	The Intangible Formless Void
Te Kore Makiki Hi Rere	The Formless Void pierced by a Line extending into Space
Makaka	The Sacred Curve
Io	The Supreme Being

The Nights (*Nga Po*), or Epochal Periods, during which *Io* evolved through these eight stages were called: *Te Po ka ura* (the night that glowed), *Te Po uriuri*, (the dark green night), *Te Po kakara uri* (the night that faintly gleamed), *Te Po aoao nui* (the night with the aroma of sprouting things), *Te Po kerekere* (the night of intense darkness), *Te Po tamaku* (the creation night).

Then, with the appearance of Io, came *Te Aio nuku* (the widespread calm). Io dwelt in harmony for countless ages during the Epochal Period called *Te Aio nuku* until the coming of the Night (Po), or Epochal Period called *Te Po tiwhatiwha* (the gleaming night) which heralded the appearance of *Te Whetu* (the world of stars).

(b) Te Aho Tuarua (The Second Strand): The Genealogy of the World of Stars

Io

Te Whetu The World of Stars

The World of Suns	Te Ra	=	Tau Ana Te Marama Floating Moons
The Big Universe	Ao Nui	=	Te Po Nui The Big Night
The Far-flung Universe	Ao Roa	=	Te Po Roa The Far-flung Night
The Bitterly Cold Universe	Ao Papa Kina	=	Te Po Papa Kina The Bitterly Cold Night
The Shattered and Expanding Universe	Ao Pako Rea	=	Te Po Pako Rea The Shattered and Expanding Night
The Separated Universe	Ao Ki Tua	=	Te Po Ki Tua The Separated Night
The Inward-striving Universe	Ao Ki Roto	=	Te Po Ki Roto The Inward-striving Night
The Remote Universe	Ao Ki Tawhiti	=	Te Po Ki Tawhiti The Remote Night
The Brooding Universe	Ao Ruru	=	Te Po Ruru The Brooding Night
The Becalmed Universe	Ao Aio	=	Te Po Aio The Becalmed Night
The Reddened Universe	Ao Whero	=	Te Po Whero The Reddened Night
The Whitened Universe	Ao Ma	=	Te Po Ma The Whitened Night
The Blackened Universe	Ao Pango	=	Te Po Pango The Blackened Night
The Budding Universe	Ao Whakarito	=	Te Po Whakarito The Budding Night
The Perplexed Universe	Ao Kumea	=	Te Po Kumea The Perplexed Night
The Ascending Universe	Ao Ki Runga	=	Te Po Ki Runga The Ascending Night
The Descending Universe	Ao Ki Raro	=	Te Po Ki Raro The Descending Night
The Universe turning Right	Ao Ki Katau	=	Te Po Ki Katau The Night turning Right
The Universe turning Left	Ao Ki Maui	=	Te Po Ki Maui The Night turning Left
The Great Sky that stands Above	Te Rangi Nui E Tu Iho Nei	=	Papa Tu A Nuku The Earth that lies Beneath

73

(c) Te Aho Tuatoeu (The Third Strand): The Genealogy of Human Beings

The Sky Father	Ranginui — Papatuanuku	The Earth Mother

| The Grim visaged Tu, god of War and Man | *Tumatauenga — Hineahuone | The Earth-formed Maid |

The Unfortunate One	Aitua
The Surprised Unfortunate One	Aitu Ere
The Enfeebled Unfortunate One	Aitu Kikini
The Deranged Unfortunate One	Aitu Tamaki
The Restored Unfortunate One	Aitu Whakatika
The Flaccid One	Te Kore
The Deeply Flaccid One	Te Kore Nui
The Long-suffering Flaccid One	Te Kore Roa
The Sapless Flaccid One	Te Kore Para
The Destitute Flaccid One	Te Kore Whiwhia
The Flaccid One destined for the Realms of Night	Te Kore Te Oti Atu Ki Te Po
The Striving One	Ngana
The Renowned Striving One	Ngana Nui
The Long-striving One	Ngana Roa
The Impetuous Striving One	Ngana Ruru
The Languid Striving One	Ngana Maoe
He with the urge to Conquer	Hotu Wai Ariki
The Questioning One	Tapatai
The Purposeful One	Tiki
The Purposeful One of the Front Pillar	Tiki Te Pou Mua
The Purposeful One of the Inner Pillar	Tiki Te Pou Roto
The Purposeful One of the Origin	Tiki Ahu Mai I Hawaiki
The Evil-spirited One	Whirotetupua
The Jaded and Tingling One	Toi
The Incoherent One	Hatonga
The Adorned and Exuberant One	Rakeiora
The Unsettled One	Tahatiti
The Son with the Heavenly Urge	Tamakiterangi
The Conquered and Evil-smelling One	Piro

* in some tribal whakapapa, Tanenuiarangi is said to be the progenitor of human beings.

| The Consumer of Man | Kaitangata — Whaitiri or Whatitiri | The Goddess of Thunder |

74

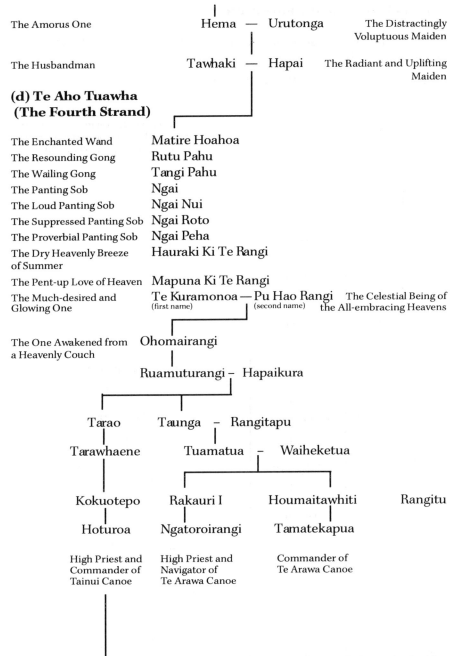

	Hema — Urutonga	
The Amorus One		The Distractingly Voluptuous Maiden
The Husbandman	Tawhaki — Hapai	The Radiant and Uplifting Maiden

(d) Te Aho Tuawha (The Fourth Strand)

The Enchanted Wand	Matire Hoahoa
The Resounding Gong	Rutu Pahu
The Wailing Gong	Tangi Pahu
The Panting Sob	Ngai
The Loud Panting Sob	Ngai Nui
The Suppressed Panting Sob	Ngai Roto
The Proverbial Panting Sob	Ngai Peha
The Dry Heavenly Breeze of Summer	Hauraki Ki Te Rangi
The Pent-up Love of Heaven	Mapuna Ki Te Rangi

The Much-desired and Glowing One   Te Kuramonoa — Pu Hao Rangi   The Celestial Being of
                  (first name)   (second name)   the All-embracing Heavens

The One Awakened from   Ohomairangi
a Heavenly Couch

Ruamuturangi – Hapaikura

Tarao	Taunga – Rangitapu		
Tarawhaene	Tuamatua – Waiheketua		
Kokuotepo	Rakauri I	Houmaitawhiti	Rangitu
Hoturoa	Ngatoroirangi	Tamatekapua	
High Priest and Commander of Tainui Canoe	High Priest and Navigator of Te Arawa Canoe	Commander of Te Arawa Canoe	

Note: The Tainui and Arawa canoes left Hawaiiki (the ancestral homeland – probably Raiatea in the Society Group, French Polynesia) circa 1000 A. D. for Aotearoa.

(e) Whakapapa of the First Author

Persons marked with an asterix are females. Tainui subtribal affiliations are noted in parentheses.

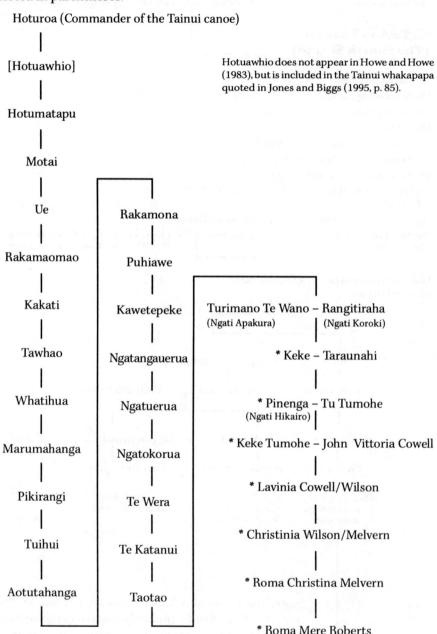

Hoturoa (Commander of the Tainui canoe)

[Hotuawhio]

Hotuawhio does not appear in Howe and Howe (1983), but is included in the Tainui whakapapa quoted in Jones and Biggs (1995, p. 85).

Hotumatapu

Motai

Ue   Rakamona

Rakamaomao   Puhiawe

Kakati   Kawetepeke   Turimano Te Wano – Rangitiraha
    (Ngati Apakura)   (Ngati Koroki)

Tawhao   Ngatangauerua   * Keke – Taraunahi

Whatihua   Ngatuerua   * Pinenga – Tu Tumohe
    (Ngati Hikairo)

Marumahanga   Ngatokorua   * Keke Tumohe – John Vittoria Cowell

Pikirangi   Te Wera   * Lavinia Cowell/Wilson

Tuihui   Te Katanui   * Christinia Wilson/Melvern

Aotutahanga   Taotao   * Roma Christina Melvern

     * Roma Mere Roberts

Appendix 2

Whakapapa of the Children of Ranginui and Papatuanuku

(abbreviated; naming only some of the seventy or more demigods and their offspring)

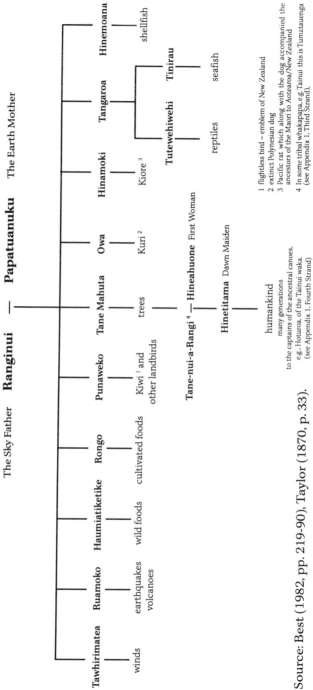

Ranginui — **Papatuanuku**

The Sky Father — The Earth Mother

| Tawhirimatea | Ruamoko | Haumiatiketike | Rongo | Punaweko | Tane Mahuta | Owa | Hinamoki | Tangaroa | Hinemoana |
| winds | earthquakes volcanoes | wild foods | cultivated foods | Kiwi [1] and other landbirds | trees | Kuri [2] | Kiore [3] | | shellfish |

Tangaroa branch:
- Tutewehiwehi — reptiles
- Tinirau — seafish

Tane-nui-a-Rangi [4] — Hineahuone First Woman

Hinetitama Dawn Maiden

Tane Mahuta line:
humankind
many generations
to the captains of the ancestral canoes,
e.g. Hoturoa, of the Tainui waka.
(see Appendix 1, Fourth Strand)

1 flightless bird – emblem of New Zealand
2 extinct Polynesian dog
3 Pacific rat which along with the dog accompanied the ancestors of the Maori to Aotearoa/New Zealand
4 In some tribal whakapapa, e.g. Tainui this is Tumatauenga (see Appendix 1, Third Strand).

Source: Best (1982, pp. 219–90), Taylor (1870, p. 33).

5   Preconquest Consciousness

E Richard Sorenson

Precursory Considerations

Anthropology as an epistemological problem. Most anthropologists are aware that what comprise the standard habits, inclinations, and activities of humankind in one culture may seem quite exotic in another. When the separateness of peoples is extreme, incompatible modes of awareness and cognition sometimes arise, as occurred between the preconquest and postconquest eras of the world. Basic sensibilities, including sense-of-identity and sense-of-truth, were so contradistinctive in these two eras that they were irreconcilable. Even core features of life in one era were imperceptible to people in the other. While such disparate cognitive separation may be rare, a single occurrence is sufficient to make anthropology an epistemological problem.

Epistemology as an anthropological problem. Moreover, when irreconcilable modes of cognition emerge within humankind, it becomes more obvious that sense-of-truth is the product of mental evolution within a particular cultural framework. Epistemology may well be a noetic discipline, but it also emerged as a cultural phenomenon from the early Western process of civilization in the Mediterranean Basin. As a product of culture, it becomes a subject for anthropological inquiry.

The quandary. When epistemology and anthropology each become a problem of the other, an inquiry oscillation emerges that befuddles thought in direct proportion to one's adherence to these modes of inquiry. The existence of such a conundrum reveals the need for inquiries into truth that are not beholden to the sense-of-truth of any one particular culture.

The Preconquest Setting

The preconquest type of consciousness detailed below survives today only in a few, now rapidly vanishing, isolated enclaves. Although those we contacted were widely dispersed, they shared a distinctive type of consciousness – one very different from the postconquest type that dominates the world today. It emerged from a type of child and infant nurture common to that era but shunned in ours.

The outstanding demographic condition required for such a life is small populations surrounded by tracts of open territory into which anyone can diffuse virtually at will. This allows those discomfited by local circumstance, or attracted by conditions further on, to move as they wish with whoever might be similarly inclined. This was the case even in the smallest of all the preconquest enclaves seen. The outstanding social condition is a sociosensual type of infant and child nurture that spawns an intuitive group rapport and unites people without need for formal rules. The outstanding psychological condition is heart-felt rapprochement based on integrated trust. This provides remarkable efficiency in securing needs and responding to nature's challenges while dispensing ongoing delight with people and surroundings.[1] The outstanding economic condition is absence of private property, which allows constant cooperative usage of the implements and materials of life for collective benefit. The human ecology engendered by the interaction of these outstanding conditions makes the forcing of others (including children) to one's will a disruptive and unwholesome practice. It was not seen.

Any form of subjugation, even those barriers to freedom imposed by private property, are the kiss of death to this type of life. Though durable and self-repairing in isolation, the unconditional open trust this way of life requires shrivels with alarming speed when faced with harsh emotions or coercion. Deceit, hostility, and selfishness when only episodic temporarily benumb intuitive rapport. When such conditions come to stay and no escape is possible, intuitive rapport disintegrates within a brutally disorienting period of existential trauma and anomie. With no other models about except those of conquerors, a 'savage-savage' emerges from the wreckage of a once 'noble-savage.'[2] These more brutal beings adjust to the postconquest milieu by adopting formal group identities. First they internalize various abstract ideas of space, boundary, and kinship introduced by their conquerors. They then use them to anchor claims of their own to turf. They devise rules and customs that clearly identify them as a distinct people with formal rights. From this process different kinds of cultural elaboration emerge in separated regions – until a harsher level of conquest presses their uniqueness to extinction.

This preconquest type of life, and its transformation, came to light unsought and unexpectedly during a comparative study of child behavior and human development in cultural isolates. It was encountered among such peoples as: Neolithic hunter-gatherer-gardeners in the Central Range of New Guinea; pagan Sea Nomads in the Eastern Sea of Andaman off southern Burma and Thailand; maritime nomads in the Sulu Sea between Borneo and the Philippines; isolated ocean-going fisherfolk in southern India; nomadic hunter-gatherers in Tamil Nadu, India; subsistence agriculturists (Tharu and Tamang, but less so Jyapu) in Nepal; forest nomads (Sikai) in the interior mountains of the Malay Peninsula on the Malaysia-Thailand border; Negrito hunter-gatherer-gardeners in interior mountains of Negros Island in the Philippines; hunter-gatherer-gardeners (Mbotgate) in the central rainforests of Vanuatu's Malekula Island; nomadic Tibetan herders of the Changthang Plateau; subsistence Micronesian atoll dwellers in traditional outliers of the Western Caroline Islands, the remote Polynesian population on Ono-i-Lau; and in isolated American Indian enclaves in Mexico and South America. Vestigial aspects of preconquest life were seen in segregated urban ghettos in Asia and Oceania. Early accounts suggest that traditional Eskimos and many North American Indian tribes possessed similar traits. The Yequena Indians of Venezuela clearly did.[3]

Most groups seen were in secluded, obscure areas. Where governments were taking charge, the preconquest type of consciousness tended to survive only in isolated fringe refuges. In New Guinea, the type was seen in finest fettle in the remotest, most isolated clusters of hunter-gatherer-gardeners verging into vast regions of uninhabited virgin rainforest at the time of civilized contact. There, despite the seemingly incessant rain, the always densely saturated air, the insular remoteness, and the absence of anything resembling modern amenities or comfort, life exuded a most remarkable, on-the-mark intuitive helpfulness and a constant considerate regard by each for all the others. These extended not just to associates and friends but to strangers too. Long before we shared a single word of any common language (indeed, in my first hours there), these forest-dwellers had instinctively tuned in to my feelings and made life easier and happier for me.

Among the Canela Indians in Brazil, the relaxed sociosensual camaraderie characteristic of preconquest rapport was seen only in the remote agricultural outliers, away from the central village. This was so, as well, for the Sikai forest nomads in the central mountains of the Malay Peninsula. In the Andaman and Sulu Seas, empathetic intuitive rapport manifested in exquisite form only among Sea Nomads roaming remote areas of their reef and isle bespattered domain. Ensconced within archaic handhewn houseboats, they steadfastly and deliberately avoided areas breached by settlement or commerce. Empathetic, integrative, intuitive rapport manifested itself in particularly high form among those who carefully avoided regions penetrated by commerce and settlement as they circulated their nomadic domain. In the Himalayas (Nepal, Tibet, and Bhutan) it was most evident among small, isolated subsistence populations in remote regions that were difficult to access.

Preconquest regions were often fringed by intervening zones of mayhem and disorder, including warfare, piracy, extravagant sexuality, and brigandage.

81

Getting through to them was often dangerous.

Groups only lightly touched by aggressive cultures retained much of their basic sociosensual child nurture and instinctive intuitive rapport. These core traits declined as the force of conquest increased. In the face of sustained demanding contact, open sociosensuality largely disappeared from view, to reshape as a confined covert type (seen inside houses, at sea on boats, in obscure nooks, and in isolated social fringes). Where preconquest populations were unrelentingly besieged by harsh conquistadorial demands, intuitive rapport sometimes suddenly give way en masse, precipating a period of acute existential crisis. Arising from such crises was the 'savage-savage' who caused much of the mayhem and disorder seen in those disturbed and dangerous zones that so often barricaded entrance to remnant preconquest areas.[4]

Liminal Awareness

Most of us know about subliminal awareness – the type of awareness lurking below actual consciousness that powerfully influences behavior. Freud brought it into the mainstream of Western thought through exhaustively detailed revelations of its effects on behavior. But few, including Freud, have spoken of liminal consciousness, which is therefore rarely recognized in modern scholarship as a separate type of awareness. Nonetheless, liminal awareness was the principal focus of mentality in the preconquest cultures contacted, whereas a supraliminal type that focuses logic on symbolic entities is the dominant form in postconquest societies.[5]

Liminally focused consciousness is very different from the supraliminal type that has almost entirely replaced it. Within the preconquest cultures observed basic sensibilities (such as of identity, number, space, and truth) shape up in unexpected ways. So does human integration. Preconquest groups are simultaneously individualistic and collective – traits immiscible and incompatible in modern thought and languages. This fusion of individuality and solidarity is another of the profound cognitive disparities that separate the preconquest and postconquest eras. It in part explains why even fundamental preconquest cultural traits are sometimes difficult to perceive, much less to appreciate, by postconquest peoples.

From the Latin language underlying our Western heritage we can understand that liminal awareness, by definition, occurs on the threshold of consciousness. This concept, though abstract, provides a useful term. In the real life of these preconquest people, feeling and awareness are focused on at-the-moment, point-blank sensory experience – as if the nub of life lay within that complex flux of collective sentient immediacy. Into that flux individuals thrust their inner thoughts and aspirations for all to see, appreciate, and relate to. This unabashed open honesty is the foundation on which their highly honed integrative empathy and rapport become possible. When that openness gives way, empathy and rapport shrivel. Where deceit becomes a common practice, they disintegrate.

Where consciousness is focused within a flux of ongoing sentient awareness, experience cannot be clearly subdivided into separable components. With no clear elements to which logic can be applied, experience remains immune to syntax and formal logic within a kaleidoscopic sanctuary of non-discreteness. Nonetheless, preconquest life was reckoned sensibly – though seemingly intuitively.

With preconquest consciousness largely unencumbered by abstract concepts, it remained unconstrained by formal categories of value and cognition (i.e., rules and stable cognitive entities). Only when awareness shifted from liminal to supraliminal did the notion of 'correctness' become a matter of concern – e.g., behaving 'properly,' having 'right' answers, wearing 'appropriate' clothes, etc. 'Improper' aspirations, inclinations, and desires were then masked as people tried to measure up to the 'proper' rule and standard. They used rhetoric and logic argumentatively with reference to norms, precedents, and agreements to gain and maintain dignity, status, and position. It was an altogether different world from that of the preconquest era where people freely spread their interests, feelings, and delights out for all to see and grasp as they lurched toward whatever delightful patterns of response they found attractive.

Spawning Preconquest Consciousness

Preconquest mentality emerged from a sociosensual infant nurture common to its era but shunned in ours. When I first went into those isolated hamlets in the deep New Guinea forests I was dumbfounded by the lush sensuality of infant care I saw in the southern reaches of what the new Australian administration called 'South Fore.'[6]

This type of nurture was studied in greatest detail among the New Guinea forest-dwelling hunter-gatherer-gardeners on the southern slopes of the Kratke Range just after Western contact in the early 1960s. They provided the initial model for liminal consciousness. Bordering them to the north were people whose adoption of sweet potato as their staple was despoiling forest lands and undercutting the free range requirement of their traditional preconquest way-of-life. Among them an indigenously emerging supraliminal type of consciousness was coming into being.

In the isolated hamlets in the southern forests, infants were kept in continuous bodily contact with mothers or the mothers' friends – on laps when they were seated, on hips, under arms, against backs, or on shoulders when they were standing. Even during intensive food preparation, or when heavy loads were being moved, babies were not put down. They had priority.

There was always a place for them against the body of a 'mother' or close associate. Loads could be shed or lightened, but babies were simply not put down, not deprived of constant, ever-ready, interactive body contact – even when the group was on the move under difficult conditions.

Babies responded to this blanket of ever-ready empathetic tactile stimulation by tactile responses of their own. Very quickly they began assembling a sophisticated tactile-speech to transmit desires, needs, and states of mind. They didn't whine or cry to get attention; they touched. While babies everywhere are liminally aware, the constant empathetic tactile contact required to produce a sophisticated type of preverbal communication is rare – except among preconquest peoples.

Eliciting delight from babies was a desired social norm, and attentive tactile stimulation was the daily lot of infants. It included protracted body-to-body

Figure 5.1 As among all preconquest children, play between this young girl and baby boy includes spontaneous episodic kissing, mouthing, fondling, and biting.

84

caressing, snuggling, oral sensuality, hugging, fondling, and kissing. The seductive aspect of the play was frequently collective as older children singly or in combination used their inventive wiles to delight a baby. In their hamlets crying might be heard in reaction to accidental pain, but I don't recall a single case of disgruntled whining or demanding crying.[7] Regarding sibling rivalry, these southern hamlets also contrasted considerably with those of the sweet potato farmers in the north. Only in their villages could sibling rivalry be seen.[8] I tried hard to find at least one occurrence in those remote forest hamlets of the south, but it did not appear.

With nourishment, comfort, and stimulation constantly on hand, infants did not have to wait helplessly to have their needs met. They had no emotional need to anchor their libidos to abstract concepts of time, place, or kinship; and abstract foundations of awareness such as these were not imprinted on their nascent consciousness.

Figure 5.2 Not put aside for sleeping, babies enjoy continuous body-contact with those who care for them – even when essential work is underway.

As babies grew, their interests widened to the materials, objects, and activities at hand. They had amazing freedom to explore momentary whims and interests. At first, they did so with one hand on the 'mother,' the other reaching out. Then they began making short sorties further and then further out from their 'mothers'; just a few steps at first, then some more. Such moving out was on their own. Though a 'mother' or a 'sibling' might nod to encourage a baby who seemed uncertain about proceeding, they did not intervene or direct the baby's interests or directions. They stayed just where they were, doing whatever they had been doing – but as bastions of security to which babies could return for comfort, assistance, or a sense of surety. Though elders did not go with babies on their jaunts, they were ever ready to assist with whatever might be brought to them. Babies joined the activities of elders; elders did not join theirs.

Not put aside when work was being done, infants remained constantly *in touch* with the activities of life around them, their tiny hands ever reaching out to whatever items or materials were in use, and onto the hands, arms, and muscles of the users. In this way even as tiny babes-in-arms they began accumulating a kinesthetic familiarity with the implements and activities of life. This familiarity, supplemented by a rapidly developing 'tactile-talk,' produced in toddlers an ability to manage objects and materials safely that might be dangerous elsewhere. When first sojourning in those southern hamlets, I was repeatedly aghast to see toddlers barely able to stand upright playing with fire, wielding knives, and hefting axes – without concern by anyone around. Yet they did not burn down their grass/bamboo abodes or chop off their toes and fingers. During all the years I spent within their communities, I never saw these babies hurt themselves while engaged in this type of independent exploration.

When tots explored outward, their antennae stayed tuned to the affect, mood, and musculature of those they left behind, thereby maintaining affective connection across space. With adults and older children constantly a source of gratification rather than obstruction, toddlers had no desire to escape from supervision. Even slight intimations of concern from those behind, such as a tensing of musculature, was enough to stop a baby in its tracks and cast about for cues. While mothers in many places feel within themselves the kind of pain that might be looming for their baby, it's not so instantly perceived. Faster than any words of warning could be formed, these New Guinea tots were already responding. No words necessary. If some subtle 'all-clear' cue did not quickly come, the infant made fast tracks to 'home base.' No reckless plunges onward, no furtive tricks to escape supervision.

Figure 5.3 Immersed within a milieu of constant, ever ready stimulating physical contact with older hamlet mates, babies automatically start sharing inner feelings openly without reserve. From this sharing, a sophisticated tactile 'language' builds up before onset of verbal speech.

When babies began acquiring verbal speech, their words and sentences floated out atop a sophisticated body-language already well in place. Even after acquiring spoken language, tactile-talk continued taking precedence in much of daily life. It conveyed affect better. It was faster and more direct. Most of all it touched more deeply and more quickly into the hearts and minds of others. Tactile-talk was affect-talk. It integrated the spontaneous affect of individuals, often many at a time. So adept did young children become at this that they would at times merge actions into wordless synchrony.[9]

With such rapport surrounding them tots could also safely enter into the rough-and-tumble play of older children. There were no games with rules, no formal skills to measure up to. Play was spontaneous, improvised, and exploratory, so small children were never in the way. Instead, their wide-eyed enthusiasm was a constant source of pleasure for the older children. The younger children were always welcome and were handled with intuitive regard and delight.

If some aggravation unwittingly occurred in the course of active play, it withered quickly within the collective empathy. Negative feelings thus faded before they had a chance to grow. Full-blown expressions of, for example, anger or sadness, were therefore very rare. That, too, contributed to the intuitive rapport that so delighted them.

Up to about seven or eight years of age, boys and girls played together, disporting in mixed groups in the gardens amid the plantings. Boys continued garden dalliance until about the age of eight or nine; then their interests shifted and their hearts turned toward exploring further regions with other boys. Small gangs went first down one trail, then another, through all the dispersed hamlet segments to the furthest gardens and beyond. Girls did not like this moving all about. They preferred the sensual relaxation of garden life, quiet, tactile play with one another and with smaller children. By 12 to 13 years of age they were merging garden sensuality

Figure 5.4 Body contact with older friends continues during active rounds over difficult terrain. This young girl, moving across a log bridge from a forest garden, did not leave in the easier surroundings of the gardening group a toddler to whom she felt heart-linked. She took him with her, on her back, just to be with him – and to show to him the 'world' she knows.

with cultivation skills so artfully and seductively that they were attracting older males.[10] By their early teens they were often married.

Boys that age continued hunting and exploring out into the forest with like-minded comrades. Acquiring much of their own food there, they often

Figure 5.5 While exploring outer trails, two young boys communicate with the affectionate tactile-talk common to exploratory preconquest children.

ate and slept together in the 'boys'-houses' they constructed or took over. During adolescence, their rapport intensified. A rapid flow of synchronous regard began uniting them even more closely as they scattered through the forest, each constantly enlivening the others by a ceaseless, spirited,

Figure 5.6 Affectionate tactile-talk turns into cooperative activity as children grow. Here, two boys enjoy the immense personal freedom that preconquest children have to spontaneously pursue, on their own terms, the economic welfare of their group. Conjoining individual inclinations and desires during hunting, these boys wordlessly integrate their separate perspectives on the changing circumstances through which they move. Spurred on by the inner pleasure such rapport brings, they merge individuality and solidarity (qualities immiscible in Western thought and languages) into a single entity.

individualistic input into a unified at-oneness. The phenomenon was alien to my Western consciousness, and so beyond the English language that there are no good words for it even in the Oxford Unabridged. So, when trying to describe that kind of unity in English, the words bump up against each other as if contradictions – as in *individualistic unified at-oneness*, a phrase self-contradictory in English, and yet another indication of the magnitude of the gap separating these two types of consciousness. The following event illustrates:

> One day, deep within the forest, Agaso, then about 13 years of age, found himself with a rare good shot at a cuscus in a nearby tree. But he only had inferior arrows. Without the slightest comment or solicitation, the straightest, sharpest arrow of the group moved so swiftly and so stealthily straight into his hand, I could not see from whence it came.
>
> At that same moment, Karako, seeing that the shot would be improved by pulling on a twig to gently move an obstructing branch, was without a word already doing so, in perfect synchrony with Agaso's drawing of the bow, i.e., just fast enough to fully clear Agaso's aim by millimeters at the moment his bow was fully drawn, just slow enough not to spook the cuscus. Agaso, knowing this would be the case made no effort to lean to side for an unobstructed shot, or to even slightly shift his stance. Usumu similarly synchronized into the action stream, without even watching Agaso draw his bow, began moving up the tree a fraction of a second before the bowstring twanged.
>
> He grasped the wounded cuscus before it might regain its senses and slipped out onto a slender branch that whizzed him down to dangle in the air an inch or so before Agaso's startled face. The startle had begun its standard transformation to ecstasy, when Usumu startled him again by provocatively dropping the quivering cuscus onto his naked foot, as he flicked a tasty beetle he'd found up in the tree into the pubis of delighted young Koniye (the youngest of the group). Doubly startled in quick succession, Agaso was wallowing in an ecstasy, then shared by all, until he abruptly realized that the cuscus might come back to life and dash off.[11] Then in a mirthful scramble they all secured it.
>
> Within that type of spirit they roasted both beetle and cuscus on an open fire (to which two friends exploring separately added grubs they'd found in a rotting log). As night came on, one-by-one, they all dropped off to sleep together, entangled in what can only be described as a contagiously subdued rapture coalescence. It took many years for me to understand the underpinnings of this guileless hypersensual interactive unity (another example of the kind of language awkwardness that arises when speaking of events across eras).

In these isolated southern groups, such rapport by exploring boys was not restricted to comrades; it radiated out to strangers, too. With heightening

90

élan, these youthful gangs would radiate into the graces of new faces in the forest. The following bit of oral history shows how a band of 'Fore' boys seduced even the aversive, warlike 'Awa,' a people from an altogether different setting, way-of-life, and language family.[12] I heard variations of this story in many hamlets throughout the Waisarampa Valley in the 1960s. It tells of the first contact between the hunting-gathering-gardening southern 'Fore' and the instinctively hostile taro-growing 'Awa' from the great grasslands of the upper Lamari Valley. It is reconstructed here from several accounts:

One day, somewhat before World War II, two bands of youths, one Fore the other Awa, were ranging out from their widely separated hamlet homes into the dense uninhabited forest ranges that stood between these different peoples. It was the first time either group had ventured out so far.

The Awa boys had darted from a side trail out onto a knife-edged promontory down which they were proceeding above the Lamari River, when they found themselves between the rear and forward elements of the Fore boys going out there too. With both front and rear blocked by Fore, and ridge sides at that point too precipitous to scramble down, they had no place to turn. They were hemmed in too closely to think of raising bows – or perhaps they were too young to think of it, or perhaps because they were so young their funny-bones got tickled, or the situation was so strange they simply went agog. For whatever reason, the antagonistic Awa nature didn't surface, and despite a gaping language barrier amity broke out.

They compared bows and arrows (the Awa had the best), then food (the Fore sweet potato was an instant hit). They examined each other's different kinds of dress and compared physiques.[13] When showers threatened, melding diverse building styles, they improvised a leaf-thatched shelter and spent the night close onto one another in the Fore sensual style. By morning they were bosom buddies.

At first light, they were up and out along the ridge on a hunt together. They showed off their different hunting styles, bagged a tree-kangaroo, cooked and ate it with the remaining sweet potato. When they separated to go back home, they made a date to meet at the same shelter at next full moon. The Awa promised to bring arrows to exchange for sweet potatoes.

Following this second meeting, two younger Awa boys, entranced by the prowess of their stronger new Fore friends, returned to stay with them in their hamlet for several days. Two Fore boys then went for a sojourn in the Awa hamlet of Yakia. They took a sack of sweet potatoes to trade for arrows.

In this way the two gangs became good friends and built a boys'-house near the famous knife-edged ridge to stay in together. Soon that site became an entrepot for Fore-Awa trade, mainly arrows for sweet potatoes. A larger house was built to accommodate the flow. The Awa boys picked up Fore words, and the Fore, ever fond of playing with new expressions, picked up theirs. Soon all were speaking a Fore-Awa blend.

Later, two Fore sisters married two of the Awa youths and took possession of the older boys'-house (which then became a women's-house). The just-built new boys'-house then became a men's-and-boys'-house (by virtue of the marriages). With wives in residence, more gardens rapidly appeared. A sister of an Awa boy married his closest Fore comrade. So another women's-house was built, which she occupied with her unmarried Awa girl-friend (the 13-year-old sister of one of the original Awa boys). She soon married one of the Fore boys.

In this way the first mixed Fore-Awa hamlet in the region came into being. As more cross-marriages occurred, a genetic merging of those Awa and Fore began.[14] More mixed hamlets came into being – on both sides of the Lamari. When the government arrived, they called those on the east side of the river, 'Awa,' those on the west side, 'Fore.'

This account shows how the sensual verve and spirited amiability of exploratory Fore boys could unite quite different peoples. From an accidental meeting began a merging of 'Awa' with 'Fore' that was later clearly seen in blood-gene distributions. The event demonstrates how the Fore hunter-gatherer-gardeners made friends, how they segmented and recombined, and how dialect chains emerged between different language families.

Noticing Preconquest Consciousness

The cognitive gap separating preconquest and postconquest life may be responsible for conquerors not recognizing it for what it was. It seems to have similarly blinkered modernized observers. For years I considered such child nurture practices an anomalous product of the remote New Guinea jungle and for a long time remained steadfastly unaware of its implications. Deeper understanding emerged at a snail's pace. Without non-dialectic techniques, understanding probably would never have occurred. Two such techniques emerged: (1) phenomenological data records made at the time of early contact, and (2) in-close, crosscultural, direct experience.

The undifferentiated phenomenological data on the film allowed analysis to by-pass the normal dialectics-based inquiry systems of our Western culture. When these are escaped, the raw pattern-recognition capability of the human mind has fuller swing. When these visual data records (research films) of New Guinea childhood were reviewed again and again, patterns of recurrence and association began emerging. Eventually they stood out clearly to reveal the sociosensual basis of New Guinea childhood nurture. With the basic patterns thus exposed, these same patterns could then be quickly recognized wherever they occurred. After sighting several similar cases in widely separated preconquest enclaves, it was clear such practices represented a widespread early norm.

With such understanding it became much easier to employ in-depth, direct experience, another non-dialectic technique. In the course of daily living in a variety of preconquest enclaves, a clear, though undefinable, commonalty of sensibility sometimes connected across cultural barriers, even in the absence of a common language. It required spontaneous, instinctive friendship beyond the level of ordinary discourse, as when a heart-felt liking for someone simply just arose.[15] As mystical as that might seem, the affect exchanges then made possible led to sustained, adaptive, experiential interactions much deeper than those enabled merely by conversation. Experiential depth is what eventually revealed the major role played by affect coordination in preconquest life. Without this nonverbal crosscultural bridge, it would not have been possible to grasp why preconquest mentality was so vulnerable to anger, deceit, greed, and aggression. Nor would it have been possible to notice crucial subtleties of sense-of-name, sense-of-space, sense-of-number, sense-of-truth, and sense-of-emotion.

Two unorthodox procedures going beyond the dialectic approach to truth of our Western culture were required to bring an important type of nonwestern consciousness to light.

Basic Features of Preconquest Consciousness

As detailed below, major areas of preconquest human sensibility diverge strikingly from what one sees in postconquest sensibility. These areas, as they are set forth here, are too abstract and delimited to be meaningful to those who see the world through preconquest eyes. They focus on interconnection, interdigitation, and interdissolution. Only for more modern minds do formal cognitive divisions become important tools.

Sense of Name

In these preconquest regions of New Guinea names were rarely binding. What one was called varied according to time, place, mood, and setting. Names were improvised, not formally bestowed, and naming (much like local language flexibility) was often a kind of humorous exploratory play. New names could be quickly coined, often whimsically from events and situations, with a new one coming up at any time. One young boy running in a peculiar way was affectionately dubbed 'Grasshopper'. It stuck. Another was called 'Kaba' (short for the prized *embokaba* beetle) because, during an episode of biting-mouthing play, a friend proclaimed his skin was as delicious as that savory beetle's flesh. One girl was called 'Aidpost' following her excitement

93

about the first one in the region; another was called 'Sleepgood' by a new friend who liked sleeping with her. A boy from a distant hamlet in the south who tagged along when I went north to the new Australian Patrol Post fled into the jungle in crouched, zigzagging panic when an object he believed to be a metal house abruptly growled and moved. His name became 'Land Rover.'

Names were nicknames. They stuck for a while, then a new one came along. Only when the new (Australian) government began insisting that they use the same name for official dealings, especially in the annual census soon instituted, did formal names emerge. Otherwise, individuals responded to whatever name they knew they might be called.[16]

Place-names were equally as flexible. They emerged from distinctive landmarks, the plants or animals that might be found there, the name of someone memorably associated with the site, or just by an interesting event that had occurred at the location. One place in the forest took its name from a boy who had fallen from a tree there. Names were often impromptu, with different names being used at different times even by close friends. Group names, too, were informal. A group might be referred to by the site its main hamlet occupied, by the name of someone in the group, or by some noteworthy event involving the group. Since groups frequently segmented and reconstituted, such names came and went and were not considered particularly significant. Not all members of a group used the same name even for themselves, much less their group of associates. Just as for individuals and places, there were numerous possibilities for naming groups, and they often had several names.

Sense of Space

Just as body language originated in empathetic responsiveness to affect, so did sense-of-space. These preconquest people had no standard way to partition lands, to measure time and distance, to project abstract boundaries onto regions, or to impose abstract spatial concepts. Geographic sensibility was simply affect relationships thrust out onto surroundings. Such geography was haphazard and rarely uniform. It fluctuated over time, from place-to-place and from individual-to-individual. Meaningfulness emerged from the affect associated with a place – e.g., comfort, excitement, enjoyment, eagerness, interest, delicious foods, good company, etc. Such 'geographical' entities had recognizable centers, but they overlapped and graded imperceptibly into one another – just as did their kinship and their languages. Such 'geography,' though clear enough at centers of rapport, was indistinct and fuzzy where affect association lessened or became ambiguous. All boundaries, spatial and otherwise, were therefore hazy, inconsistent, and ambiguous.

Navigating such affect-space is not at all like barreling down the Beltway to Bethesda or even going to Mars. Feelings mattered, not hours, kilometers,

94

or abstract directions. When I meandered through the forests within the affect-space of New Guinea friends, one and then another would branch to complex, divergent different paths, regrouping variously along the way – because that's how their affect-geographies were panning out that day. At first traveling in affect-space seemed entirely unworldly – much too indirect, labyrinthine, snail-paced, and intellectually disorderly. I conceived space through maps and compasses, schedules and boundaries, and was geared mentally to a Euclidean sense-of-space. I was map cognitive. Among these people, feelings about locales were what mattered, and it was feelings that defined them. Arbitrary geographical divisions were devoid of such meaning, so had no relevance to them and were unrecognized. A locale's name varied according to the numerous affect relations different people had with it. There were no abstract sectionings of space, no geometric projections onto space, no projected boundaries to undo their sense of interdigitation.

To get directions to go somewhere required shared knowledge of local place names. Due to the deeply dissected, convoluted, densely forest covered mountain setting, no locales were reachable except via obscure winding jungle trails on which any sense of direction was very soon befuddled. There were no direct ways to go even out to somewhat distant gardens. When asking how to go somewhere, a string of local names is what I'd get, and not always the same ones. Even simple abstractions (like right and left or east and west) did not enter in. Instead of saying turn right at some forking of the trail, they would say 'take the path to wherever.' And so forth. Locations could be pointed at, if visible – much as one might point to a person or a house. But to point was not to tell you how to get there. They might point at some landmark in the distance, such as a mountain, and tell you that the place you asked about was behind it. If they thought you knew how to get to some mutually recognized place on the mountain, they would then spit forth the string of trail-connected names beyond (if they knew them).

Just how strong a general sense of location existed was not easy to determine. Pointing toward things not visible was not usually on the mark as when following a winding, forest obscured trail (remember, I had a compass), unless the site was very near. So when going beyond a place I knew, I had to go with local friends familiar with the route. To go further I had to hope they had a friend out there who could show the path onward to the next. When going through a series of such regions on a protracted regional survey, I had to find new guides in each new area of settlement. This more extensive type of traveling required following kinship and dialect chains across the region – sometimes even just to go ten miles, as flies the crow.

When I first went into the region I was still a somewhat cocky Westerner with little crosscultural sensibility. I repeatedly tried to get my point across with maps and compasses and even aerial photographs. All useless. Every time I tried to explain *a* to *b* directness, boundaries, or standard measures, though they seemed eager to get the point. They eventually just went blank.

Some concluded I was playing word games and would simply laugh. In those days the territory was mapped only in the very crudest sense (from hastily produced World War II aerial photographs without ground information). So reliance on local friends was the only way I could find my way around. My overwhelming daily problem was how to guess which local friends might have the most favorable socio-geography for where I had to go that day. It was grievously perplexing at first – then it became a deeply moving introduction into the world of affect-geography.

Sense of Number

Counting, like boundaries, took on importance only where supraliminal consciousness was developing, i.e., in the agricultural regions of the north where sweet potato had become the staple. In the forests of the south, where liminal consciousness was most highly evolved, few could count above five without great effort. They had no precise names for higher numbers, and scarcely any for the lower digits. The word for five was a cognate of their word for hand. Some understood that several hands meant larger quantities; but beyond two hands (ten) the word was usually 'many.' Sometimes a foot would be added, or a nose. One friend added his penis in a humorous demonstration of the foolishness of taking the task of counting seriously. When it was erect, he said, it was worth even more. Quantity was impressionistic, not numerical. What mattered was the magnitude of collective joy produced – not how many items could be counted. Depending on taste and circumstance, a single unit might be more important than many units at another time or place. Plants and animals collected during hunting-gathering were rarely of the same size and kind, so counting rarely had much point. Counting was indeed like mixing penises with toes, and just as foolish, which was the point my friend was trying to make.

A more precise sense of counting developed only in the north where pigs had become a means of value exchange between groups needing allies. Adult pigs were rather much the same size, so they lent themselves to counting. Sweet potato cultivation meant that many pigs could be raised. These pigs were then used to forge and confirm political and defense alliances. Counts firmed up these types of relationships. Higher counts conferred status and thus political power. Where pig counting became a general practice, the number bestowed at pig exchange feasts affected availability of wives, security of settlements, rights to land, and trade relationships. As pig feasts became more lavish, so did counting. Where fifty pigs might be presented at a feast, two fingers worth of two hands (twenty) or a hand's worth of two hands (fifty) were widely understood.

As detailed above, sociosensual child nurture spawned body language based on tactile exchanges of affect. Infants were quick to notice that the happiness of others made their own lives happier and richer, so they responded accordingly. Soon they realized that the more accurately and fully they conveyed their inner needs and interests, the more quickly rewarding responses were forthcoming. So they displayed true feelings without artifice, as openly and clearly as their tiny frames permitted. The more skilled they were, the happier they were; indeed, the happier were all.

Therefore 'tactile-talk' was 'affect-talk,' and 'affect-talk' was 'truth-talk.' It was so compelling that even after learning verbal speech children continued bouncing inner passions back and forth in 'affect-talk.' The messages were more emotionally rewarding. They moved more quickly and more accurately and were usually more deeply evocative. Spoken words did not have the same instant sensuality and were thus more remote from lives sentiently focused. Affect-talk was truth-talk because it only worked when personal feelings were above board and accurately expressed, which required transparency in aspirations, interests, and desires.

With body language based on full-time accurate truth, infants became candid and open, and remained so as they grew. When I first went into their hamlets I was astonished to see the words of tiny children accepted at face value – and so acted on. For months I tried to find at least one case where a child's words were considered immature and therefore disregarded. No luck. I tried to explain the idea of lying and inexperience. They didn't get my point. They didn't expect prevarication, deception, grandstanding, or evasion. And I could find no cases where they understood these concepts. Even teenagers remained transparently forthright, their hearts opened wide for all to gaze inside.

Recognition of Emotion

Such an open life shapes awareness of emotions, which was seen in their responses to a standardized set of photographs of basic emotions.[17] Individuals from the most isolated regions became highly agitated when shown photographs of anger. Some went dumb, others became tongue-tied, many trembled, some perspired profusely or looked wildly about. Those from remotest hamlets reacted most dramatically. Not just confounded, they were fearful too. It was an astonishing and gripping spectacle.[18]

In those isolated hamlets of the south emotions such as anger, if inadvertently induced by rough-and-tumble play, quickly faded in the ambiance of constant empathetic rapport and tactile stimulation. Getting angry among confreres was like one hand getting angry with the other. So they were not accustomed to full-blown expressions of negative emotions. When confronted with our photographs of full-blown anger, many were stunned, frightened, and disoriented. Even in photographs not intended to show anger, they sometimes noticed subtle traces that are so common in the West that they are not even considered anger there.

They had other reasons to be frightened of negative emotions. They had no formal social structure, therefore no stable social safety net to hold them all together when affect-rapport gave way. When it did, as in the 'time-of-troubles,' they were bereft, existentially desolated.

Collapse of Preconquest Consciousness

The time-of-troubles in New Guinea was regional. In smaller preconquest isolates such disorders were sometimes confined to single tiny islands, even villages, even segments of the village population (e.g., teenagers often seemed particularly susceptible). Nonetheless in all cases the subtlest affect exchanges faded first with intuitive rapport going into irreversible collapse much later.

After loss of intuitive rapport, the sensually empathetic instincts governing sociosensual nurture became cruder and were less often on-the-mark. In large regions a grand cultural amnesia sometimes accompanied this collapse. Whole populations would forget even recent past events and make gross factual errors in reporting them. In some cases they even forgot what type and style of garments they had worn a few years earlier or (in New Guinea) that they had been using stone axes and eating their dead close relatives a few years back. Initially I thought they were dissimulating in an effort to ingratiate or appear up-to-date, but rejected this thought almost immediately. They were simply too unassuming and open in other respects for such a theory to hold up. And when I showed photographs I'd taken a few years earlier, they would brighten up, laugh, and eagerly call their friends as they excitedly began relating their reviving recollections.

The periods of anomie sometimes alternated with spates of wild excitement leading to a strange mixture of excess and restraint.[19] It was during such disorders that abstract concepts of rights, property, and possession began emerging. So did formal names for people, groups, and places. These were then used argumentatively in defense of rights, property, and possessions. Negative emotions were applied to strengthen argument. Eventually they became structural aspects of society. As the art of political manipulation emerged, the selfless unity that seemed so firm and self-repairing in their isolated enclaves vanished like a summer breeze as a truth-based type of consciousness gave way to one that lied to live.

A similar type of turmoil and transformation began occurring on small islands in the eastern Sea of Andaman somewhat after the Vietnam War.

South East Asia was then rapidly developing economically, and the dazzling scenery, fine beaches, and crystal waters of many of those islands attracted an explosively abrupt tourism trade. As it gathered pace, the intuitive rapport that was still extant on many islands first began to waver, then to oscillate. In some cases a half-way house adjustment would occur, and then another, both without serious psychological disability. However, in cases of accelerated change, a whirlwind psychological debility would sometimes suddenly break loose. The following, abstracted from my field notes, is a firsthand description of one such case:

I'm out, back from the Andaman where I've just been through an experience I'll not soon forget. Only by pure chance did I happen to be there when their extraordinary intuitive mentality gave up the ghost right in front of me, in an inconceivable overwhelming week. I'm almost wrecked myself, in a strange anomie from having gone through that at too close a range, and from staying up all night too many times to try to understand just what was going on. I never was much good at keeping research distance, always feeling more could be learned close in. And I'd come straight into the Andaman from two months of tantric philosophical inquiry in a Tibetan monastery. Perhaps that tuned awareness up a notch too much.

There really was no way to have predicted that, just after I arrived, the acute phase of their ancient culture's death would start. To speak abstractly of the death of a way-of-life is a simple thing to do. To experience it is quite another thing. I've seen nothing in the lore of anthropology that might prepare one for the speed by which it can occur, or for the overwhelming psychic onslaughts it throws out. Nor does my profession forewarn of those communicable paroxysms that hover in the air which, without warning, strike down with overwhelming force, when a culture's mind gives way.

Yet this is just what happened when the traditional rapport of those islands was undone, when the subtle sensibility of each to one another was abruptly seared away in a sudden unpredicted, unprecedented, uncognated whirlwind. In a single crucial week a spirit that all the world would want, not just for themselves but for all others, was lost, one that had taken millennia to create. It was suddenly just gone.

Epidemic sleeplessness, frenzied dance throughout the night, reddening burned-out eyes getting narrower and more vacant as the days and nights wore on, dysphasias of various sorts, sudden mini-epidemics of spontaneous estrangement, lacunae in perception, hyperkinesis, loss of sensuality, collapse of love, impotence, bewildered frantic looks like those on buffalo in India just as they're clubbed to death; 14 year olds (and others) collapsing on the beach, under houses, on the pier, in beached boats as well as those tied up at the dock, here and there, into wee hours of the morn, even on through dawn, in acute inebriation or exhaustion. Such was the general scene that week, a week that no imagination could have forewarned, the week in which the subtle sociosensual glue of the island's traditional way-of-life became unstuck.

To pass through the disintegrating social enclaves was to undergo a rain of psychic blows, a pelting shower of harrowing awarenesses that raised goose flesh of unexpected types on different epidermal sites along with other kinds of crawlings of flesh and skin. There were sudden rushes, both cold and hot, down the head and chest and across the neck, even in the legs and feet. And deep inside, often near the solar plexus, or around heart, or in the head or throat, new indescribable sensations would spontaneously arise, leave one at a loss or deeply disconcerted.

Such came and then diffused away as one passed by different people. Sensations would abruptly wash in across the consciousness, trigger moods of awe, or of sinking, sometimes of extraordinary love, sometimes utter horror. From time-to-time nonspecific elemental impulses arose just to run or dance, to throw oneself about, to move. All these could be induced and made to fade and then come back, just by passing through some specific group, departing, and then returning, or by coming near a single friend, moving off and coming back. That this was possible so astonished me that I checked and checked and checked again.

Such awarenesses, repeatedly experienced, heap up within the brain. Eventually the accumulation left me almost as sleepless and night-kinetic as they had become. I did discover that with body motion, mind becomes less preoccupied within itself, therefore less distressed. With kinetic frenzy mind-horror lessens very much. But it left them exhausted during the day, somnambulant, somewhat zombie-like. When night returned, the cycle would re-begin, as if those nocturnal hours, when they would otherwise be sleeping, were the time of greatest stress.

Though the overt frenzied movements could be observed by anyone, the psychic states that so powerfully impelled them were not easily detectable to outsiders. It seemed as if one had to have some personal rapport within the lifeway before the mental anguish could be sensed. Then it would loom, sometimes overwhelm. One Westerner looking casually on said, 'How exotic to see these uneducated types staying up throughout the night, dancing strangely, relating to each other in nonproductive ways. This place must be an anthropological paradise.' Tourists happening on the scene thought it a fillip to their holiday. Intimacy and affection seem prerequisite to connecting with these inner surges of human psyche, even overwhelming ones.

Eventually I retreated, mentally exhausted, cognitively benumbed, emotionally wrung out. I tried to thwart that siege (when I finally recognized it for what it really was) by getting key people out. A useless foolish gambit; for no one would leave the spot, as if they were welded to it, as if it held some precious thing they very greatly loved, which they neither would nor could abandon.

When the mental death had run its course, when what had been was gone, the people (physically still quite alive) no longer had their memory of the intuitive rapport that held them rapturously together just the week before, could no longer link along those subtle mental pathways. What had filled their lives had vanished. The teensters started playing at (and then adopting) the rude, antagonistic, ego-grasping styles of the encroaching modern world, modeled after films and then TV. Oldsters retreated into houses, lost their affinity to youngsters, who then turned more to one another, sometimes squabbling (which did not occur before).

It seems astonishing that the inner energy of such passings is so undetectable to minds not some way linked to the inner harmonies and ardors of the place. Research-distance yields abstractions like 'going amok,' which could have been easily applied that week, or 'revitalizing movement,' which also could have been (in a perverse kind of way). It seems that only by some mental coalescence with the local lifeway can one access its deeper psychic passions, not just those of adolescence, but graver ones like those which for a time were released in inconceivable profusion, when the collective subtle mind of the islands, built up over eons, was snuffed out.

Similar processes, perhaps not always so dramatic, seem to occur when any domineering or abstractly focused alien culture (whether Western, Sinic, Indic, or Islamic) impacts on a preconquest people. To the degree that the in-depth readjustment requires new relationships between the awareness and manipulation centers in the cerebral cortex and the centers of emotion in the mid and lower brains, they represent physiological as well as psychological change and therefore raise important questions about the promise and condition of the state of humankind.

Resketching the Civilizational Process

The details set forth above show how preconquest consciousness can be transformed into a postconquest type. They also show how an integrative human mental evolutionary development was destroyed by the emergence of an adversarial one. Such knowledge enables a re-examination of the civilizational process from a pre-civilizational perspective. Indeed, in the face of these insights such re-sketching virtually suggests itself. Since all four major civilization developments of the world (Western, Sinic, Indic, and Islamic) have conquistadorial features, a sketch of one makes the basic point. We know that pre-civilizational Mediterranea had a sparse and dispersed population with tracts of lands unusually suitable for onset of agriculture.[20]

101

So, let's sketch out how our Western Civilization is most likely to have emerged from its birthplace there.

It is common knowledge that agriculture enables larger populations. We also know that larger populations sometimes outstrip the natural resources they depend upon (much like what happened with sweet potato in New Guinea). In primeval Mediterranea agricultural innovation would have come on come on spottily at first, here and there, not everywhere at once; in some places it started a millennium later. Where regions became congested, and new land resources scarce, the free-range requirement of preconquest life disappeared – slowly at first since surrounding virgin lands would for quite some time be able to absorb pressed peoples. Eventually, however, there would be confinement, confrontation, and conflict. At that point in the evolution, a psychological transformation commenced, one that focused with growing intensity on emergent cognitive abstractions and symbols by which to anchor claims to property. As these took hold, possessiveness evolved as a basic human trait.

As possessive populations continued to increase, larger bands of emergent postconquest people moved more frequently and more forcibly into neighboring preconquest regions. This produced a faster mental transformation due to the nature of the impact of aggressive miens on preconquest people: It first paralyzed their intuitive rapport and then disabled it. Where exposure to conquistadorial temperament was light, or episodic, a relatively nontraumatic adjustive transformation was possible. In the face of sustained powerful exposure to anger, deceit, or greed, preconquest mentality collapsed. In the traumatic existential period that caused, instinctive compassion gave way to savagery, generosity to greed, and heart-felt harmony to basic sexuality. A 'savage-savage' arose from the ashes of the 'noble-savage.' Brigandage and piracy became adjustive practices. Claiming land tended to be declamatory and demanding, often backed by arms. To tell a brigand from landowner might well require waiting to see who won. Once domain was securely established, settlements were possible, indeed required for defensive reasons. With settlement, wealth accumulation became possible.

With a plentiful supply of savages, pirates, and brigands in this early period, and with landowners being from much the same mold, property and wealth had to be defended. Warriors were required. Then armies. When they were not equal to their task, defensive edge could be acquired by alliances forged and stabilized through formal wealth exchanges that required counts and records. As increasingly sophisticated means of accounting and record keeping emerged, rights and title could be sustained by reasoned argument.

As wealth grew, so did armies. City-states soon had to conquer weaker neighbors to get wealth enough to themselves stay independent. Some discovered that people who had no wealth at all could be forced to produce it by enslavement or taxation. Conquistadors then moved out more broadly into preconquest regions to force ever larger populations to create material wealth and to keep it moving into their treasuries. Region after region lost their preconquest consciousness in this wave of conquest. When preconquest empathy and instinctive unity were gone, legal codes and law enforcement practices became necessary – not just to keep the peace in conquered lands, but at home as well. A careful reading of the history of forms of government from the very first states yet known (in the Nile Valley and southern Mesopotamia around 3200 B.C.) suggest this basic situation pertained widely, e.g., in the ancient states of Sumar, Egypt, Persia, and Assyria; the Byzantine and Caliphate empires of the Middle East; in the Han, Tang, and Ming dynasties of Imperial China; and in the classical states of Greece and Rome and their European and American descendents.[21]

Literary accounts of the early Mediterranean world leave little ambiguity about this process once it started. Herodotus, Thucydides, Xenophon, Caesar, and later Machiavelli, among others, reveal a conquest-oriented ethos in the emergent Western world. The poetry, plays, and orations of the early period poignantly depict the human consequences of conquest (*viz.*, Euripides, Sophocles, Aeschylus, Homer, Cicero).

As this civilizational process continued, in the pattern of its onset, philosophies of governance emerged. They were first a means to anchor conquest, then to manage seized property and wealth according to the wishes of the conquerors. Formal ideologies to conjoin governed peoples emerged. Loyalty to an abstract idea of nation began grasping hearts and minds. Since states that managed resources rationally became stronger, reasoned argument became a power tool. While truth in conquered territories could be arbitrarily imposed, in keeping with the nature of conquest, states that managed resources rationally became stronger. Reasoned argument developed. Such refinements as the zetetic, elenctic, and meiotic modes of dialectic reasoning emerged and were eventually formalized in the dialectic systems of Socrates and Aristotle. Since a conquest ethos lay at their root, it should not be surprising that the dialectic form was conquistadorial as well. It enabled one to dip into the kaleidoscopic maelstrom of direct sentient experience, drag out chunks, and make latent mental entities of them – as if by such capture, as if by such conquest of the senses, a higher reality was bestowed. It produced a means by which the elements of the sentient world could be materialized, conquered, and controlled according to the interests and desires of established rulers.

Despite the worldly strength bestowed by this approach to truth, surgings of that older psychic unity would unpredictably reappear, *viz.*, the Eleusinian and Dionysian mysteries, the more arcane philosophies of Christian love, and later, when no longer discouraged by immolation, shunning, and the like, various secular writings that touch into the long covertized sensual aspects of preconquest life (which to some degree probably had been going on all the while in various secluded places such as hideaways, nooks, courtly bedrooms, or even barnyards). These resurgences were remarkably akin to those erratic wellings up of sociosensual inclination I saw when collapsed preconquest communities began restabilizing in a postconquest mode. They leaked out spontaneously and unpredictably as if from some panhuman reservoir so deep it could neither be undone by existential terror nor seduced by worldly thoughts of ownership and power.

If this sketch inspired by observation of today's preconquest remnants seems too bold, consider this more noetic thought: From whence come those words that idolize our esteemed ideas of civilization? That intriguing question cannot be dealt with here, except perhaps to note the obvious need to use the thought processes bequeathed to us by our civilization even to engage the question. A step back in time to earlier this century may provide some flicker of illumination. Read R. R. Maret's scholarly foreword to White's (1922) book, *The Sea Gypsies of Malaya*, an example not unlike many of its genre. I mention this one because, from my own direct experience in the subject, it helps me see what happened.[22]

Maret's foreword is an erudite introduction and critique actually meant to help White. Maret, the distinguished arm-chair Oxford anthropologist, was well established at the pinnacle of the sense-of-truth created by Western Civilization. White had no such pretensions. Yet his thoughtful and reflective accounts of the Moken people and encyclopedic revelation of their setting are products of an open mind shaped by years of direct hands-on experience. He had close friends among the Moken and interacted with them on their terms.

Maret's foreword is modest, even self-effacing, as befits the genre. It is largely friendly and supportive and certainly well meaning. Nonetheless, it imposes onto White's thoughtful observations an analysis in the didactic argumentative academic mode by which truth gets recognized and established in the West. In a sense, it is a silk-gloved academic conquest of White's work carefully and eruditely set forth in fine academic style. But it informs us not a whit about the Moken, even leads us astray from them (admittedly easier to see more than a half century later). Since Maret is so clearly a well-meaning and thoughtful person, one can only wonder how this could have happened. Close examination reveals a reliance on the standard form evolved from the conquistadorial sense-of-truth bequeathed by the Western civilizational process. It is actually academic domineering under the guise of urbane, polite critique. It tells us nothing of how the Moken think or what they really are. Its main achievement is to reinforce the sanctity of the Western mode of thinking in the face of Moken challenge.

White's non-academic words, on the other hand, are a product of many years of in-close human contact with people he came to like. He speaks reflectively and from the heart. Though what he says is interlaced with guileless commonplace comparisons with his own background, he sets those out so unabashedly and straightforwardly that they provide a bridge that helps us better sink into meanings that are Moken. There's no bridge at all in the logically delivered, academically profound conquistadorial commentary by the distinguished armchair don.

Basic Problems in Crosscultural Observation

The negative emotions of supraliminally focused potato farmers in New Guinea devastated the sociosensual rapport of liminally focused hunter-gatherer-gardeners whose open range they began seizing for private benefit – *automatically, without awareness they were doing so*. Western visitors, merely by their presence, paralyzed the cognitive processes of liminally focused Sea Nomads in the Sea of Andaman – *automatically, without awareness they were doing so*. These examples illustrate the first basic problem in crosscultural observation: people from one culture can be grossly unaware of the transformational impact they have on people from a different culture.

When I was first exposed to sociosensual cultures, I saw neither their underlying sociosensuality nor the intuitive rapport it spawned. Never mind that these features were the principal game of life – in those days they were opaque to me just as much as to any other outsider. Even after a year in residence with such people I had only gained an unarticulated, marginal awareness. It took repeated exposure to several preconquest cultures over decades before I had any real local indigenous sensibility. This illustrates the second basic problem in crosscultural observation: inability of people from one culture to see the fundamental dynamics of another culture when they fall outside the observer's own cultural experience.

When I first entered the isolated hamlets of the New Guinea forest, the remote atolls of Micronesia and Polynesia, and finally several other sociosensual cultures across the world, I was at first nonplused by what were openly erotic aspects of infant nurture. Due to my Western cultural conditioning, I averted gaze, avoided notice, kept it at arm's length, failed to give it recognition, or even to talk or write about it. Only after years of fieldwork in these regions did I become sufficiently blasé to cease my reflexive avoidance. This illustrates a third basic problem in crosscultural observation: the tendency to avoid noticing major features of another culture when they are incongruent with unspoken codes of probity inculcated by one's own culture.

In the eastern Andaman, before many of the traditional isolated islands were suddenly and unexpectedly targeted for tourism, traditional empathetic inclinations remained well developed and in tact for many groups. When these populations instinctively sensed that childhood genital tactility perturbed their new visitors, automatically, seemingly without thought, they modified just those aspects of behavior that seemed to discomfit their guests. Soon childhood genitality was no longer seen when visitors were about. On nearby islands that had not attracted tourists, these erotic aspects of child nurture remained out in the open for all to see. On my first visits to the more isolated isles of the eastern Andaman, just as happened in New Guinea, the erotic aspects of child and infant nurture started fading. Being more sophisticated then, I took special care to keep my cultural ethos masked on some islands and unmasked on others. The erotic aspects began disappearing from view where I did not mask my hometown Western ethos, but they remained visible and very much in the open where I masked that conditioning. Where I masked and then unmasked, the eroticism started vanishing and then returned, slowly at first, but eventually to the extent I had seen at first contact. This illustrates a fourth basic problem in crosscultural observation: preconquest peoples, indeed any empathetically oriented people, will suppress even major behavioral traits to avoid discomfiture to others.

Reflections

For several years after I began contacting preconquest peoples like those described above, I considered their type of consciousness an oddity, a kind of naive primitive emotionality, one perhaps suitable only for small, isolated groups, but certainly for no one else. It took a long time for me to realize that they had evolved their own sophisticated type of cognition that was simply different from what I (or anyone I knew) was used to. And I came to realize that such mentality could not be considered primitively ignorant if only because it was so sensitively intelligent and beneficially responsive. It moved more facilely, more harmoniously, and more constructively than do the mentalities associated with today's postconquest world. Furthermore, it provided for an astonishingly rewarding and zestful life.

This sophisticated development of human mentality may be realizable only in preconquest settings like those described above. There is no evidence that it is a universal, benevolent nature common to all early humankind. It would be unreasonable to assume that human mentality evolved the same way everywhere during prehistoric times. Less altruistic types also evolved. It appears that at least one such combative type in Mediterranea progressively demolished its earlier preconquest type of life.

The preconquest mentality discussed here emerges only where infants have no need to weld libido to abstract concepts of identity, regularity, or association. Under such conditions the logical sense-of-truth of our Western 'Age of Reason' simply remains outside their realm of reason. Instead of applying rules logically sorted out (to know just where they stand or how they must fit in), these preconquest infants boldly thrust their sentient interests and awarenesses into an empathetic experiential maelstrom. The boundary-resistant, fluctuating pulses of cognition they experience there leave logic at a loss, therefore undeveloped. This may seem primitive, even a madhouse to those whose sense-of-reason is built on clear concepts logically examined. Yet a remarkably harmonious, on-the-mark intuitive rapport was the lot of these preconquest peoples. Such nonlogical rapport presents serious problems both for epistemologists and anthropologists, as it does for modern 'common folk.' For many years, my logical mind considered such cognitive separations insurmountable. Now I think that they only are when inquiry is held too rigorously within a single culture's ethos and system of belief.[23]

Questions going far beyond the quandary stated at the beginning of this chapter are raised. As fascinating as we may find the impact of conquering cultures on preconquest groups, it pales before the challenge to epistemology posed by the existence of a system of cognition not based on symbolic logic. We of Western training may find it virtually impossible to see how truth can be demonstrated without recourse to symbols that are logically controlled. When I first came face-to-face with these experientially-based modes of cognition wherein logic was irrelevant, they slid right past me. I did not even see them. Even when I did begin to catch on, I tended to doubt such perceptions once I was again within the confines of Western culture. It took years of repeated, even dramatic exposure before these initially fragmentary mental graspings were able to survive re-immersion in Western culture. Experiences repeated, however, eventually make their mark and I began to question whether symbolic logic was actually the only means to get at truth. Now I rather think that alternative routes to truth may exist within the immediacy of a type of experiential awareness that perhaps moves in extra-sentient directions not yet brought into the realm of our modern sense-of-truth.[24] My slowness in this matter leads me to believe it may take modern humankind some time to identify and make use of these perhaps more rarefied mental capabilities.

If such capabilities could indeed be realized, what practical significance might they have on the world as it has currently evolved? Integrative (as opposed to adversarial) approaches to truth might benefit a population that is becoming increasingly congested in its planetary home. Freeing epistemology from the so-called 'Age of Reason' might even bring scholarly benefits, such as opening areas of inquiry notoriously resistant to logical investigation, e.g., the visionary quests of sorcerers, the meditational insights of lamas, or just those evanescent understandings people sometimes grasp in that never-never land between sleep and waking. It might also help us understand those awareness flows that can occur across seemingly impenetrable cultural and cognitive barriers, as, for example, when liking is astir. Inquiry into such matters has long resisted both syntax and logic as well as the crucial pillars underlying them: e.g., quantification, measurement, and classification. A new way of looking would seem required.

Finally, in the ultimate analysis, we do not yet have a way to know if the postconquest type of consciousness that dominates the world today represents a positive or negative shift in the evolution of mentality. This question of fundamental values bears on all of humankind and on the future of humanity. Thus, of all the questions raised, it is the one that most demands an answer.

Notes

An earlier version of this essay under the title 'Cross-Cultural Epistemological Conundrums' was presented at the 70th Annual Meeting of the American Philosophical Association (Pacific Division) in Seattle, Washington, 3-6 April 1996. Older research material, drawn in to support the findings presented here, appears in a series, titled 'Sensuality and Consciousness,' published by *Anthropology of Consciousness*. Copyrights © 1995, 1996, 1997, Dr. E Richard Sorenson.

1. For a particularly dramatic case of integration with nature's forces that occurred in the eastern Andaman see Sorenson (1995).
2. The 'savage-savage' emerged in a time-of-troubles in which generosity gave way to grasping, instinctive sharing to instinctive hoarding, instantaneous friendship to calculated politics, automatic benevolence to selfish calculation, and spontaneous amity to warfare. The generous libidos of the spirited exploratory youths of preconquest communities were then transformed into the suspicious militancy of warriors shorn of generalized intuitive rapport. Such transformations reveal the vulnerability of the sophisticated nonwestern type of intelligence that evolved in preconquest settings.
3. I did not personally observe the Yequena in Venezuela's Coroni River region; however observations by Jean Liedloff (1975) show harmonious behavior and child nurture almost identical to what we saw, first, in those most isolated enclaves in the Central Range of New Guinea at the time of contact and, then, in less dramatic form in other preconquest groups where consciousness remained focused liminally.
4. The dynamics by which the 'savage-savage' emerged from a 'noble savage' is presented in Sorenson (1997).
5. There are relevant works in Western science that comport with existence of liminal areas of consciousness which were completed before the concept of liminal consciousness was publicized. While these scientists were, therefore, not in a position to refer to liminal consciousness as such, their work nonetheless provides material on some of its physiological and psychological underpinnings. The grandest operational field for liminal consciousness was opened up by the now classic neurophysiological work of MacLean (1993). In his physiology of the development of mentality he shows neurological connections between the limbic system of the midbrain and the cerebral cortex that provide considerable scope for the

interplay of consciousness within nonverbalized realms touching on emotions, immediacy and sexuality – all vital aspects of liminal consciousness. Adams' (1993) studies of the parieto and occipital lobes of the cerebral cortex suggest physical sites for the kind of liminal consciousness we saw in preconquest peoples. Though Adams is materialistic in orientation, the 'gut-feelings' of which he speaks are within the realm of consciousness since, if they were outside, we wouldn't know we had them. The same is true of emotions. Such aspects of consciousness fall well within the parameters of liminal consciousness. Tononi (1991) revealed physiological sites in the brain that are consistent with a liminal type of consciousness. He shows that qualities such as shape, size, proximity, alignment, and motion (all important elements of liminal consciousness) are managed by the visual (not the verbal) cortex. Berger and Luckmann (1966), in a study of the social structure of reality, speak of a 'primary socialization' that is worth examining in connection with the instinctively consensual socialization that occurs among preconquest peoples. They also speak of 'secondary socialization' which seems not to exist in these preconquest populations, at least on the instructive or coercive level. It is important to realize that Berger and Luckmann are particularly concerned about the importance of 'mental hygiene' as remedial socialization which they consider a necessary ingredient for human alliance. The fascinating aspect of such 'hygiene' is that, among the preconquest peoples, it occurred spontaneously without duress in the realm of consensual liminal sensibility. Laughlin (1994) establishes a context for liminal consciousness in his biogenetic structural account of Tibetan Yoga. He speaks of 'sensorial space' as the introspectively perceived output of 'sensorial dots' that provide for immediate perception of sensorial events. This type of immediacy is the hallmark of the liminal consciousness seen in the preconquest populations studied.

6.   The initial observations of infant and child nurture practices that gave rise to their liminal type of consciousness (and sense-of-truth) were presented before the effect of such practices on consciousness development was understood (Sorenson 1976, 1979). While those details are correct, only after additional experience among several preconquest peoples did the nature of the mentality involved become clear. The initial presentation of the relationship of infant handling and child rearing practice to basic mentality among these aboriginal groups was first presented in Sorenson (1996).

7.   Only in the southern communities where play with infants was sensually interactive were crying and affect-withdrawal rare. In the supraliminally focused sweet potato communities of the north such traits were often seen.

8.   Only in these southern hamlets was sibling rivalry not seen. Among the sweet potato farmers in the north sibling rivalry could frequently be seen.

9. There were no funds for filming in the eastern Sea of Andaman. However, much the same sort of synchrony was filmed among young Canela Indian children in Brazil. Several sequences of synchronous activity were assembled for a report film on the subject (Sorenson & Crocker 1983).

10. In areas where hunting-gathering was emphasized, girls and women also collected wild foods in the forest with the same synergistic sensuality that enlivened garden life in communities more horticulturally focused. In both cases sensual seductiveness increased in the face of choice foods.

11. Synchronous cooperation punctuated by playful surprise triggering ecstasy was an outstanding feature of the forest-dwelling hunting-gathering-gardening youths. It kept their collective hearts synchronized and elated.

12. The names 'Awa' and 'Fore' were imposed by Australian government officials later. No such regional, linguistic or ethnic names existed among the original Neolithic population. The situation was of customs, languages and practices adapting into one another along lines of contact without distinct separations or identities. The 'Fore' got their name by virtue of Western consciousness, when, from the high overlook at Moke between what became the northern and southern Fore regions, the Australian officer-in-charge of the initial exploratory patrol gazed across the vast panorama of the Puburamba and Lamari Valleys down below and onto the dramatic grassland slopes rising up beyond the Lamari River. He asked who were the people were living there. He was told *'fore kina.'* In the local language that meant 'the people living down below.' He knew that *kina* was the local name for 'people' and so recorded them as 'Fore.' Those 'people down below' encompassed a genetically diverse collection of hunter-gatherers, protohorticulturalists and full-time agriculturists speaking different languages and dialects. When the Lamari River later became the border of an administrative district to the east, those on the east side of the river were designated 'Awa' by officials of that new district. Though they considered themselves 'one-talks' with their brethren on the west site, they were said to be 'Awa' and to speak the 'Awa' language while those on the west side continued to be called 'Fore' and were said to speak the 'Fore' language. Formally these two languages belong to different language families. But due to dialect chaining across the region, the inhabitants of those hamlets in fact spoke a fusion of them both which they considered 'their language.' Depending how a linguistic investigator asked his questions, or what kind of an interpreter he had, a hamlet could be assigned to Fore by one investigator and Awa by another. Those called 'Fore' did not object, because they were flexibly accommodating regarding names. In the absence of any other regional or ethnic reference, academics, entrepreneurs and missionaries adopted the usage (and boundaries) established by the government. Thus was the ethnic and linguistic map of the region constructed. At first the 'Fore' used their new identity only when dealing with the government. Then they began

referring to themselves as 'Fore' to all Westerners; then to individuals from other regions in New Guinea; and finally among themselves. A finer-grained geography was created as subregions were named and mapped by subsequent Patrol Officers in similar fashion. Although the Western sense of geography did not correspond to the original local sense, these new names gained currency as government activity increased, and most dramatically when annual censuses were instituted. Individuals were then required to annually re-present themselves at the same established census site each year. As they did so, year-after-year, their sense of affiliation with that region (and its name) got stronger. When schools were later introduced, these regional names were passed on to the young as the 'Fore' geography. The Fore people, the Fore territory and their regional subdivisions (like many others in New Guinea) were in this way formally established.

13. The Fore *watimagi* is a wing-shaped carved-wood display platform on which the maturing penises of Fore adolescents were laid out to view. The Awa *tonana* is a band secured around the hips beneath a copious grass skirt to keep adolescent penises obscured and down. These two items of apparel represent major crosscultural differences in treatment of adolescent genitality. Fore boys didn't wear *watimagi* when active, and so and had none when they met the Awa, but their grass skirts were puny by comparison. At least one Awa boy was wearing his *tonana* when the two hunting groups met (Fore were still mirthfully commenting on this in 1963).

14. This was subsequently demonstrated in an ecological/genetic study which also shows that a similar process occurred widely throughout the highlands among many different peoples speaking many different languages (see Sorenson 1976, chapter 5).

15. For a particularly revealing case of such instinctive friendship among aboriginal Moken Sea Nomads in the Sea of Andaman see Sorenson (1998).

16. It was very different in communities to the north where consciousness was becoming supraliminal. Names lasted longer there, and initiations had begun bestowing initiation names – an emergent form of formal name. Claims on property were firming up, and kindreds had begun to formalize. Names of groups and sites were becoming more significant and more durable. Places started being named for the kinship group living there – opposite to the practice in the distant south where groups were more often referred by the name of the site on which they happened to be living. Similarly where abstract thought and arguments were emerging, names were firmer – for people, sites and kindred.

17. These photographs were first standardized in Westernized populations. For the initial report of this inquiry into the recognition of emotion across cultures see Ekman et al. (1969). For a report focusing on the crosscultural differences encountered see Sorenson (1975).

18. Individuals from the agricultural regions were much less sensitive. Unlike the hunter-gatherer-gardeners of the south, they were not distraught by photos showing full-blown negative emotions.

19. For details on this pattern of excess and restraint see Berndt (1962) and C. H. Berndt (1953). For details on the 'time-of-troubles' see Lindenbaum (1979, 1971), R. M. Glasse (1969), S. Glasse (1964), Glasse and Lindenbaum (1969).

20. That the earth was lightly populated principally by nomadic peoples before the rise of civilizations is generally accepted in anthropology. For a recent comprehensive summation of the socio-ecological development of the world in the 13,000 years since the most recent Ice Age see Diamond (1997). On a broad canvas, he traces a world that moved from universal nomadism to virtually universal settlement largely as a result of agriculture. For it was with agriculture that came stored resources, large populations, surplus labor, centralized power and all the other, some not so pleasant, trappings of civilization. Agriculture came on spottily, here and then there, some places being more easily adaptable to early tilling than others. Of the plenty of good potential agricultural regions in the early world, Diamond explains why the fertile crescent of the Mediterranean Basin (from Gibraltar to the Middle East) was one of the best (its climate, topography and the opportune diversity of its plants and animals). This is the area I refer to here as Mediterranea. It includes all the regions draining into the Mediterranean and is where Western Civilization had its earliest beginnings.

21. For a comprehensive presentation of the history of governments beginning about 3200 B.C. see Finer (1997).

22. This insight comes from numerous in-close personal contacts with both the land-oriented Sea Nomads that White (1922) contacted as well with the aboriginal type he did not. The latter avoids contact with postconquest people. For an unusual account of a month in residence on a Moken nomad craft of this latter shyer type see Sorenson (1998). This more aboriginal type scrupulously evades contact with commerce, avoiding even those semi-acculturated Moken, using obscure routes to bypass areas harboring these modern perturbations to their gentle lifestyle.

23. In this connection it is illuminating to peruse Sheets-Johnstone's (1996) elaborately reasoned analysis of the effect of a culture's symbolism on what researchers in one culture say about people in another. She critiques two major research bodies that distinguish Neanderthal from *Homo sapiens*. Asking whether we can justly say we know Neanderthals if we know them in anything other than 'in their own terms,' she makes a compelling argument for techniques of inquiry that bridge awareness differences among various forms of humanity. She argues:

> Words or phrases such as 'symbolism,' 'symbolic behavior,' and 'symbolic codes' have a patently compelling aura about them – they

are honorific, they straightaway signify intellectual acumen – and on first glance, we may think we understand what is being said. When we carefully examine what is being said, however, dear, reasonable meaning is nowhere to be found, either in the terms or phrases separately or as a unit (op. cit., p. 37).

24. For variations on the importance of experience see Blair and Prattis (1997). They deal comprehensively with the effect of experience on consciousness and of cognition on awareness in an anthology setting forth perspective-altering experiences that have influenced anthropologists. They also touch on logico-centric rationalism versus erocentric experience, feelings versus rationalization and the impact of mythos, eros and logos on mentality. In his own chapter in the anthology Prattis counterpoises dialectics and experience within the poetic dimensions of experience. Young and Goulet (1994) bring a variety of accounts together detailing the impact of extraordinary experience in crosscultural encounters. They leave little doubt about the importance of personal experience in crosscultural understanding. Laughlin (1994) shows the crucial importance of transpersonal experience in the understanding of Tibetan Dumo Yoga practice: A clear example of the need for modes of inquiry that go beyond current techniques of logic and language.

References

Adams, Walter R. (1993), 'The Parietal and Occipital Lobes and the Development of Consciousness: Some Preliminary Thoughts,' *Anthropology of Consciousness*, Vol. 4, No. 3, September, pp. 19-22.

Berger, Peter L. and Luckmann, Thomas (1966), *The Social Construction of Reality: A Treatise in the Sociology of Knowledge*, Doubleday: Garden City.

Berndt, Catherine H. (1953), 'Socio-Cultural Change in the Eastern Central Highlands of New Guinea,' *Southwestern Journal of Anthropology*, Vol. 9, No. 1, Spring, pp. 112-38.

Berndt, Ronald M. (1962), *Excess and Restraint: Social Control Among a New Guinea Mountain People*, University of Chicago Press: Chicago.

Blair, Derek and Prattis, J. Iain (1997), 'Opening Ourselves up to the Voyage of Anthropological Practice,' in J. Iain Prattis, *Anthropology at the Edge: Essays on Culture, Symbol, and Consciousness*, pp. 99-126, University Press of America: Lanham.

Diamond, Jared M. (1997), *Guns, Germs, and Steel: The Fates of Human Society*, W. W. Norton: New York.

Ekman, Paul; Sorenson, E Richard; Friesen, Wallace V. (1969), 'Pan-Cultural Elements in Facial Displays of Emotion,' *Science*, Vol. 164, No. 3875, 4 April, pp. 86-8.

Finer, Sammy E. (1997), *The History of Government from the Earliest Times*,

Oxford University Press: Oxford.

Glasse, Robert M. (1969), 'Marriage in South Fore,' in Robert M. Glasse and Mervyn J. Meggit (eds), *Pigs, Pearlshells, and Women: Marriage in the New Guinea Highlands*, Prentice-Hall: Englewood Cliffs.

Glasse, Robert M. and Lindenbaum, Shirley (1969), 'South Fore Politics,' *Anthropological Forum*, Vol. II, No. 3, November, pp. 308-26.

Glasse, Shirley (1964), 'The Social Effects of Kuru,' *Papua and New Guinea Medical Journal*, Vol. 7, No. 1, December, pp. 36-47.

Laughlin, Charles D. (1994), 'Psychic Energy and Transpersonal Experience: A Biogenetic Structural Account of the Tibetan Dumo Yoga Practice,' in David E. Young and Jean-Guy Goulet (eds), *Being Changed by Cross-Cultural Encounters: The Anthropology of Extraordinary Experience*, pp. 99-134, Broadview Press: Peterborough.

Liedloff, Jean (1975), *The Continuum Concept*, New York: Addison-Wesley.

Lindenbaum, Shirley (1979), *Kuru Sorcery: Disease and Danger in the New Guinea Highlands*, Mayfield: Palo Alto.

— (1971), 'Sorcery and Structure in Fore Society,' *Oceania*, Vol. 41, No. 4, June, pp. 277-87.

MacLean, Paul D. (1993), 'On the Evolution of Three Mentalities,' in James B. Ashbrook (ed.), *Brain, Culture and the Human Spirit: Essays From an Emergent Evolutionary Perspective*, pp. 15-44, University Press of America: Lanham.

Prattis, J. Iain (1985), 'Dialectics and Experience in Fieldwork: The Poetic Dimension,' in J. Iain Prattis (ed.), *Reflections: The Anthropological Muse*, pp. 266-81, American Anthropological Association: Washington.

Sheets-Johnstone, Maxine (1996), 'Tribal Lore in Present-Day Paleoanthropology: A Case Study,' *Anthropology of Consciousness*, Vol. 7, No. 4, December, pp 31-50.

Sorenson, E Richard (1998), 'Sensuality and Consciousness VI: A Preconquest Sojourn,' *Anthropology of Consciousness*, Vol. 9, No. 2, June, forthcoming.

— (1997), 'Sensuality and Consciousness V: Emergence of the "Savage Savage",' *Anthropology of Consciousness*, Vol. 8, No. 1, March, pp. 1-9.

— (1996), 'Sensuality and Consciousness IV: Where did the Liminal Flowers Go ?', *Anthropology of Consciousness*, Vol. 7, No. 4, December, pp. 9-30.

— (1995), 'Sensuality and Consciousness III: To Dance with Nature's Forces,' *Anthropology of Consciousness*, Vol. 6, No. 2, June, pp. 1-14.

— (1979), 'Early Tactile Communication and the Patterning of Human Organization: A New Guinea Case Study,' in Margaret Bullowa (ed.), *Before Speech: The Beginning of Interpersonal Communication*, pp. 289-305, Cambridge University Press: New York.

— (1976), *The Edge of the Forest: Land, Childhood and Change in a New Guinea Protoagricultural Society*, Smithsonian Institution Press: Washington.

— (1975), 'Culture and the Expression of Emotion,' in Thomas R. Williams (ed.), *Psychological Anthropology*, pp. 361-72, Mouton: The Hague.

Sorenson, E Richard and Crocker, William H. (1983), *Behavioral Synchrony in Childhood I: The Canela of Brazil*, Research Report Film (work print), The National Human Studies Film Center: Washington.

Tononi, Giulio (1991), 'Modelling Perceptual Grouping and Figure-Ground Segregation: How the Brain May Avoid Some Computational Pitfalls,' in International School of Neuroscience, Fidia Research Foundation Staff (eds), *Proceedings of the Course on Neuropsychology: The Neuronal Basis of Cognitive Function*, Vol. 2, September, pp. 44-53, Thieme Medical Publishers: New York.

White, Walter G. (1922), *The Sea Gypsies of Malaya*, Seeley Service: London.

Young, David E. and Goulet, Jean-Guy eds (1994), *Being Changed by Cross-Cultural Encounters: The Anthropology of Extraordinary Experience*, Broadview Press: Peterborough.

Part Four
Shamanistic Mediation of Meaning

6 Shamanistic Knowledge and Cosmology

Michael Ripinsky-Naxon

> For the eye must be adapted
> to what is to be seen.[1]
> Plotinus

The Concept of Shamanism

In an article published a few years ago, I proposed that shamanism was not merely a religious practice or a rite, but a system of beliefs with its own specific cosmologies, and thus a religious complex in its own right (Ripinsky-Naxon 1992). This statement requires further clarification, however, for shamanism is almost always integrated with another religious modality that is more nebulous and abstract in its philosophical scope. In a functional sense, when coexisting together with a pronounced form of shamanism, the supplementary modality may be regarded essentially as an ideological system consisting of sociohistorical myths – for example, theology, hagiography, geopolitical dogmas, the Greek state religion (as opposed to the core folk beliefs and practices), and so forth – and having most likely, but not universally, a ritual complex associated with it. Not necessarily derived from personal religious experience, this religious modality weaves through the cultural fabric, underscoring the sociopolitical matrix, and may itself function as an integral part within it. More importantly, as a coexisting ideological system, 'Religion gives the impetus to the entire shamanic scenario' (Hultkrantz chapter 7, p. 169), including its rituals. At the same time, trance and ecstasy give purpose to the techniques and drama of shamanism, formulating its principle aim, and forming the essential components in its fundamental structure.

Thus, shamanism forms a religious belief system based on religious experience and sacred myths, as well as on rites that find expressions through culturally-specific shamanistic techniques, in which trance or ecstasy play a prominent role. Through these rituals, shamanism fulfills a valuable cultural need by confirming the operational validity of the prevailing cosmology. Therefore, on an ideological, normative (cultural) level, both systems supplement one another, while on an emotional, personal (affective, psychological) level, they are complementary, providing a broader scope for certain emotional and symbolic outlays. Together, both form a dynamic, binary system of interactions between the more abstract religious modality and the validating shamanistic cosmology (see figures 6.1 and 6.2).

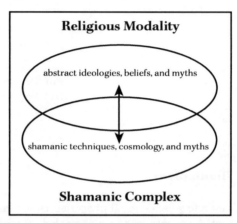

Figure 6.1   A model of a cultural binary system of religious modality and shamanic complex interactions.

The development of shamanism and hunting magic was almost inevitable. I am not treading the path of cultural determinism, but merely pointing out that a pre-existing set of conditions can ultimately give rise only to a finite number of possibilities, favoring some at the expense of others. Shamanism and hunting magic constituted a natural step (not the only step) in a world where food resource was, and is, one of the main keys to natural selection (Ripinsky-Naxon 1992, p. 38). Subsistence patterns based on hunting and gathering among the mobile communities of early humans, organized along the lines of extended family units, led to role differentiation and the division of labor between the sexes, as well as among the different age groups. Introspective and reflective consciousness, already innate by then, allowed for cognitive discrimination and abstract modes of thought. These neuropsychological changes, most probably, prompted the development of cognitive processes enabling symbolization and the use of metaphors. Such a transition may be inferred from the apparent awakening to the immense potential benefits to be derived from the observation and understanding of the natural environment, as opposed to mere passive acceptance of it. Finally, the transfer of this type of knowledge from one generation to another took the form of a ritual enhanced with accrued behavioral traits proven valuable for individual, as well as social, survival. More importantly, humans were learning to utilize their developing physical traits and transforming 'social psyche' (consciousness beyond the ego) as basic adaptive tools – a factor critical in the ongoing processes of bioevolution and culture change. As a result of the necessary development of adaptive mechanisms favoring survival, especially in view of intensified hunting, the tolerance for physical deprivation and other discomforts acquired a positive value. These traits entered into the shaman's craft by being first incorporated into and then expressed through the systems of shamanistic initiations.

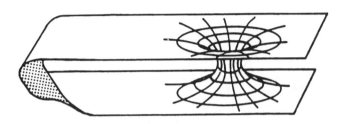

Figure 6.2 Graphic vortex representing religious modality and shamanic complex functionally integrated in a unified cultural dimension.

Clearly, throughout history, the shaman's practices have proved beneficial to the lives of hunting and gathering people. The adaptive features of shamanism enhance the life of a community that subsists by hunting animals and gathering wild plants. It is evident that such practices were integrated as a normative complex into a particular sociocultural unit. Thus, a social need (cause) is perceived as being transformed into a new culture complex (effect). Unfortunately, such unmitigated views tend to impart the gloss of dialectic materialism and economic determinism to the process of culture growth, while culture change, in turn, is viewed unrealistically as being a primary function of a social need. A close analogy may be found in the simplistic contention that the origins of agriculture and animal domestication emerged from man's rising food requirements.

Undeniably, shamanism forms an important cultural adaptive mechanism. However, it must not be interpreted solely in pragmatic terms. If one examines shamanism merely through the varnish of its exterior, ethnocentrically dismissing the shaman's helping spirits and not allowing for the existence of the Otherworld, then the meaning extracted from the entire phenomenon can hardly be perceived in other than social and functional terms (cf. Hamayon 1993, p. 3). By negating its spiritual side, one loses sight of its more profound import. To contact the spirits, to grasp the essence of shamanism, one must perceive it from the interior, travel whither the shamans go, and experience a shamanic journey. One cannot comprehend the actual nature of shamanism without a direct reference to ecstasy or trance-induced experience. In a séance, involving a trance technique and not merely visualization, the shaman journeys to the Otherworld and interacts with the helping spirits in order to heal and divine. I quite agree with Hultkrantz

Table 6.1:

A polarized schema of shamanistic ontology

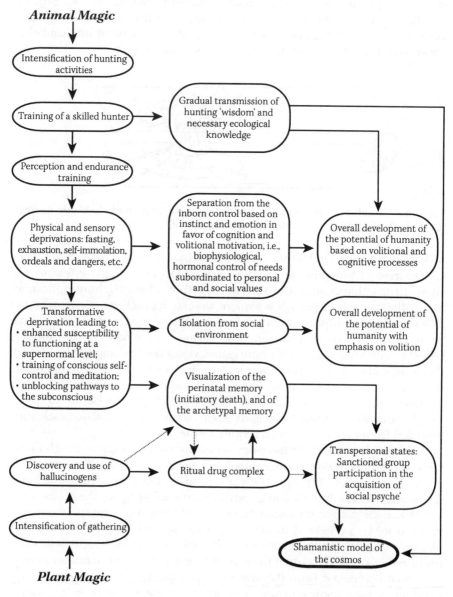

Source: Adapted and revised from Ripinsky-Naxon (1992)

(chapter 7, p. 170) when he states: 'Contact with the spiritual world can only be attained in ecstasy or trance,' and again, '... shamanism and shamanic rituals cannot be understood without the ecstatic experience of the shaman ...' The esoteric and preternatural aspects related to healing and communication with the spirit world establish claims of great significance for the origins and ontology of shamanism (see table 6.1).

The psychodynamic processes activated through the ritual techniques of ecstasy were facilitated by the discovery of hallucinogenic plants (see figure

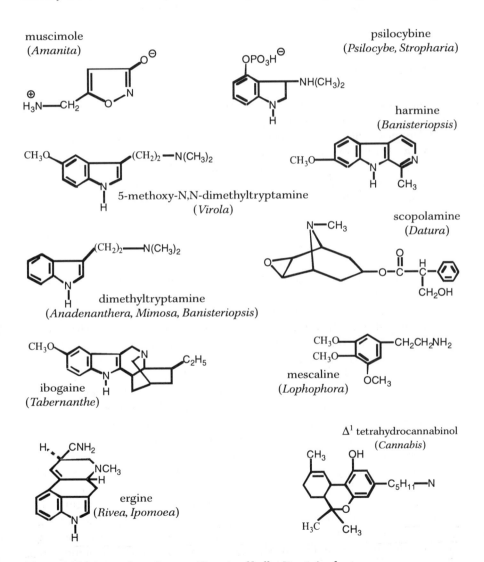

Figure 6.3 Main psychoactive constituents of hallucinogenic plants

6.3). Enhanced consciousness and cognitive abilities prompted the creation of models by conceiving structural and organizational paradigms for the cosmos.

By understanding the cognitive experiences that interrelate the various dimensions of supernatural reality with those of the ordinary one, we can grasp better the ethnogenetic factors behind processes that we perceive as culture change (cf. Ripinsky-Naxon 1989; 1993, pp. 105-6). Henceforth, the origins of shamanism need to be considered in the light of the shaman's adaptive role, as well as in the light of the symbolic and spiritual function of the shamanic figure.

The Binary Nature of Shamanism

Two classes, or categories, of plants must be recognized as forming a binary system in the pharmacopoeic repertoire of the shaman. The first may be placed in the category of entheogens: psychotropic plants that induce ecstasy, vision, and trance, and are considered sacred. The shaman utilizes them for embarking on a soul-journey to the spirit world. Hence, wherever found, the ritual plant complex forms a major component in the primary phase of the shamanic ritual. This phase becomes a prerequisite to the secondary phase that is concerned with finding the cure. The second floristic group consists of healing, or medicinal, plants that the shaman uses to effect a cure. These may be known to him empirically or revealed by the helping and familiar spirits encountered on a shamanic journey. Such plants become elements of the shamanic seance as a result of the shaman's encounters in the spirit world, facilitated, in the first instance, by the sacred plants. Hence, the medicinal plants are components of a secondary order.

We may be inclined to see some basic differences that must understandably exist between shamanic healing practices in the neotropical regions, such as the Amazon valley, and those of the Arctic and Siberia. Undeniably, tropical biodiversity produces wealthier storerooms of medicinal plants than does the sparser floral diversity of Siberia or the Arctic. Hence, the healing ritual drama of a Siberian, Saami, or Eskimo shaman is, to a comparative degree, more dependent on ecstatic techniques than that of a shaman from the Amazon, who has a vast store of botanical pharmacopoeia at his disposal. This is not to say that Amazonian shamans do not enter trance or go on soul-journeys. However, they are compelled to do so less frequently in order to heal better known or more ordinary symptoms. They are able to utilize the known properties among the abounding medicinal plants. The indigenous Central and South American healing tradition, *curanderismo*, must be a natural outgrowth of the secularization of various local shamanic healing techniques based on the shaman's corpus of knowledge of medicinal plants.

124

The principle of polar biunity is manifested also in the figure of the shaman. In certain cultures, there exist shamans and shamanesses who claim gender transformation and manifest a symbolic sex change. On much rarer occasions – for example, in Malay – they may actually undergo an anatomical change. As a result of their psycho-physiological predispositions (bisexuality) or androgynous physical characteristics (hermaphroditism), these shamans appear to combine in their persons the feminine (earth) and the masculine (heaven) principles. In other words, they represent the complementarity of bipolar unity, the union of opposites. The unification of polarized principles in the shaman satisfies the condition needed for recreating anew the unification between Heaven and Earth (Ripinsky-Naxon 1997, pp. 47-53). Consequently, such an individual is viewed as the intermediary, the intercepting axis, between the heavenly and the worldly realms, a nexus for the divine and the human. This androgynous state may be experienced through rituals and ecstasy, and is a condition for transcending the secular existence.

The principle of duality (e.g., sky = male, earth = female; light = male, darkness = female), although an inherent part of shamanistic cosmology, does not necessarily imply that the shaman's worldview is dichotomous. The existence of corresponding states of reality, or other 'dimensions,' is not necessarily viewed as dualistic divisions of the universe, but rather as integrated parts of a single unified whole. This concept acquired a more balanced and profound mystical significance in many cultures when it had become manifest as the principle of polar biunity (e.g., light-dark, benign spirit-malevolent spirit, male-female). The struggle between the jaguar and the serpent is a good example of polarized cosmic forces in the Maya universe. It is worth speculating here about the role of hallucinogenic agents in the etiology of such images of reality. With the ingestion of mind-altering substances, an inner personal conflict (IPC) may be brought to the foreground, prompting certain psychic states that may range from euphoria to withdrawal. Such experiences are capable of producing an acute sense of polarized reality. When projected onto a larger scale of psychocultural phenomena, they may even become an integral part of a cultural worldview.

The basis of human experience rests on the union of polar dualities, which is not only fundamental in the discernment of everyday existence, but is also believed to underlie all universal processes, affirming the principle of the absolute. The human mind is imprinted with the conviction that binary opposites, which characterize the direct and experiential reality of the individual, derive their essential attributes from absolute reality, where such opposites are also believed to exist. The efforts to cross over the boundaries of opposites transport the individual outside his or her personal condition, and allow for the experience of the mystical (Ripinsky-Naxon 1997, pp. 47-53, 61-3).

125

Shamanic Acquisition of Knowledge

In the course of its long history as a cultural feature among mankind, shamanism endeavored to unravel the universal enigmas: the origins of the cosmos, the earth, men, animals, and plants. It ventured to illuminate the proverbial, existential quest for the meaning and the sense of life and death. Shamanism shaped the qualitative aspects of religious epistemology by providing a technique by which a select number of individuals could acquire the esoteric knowledge of the supernatural order. The visions of the cosmic worlds were perceived by means of the psychodynamic processes activated through the ritual techniques of ecstasy, which have been frequently induced by the use of hallucinogenic plants. Essentially, the 'supernatural' experience of the cosmic order was only a reflection of the sociocultural system known at a particular phase of cultural development, while the secular knowledge of the supernatural was the shaman's version of his visionary experience. In the process, the physico-biotic environment was observed, and the ways of plants and animals were studied, as were the movements of the celestial bodies and the properties of metals. The healing potencies of the divine plants came to be understood, and meanings were given to dreams and visionary experiences. Thus, the beginnings of rationalistic epistemology unfolded.

The signification of a need in a particular society to relate causality (input) to the shaman's worldview and to offer a response through the mode of a visionary context (output) is the nexus of cause and effect, interfacing as a complex system in a dynamic process that we perceive as culture change. This process is, in itself, only an abstract modality, and, among others, a culturally accepted product of quite early and extensive experimentation with the ethnoflora (Ripinsky-Naxon 1989, p. 222; 1993, pp. 105-6; 1996, in press). Many of the conclusions reached by Reichel-Dolmatoff – based on his extensive field work experience among various indigenous groups in the Amazon – support our understanding of the subject. Thus:

> The quest for meaning is more or less formalised in all societies ... The mechanisms leading to this goal are remarkably similar the world over: sensory deprivation, meditation, hallucinatory states induced by drug intake or by endogenous means, etc. etc. The techniques are similar: controlled breathing, sexual continence, dieting, prayers, light/darkness manipulation ... can be found in most societies: in Tibet and on the Amazon, in Montserrat and in Ise. There is nothing 'mysterious' about all these basic practices and mental processes. The existence of altered states of consciousness, of other 'dimensions' is not necessarily seen as dualistic division of the universe but rather forms part of a single system. Our perceptual, phenomenological world is divided into innumerable named categories, but in order to guarantee survival (on the individual, social, ecological, etc. level) man must learn about meanings and these

meanings are found in a parallel, sometimes mirror-like extension which is readily accessible through the above-mentioned mechanisms. An Amazonian shaman would say: 'Just disconnect!' (without having read E. M. Forster). For example: in ordinary reality a fish is a fish and people know a great deal about fish runs, about how to catch fish, how to prepare it, etc. But when met in that other 'extension' the same fish will talk and will say: 'My name is so and so; I am a woman; I shall teach you when and how to catch me and when not to go fishing. I shall teach you how to make me "edible"' etc. etc. So the quest for meaning makes human existence possible because meanings, formulated by shamans, are ecologically and psychologically very important. In this sense shamanism represents an extremely important adaptive mechanism, based upon a great deal of scientific knowledge and psychological insight (Reichel-Dolmatoff 1990, personal communication).

The shaman's intellectual abilities are of real importance to the community, particularly as they apply to issues involving the culture-environment system. Equipped with an impressive corpus of empirical knowledge (ethnoscience) and a profound grasp of human behavior, the shaman fulfills the vital role of a psychocultural adaptive mechanism, not merely as a healer of diseases, but as a harmonizer of social and natural dysfunctions and imbalance. The shaman acts on behalf of the community or an individual. In an ecological sense, he is the restorer of a natural order and a psychocultural balance by mitigating dysfunctional conditions in society and environment. In a religious sense, the shaman is the *illuminatus* and the procurer of the light of ritual enlightenment. One constant element is pervasive in all shamanic complexes: the shaman's function as a healer. He strives for harmony and balance not only in nature, but also in society. In view of his ecological significance, the shaman's role as an agent in transcendental and existential realities tends to be underplayed by those who regard cultures as systems of more pragmatic and functional configurations. The importance of the latter is undeniable, but to de-emphasize symbolic (religious, spiritual, etc.) considerations is to misunderstand the full integrative potential inherent in shamanism as a dynamic factor in the cultural process (Ripinsky-Naxon 1993, p. 9).

In South America (e.g., among the Culina, the Siona, the Shipibo-Conibo, and the Matsigenka), the shaman's social role is validated by the attainment of power. His ability to abolish boundaries and unify opposites serves as a cultural mechanism of control, especially in the absence of formal political systems. The nature of power represented by the shamans in these cultures marks a distinction between inordinary and the ordinary individual, between this World and the Otherworld. This power can be defined in terms of three categories: (a) mastery of the ecstatic techniques, (b) acquisition of spirit helpers, and (c) the acquisition of ritual songs. Of course, (b) and (c) are predicated on (a) the ecstatic experience, which validates the acquired power. As may be expected, songs, music, and dance constitute pivotal elements in the display of power during shamanistic ritual dramas. Thus, shamanism in South America offers kinetic techniques enabling the practitioner to restore into proper balance various natural, social, and individual dysfunctions. The shamanistic ritual creates a culturally acceptable means of reentry and validation of occurrence. The ritual works because 'Its efficacy lies in its power as metaphor to express and alter the human experience by altering perception.' And the shaman derives power from the ability to unify polarities, 'from his ambiguity, since he does not fit into the mutually exclusive categories that organize the world' (Langdon 1992, p. 12).

Consequently, one must not underestimate the effect of shamanistic beliefs – hence, the role played by hallucinogens – in human attempts to organize the universe into a meaningful order. Under the influence of the psychoactive alkaloid harmaline, for example – found in the *Banisteriopsis* plant of the Amazon – the different religio-philosophical attitudes strove to unravel the cosmic arcana and bring structure and organizational sense into the frustrated intellect. This they accomplished by constructing the *imago mundi* – the archetypal image – in accordance with a cosmic blueprint manifest in the transcultural acceptance of the divine paradigm, along the recognizable guidelines of psychotropic experiences. Through the understanding of the cognitive experience, interrelating the various facets of supernatural reality with their ordinary counterparts, a much fuller insight can be gained into the causalities underlying the origins and the development of a cultural trait. In other words, one should consider the extent to which the shaman's techniques have depended on hallucinogenic substances in his or her formulation of supernatural and physical worldviews. Only through such an understanding, can we develop a more profound appreciation of the interconnecting dynamic processes that weave each cultural experience. A good illustration is offered by the nexus formed between the ritual drug complex and the beginnings of agriculture, alchemy, and even metallurgy – particularly of gold (Ripinsky-Naxon 1993, pp. 106, 181-6). Pre-Hispanic gold artifacts, especially from Panama and Colombia, offer a wide array of intriguing specimens to this effect. Several scholars observed the shamanistic symbolism of goldwork in the New World (e.g., Schultes & Bright 1981, pp. 37-43; Reichel-Dolmatoff 1981, pp. 17-33).

Mythic tradition serves as an umbilical line between the past and the present, and between the sociocultural unit and its physico-biotic environment. The myths describe the formulation, in a mythical past, of the sanctions and prescriptions governing the drug ceremonial. They also infer guidelines for the processes relating to the training of shamanistic initiates, which may involve many months or even years of disciplined apprenticeship under the tutelage of an experienced shaman. The neophyte learns vital knowledge of his people, including that of the flora and the fauna, origin myths and traditions, genealogies, drug use, and the appropriate rituals; not to mention gaining skills with hallucinogenic drugs, which are considered the essential channels of communication with the Otherworld.

It is to such mythic times, during which the plant hallucinogen was allegedly obtained, that the origins of shamanism are attributed by the Tukanoan Indians of the northwest Amazon (Reichel-Dolmatoff 1979, p. 29; 1987, pp. 5, 7). Besides etiologic reasoning, we find constructs of religious philosophy and metaphoric syllogism attached to the purpose of the ritual. Its intent, according to shamanistic concepts, is to effect transitions – alchemical transmutations, of sorts – during the times of critical events, such as the rites of passage surrounding birth, death, puberty, etc. Even certain sequences in the ritual preparation of the hallucinogenic potion from the vine *Banisteriopsis* spp. signify major occurrences in the lives of the Barasana Indians of Pira-paraná river. The process of sifting the crushed stem fiber with its psychoactive alkaloid content through a rattan sieve symbolizes the process of birth among these tribesmen. By re-enacting the transformations that the participants are compelled to experience, the ritual provides the facilities to precipitate such transitions by abetting the acolyte in the confrontation and passage through the individual crisis (IPC). For 'life is livable only when its threatening annihilation is mediated by ritual' (Reichel-Dolmatoff 1987, pp. 11, 13, 16, 21).

Symbolism of the Shamanic Journey – The Old World

Among many people of northern Eurasia, the universe is conceived as a living organism. In Siberian cosmology, it is sometimes associated with animal concepts. For example, to the Tungus (Evenks), the elk symbolizes the Middleworld, while the bear is connected with the Master of the Animals or the ethnogenetic father of their people. Just as in the transcendental reality of the Urubu Indians in the Amazonian tropics, the Tungus universe has a tripartite structure of the Upper, Middle, and Lower worlds, each representing an *imago mundi* of the other two. The cosmological tradition of the Siberian Samoyeds actually holds the polar star to be not merely an astral body, but also the 'Sky Nail' from which the heavenly drapery is suspended at the apex like a yurt hanging from a nail at the top of a pole. The Mongols, for whom the constellation of the Great Bear and the planet Venus are infused with important shamanistic meanings, refer to the polar star as the 'Golden Nail' and depict Venus on the cosmic diagrams of many a drum of the Altaic shaman. At the same time, they believe that the earth is imbued with forces of good and evil.

The Upperworld of the Tungus shaman is inhabited by powerful supreme spirits who preside over natural events, the taiga (the vast Siberian forest), animals, and men. The visible blue sky is the taiga counterpart in the

Upperworld, and the Great Bear constellation is represented by the cosmic elk, Kheglen. The concept of a deity (as opposed to a spirit) is rather vague, as shown by the personification of the solar deity, Dylacha, who mirrors in the Upperworld the earthly toil and labor of mankind. Other deities play minor roles and, as abstract concepts, are also poorly developed. Where a Mistress of the Universe exists, she is also the mother of people and animals, like the important Mistress of the Animals. The Middleworld is divided into human and animal groups; Eksheri, Master of the Animals, rules over the taiga, and Amaka over everything involving people. The Lowerworld, with seven planes or levels like the Upperworld, often consists of mirror and converse images of this world, as is depicted so vividly in the Celtic tradition. The rivers may flow to, not from, their sources; day corresponds to night; humans in the realm below may fall prey to creatures they hunted in this world. The Tungus believe that living things exist also as non-living, and substances 'flowing' from the Lower to the Middle world are changed in essence by becoming invisible. And, just like the Upperworld, the Lower one contains seven planes, or levels (Anisimov 1963, pp. 160-8; Vasilevich 1963, p. 48).

Symbolism of the Shamanic Journey – The New World

'I come to you because I desire to see,' is what an aspiring Iglulik Eskimo says when asking a master shaman for an apprenticeship. 'One who has eyes,' or *elik*, is the simple term used to refer to a shaman among the Copper Eskimo. 'The gift of seeing' comes usually with the empowering 'gift of songs.' 'Thirty years after my birth was the time,' recalls Isaac Tens , a Gitksan shaman:

> I went to my hunting grounds on the other side of the river.... The voices followed in my tracks and came very close behind me. Then I wheeled round and looked back. There was no one in sight, only trees. A trance came over me once more, and I fell down, unconscious. When I came to, my head was buried in a snowbank. I got up and walked on the ice up the river to the village.... My flesh seemed to be boiling.... My body was quivering. While I remained in this state, I began to sing. A chant was coming out of me without my being able to do anything to stop it. Many things appeared to me presently: huge birds and other animals.... These were visible only to me, not to the others in my house. Such visions happen when a man is about to become a *halaait* [shaman]; they occur of their own accord. The songs force themselves out complete without any attempt to compose them. But I learned and memorized those songs by repeating them (Barbeau 1958, pp. 39-41).

The shaman may be guided on his way by songs or he may acquire new songs in the course of his journey. It is in shamanic travels such as these that he acquires the power to retrieve souls and heal the sick. The shaman's archetypal journey to free a captured soul may correspond metaphorically to a uterine voyage in which the vagina signifies the transformational road to the spirit world and its inhabitants whose house may also be the uterus. Among the Cuna Indians of Panama, this is understood to be the case. In childbirth, the mother may suffer complications that are diagnosed to be the result of her soul's capture by Muu, the spirit responsible for the formation of the fetus in the womb, as well as for its potential attributes. Their shamans use chants to cure this type of malady and, by means of these songs, they create a manifest language in which all kinds of psychic states can be expressed and thus assist the sick person's progress in the preferred direction of the recovery path. In his structural analysis of the Cuna shaman's chant-poem, Claude Lévi-Strauss (1963, pp. 191, 193) describes it as 'appropriate' for creating the 'lived experience' of the ailing body by 'a more and more rapid oscillation between mythical and physiological themes, as if to abolish in the mind of the sick woman the distinction which separates them.' Moreover, the songs

> relate in detail a complicated itinerary that is a true mythical anatomy, corresponding less to the real structure of the genital organs than to a kind of emotional geography [supplying a] picture of the uterine world peopled with fantastic monsters and dangerous animals [in the likeness of] hell à la Hieronymus Bosch (Lévi-Strauss 1963, p. 195).

Shamanism and sexuality are also closely linked among the Desana Indians of the Amazon (as well as among many indigenous groups in Siberia). Master of the Animals is 'a phallic forest spirit,' who resides in a rocky outcrop believed to be hollow 'like a huge womb-like longhouse.' In the preparation of the potent hallucinogenic potion *yajé* (*Banisteriopsis* spp.), the Desana shamans see explicit allusions to the sexual process as an act of creation. The different colors, seen as dominant in the visionary experience, coincide with different 'dimensions.' Thus, yellow is the carrier of female fertility, and red of male. The vessel used for the preparation of the plant hallucinogen is considered to be analogous with the vagina and the uterus, while the rod used for stirring corresponds to the penis. Pottery making, in itself, is viewed as a transformational process that is archetypal of the transitions of life. The finished clay vessel, representing a woman, is decorated with various shamanistic symbols, among which the Y-shaped motif signifies the clitoris and, probably, also the labia of the vagina. The pottery designs are painted by the women in the same manner as their own body ornamentations around their waists - that is, in a string-like fashion. The foot of the vessel, used in *yajé* preparation, is decorated with the U-sign, which stands for the 'Tunnel' - or the vaginal passage through which the participant proceeds toward 'the body of the vessel in order to be reborn.' The initiate dies symbolically when he drinks yajé (*ayahuasca*), and is returned to the womb - that is, to the vessel containing the drink. Like the Y-symbol, the U-sign stands in a metaphoric relationship to the bone-soul concept that is found in the Desana rebirth cycle. During the human gestation period, the womb is regarded as a hexagonal (quartz) crystal. Hexagons define existential space of transformation and origin points of sacred objects and people. Hence, childbirth is viewed as the newborn's transformative passage between uterine walls made of crystal planes (see figure 6.4).

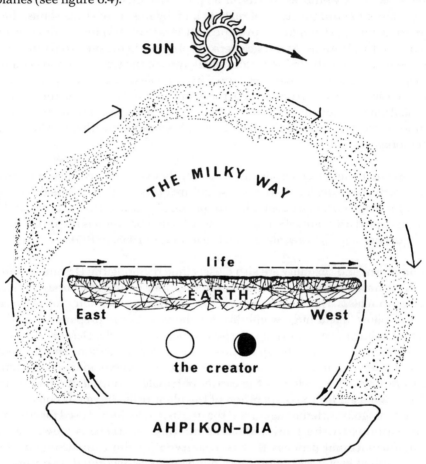

Figure 6.4   The structure of the Desana cosmos (Reichel-Dolmatoff 1971, p. 44).

In shamanistic initiations, the Desana add pulverized segments of small stalactites to the hallucinogenic Virola tree snuff. The stalactite is called 'sun-penis' (*abé yeru*), and the snuff is a 'divine semen' administered through a bone of the powerful Harpy Eagle – a shaman's avatar. The bone represents a passage for seminal fluids. The eagle's off-white down feathers are symbolic extensions of semen. Swallowing the downy feathers during initiation ceremonies becomes the allegory of impregnation. To illustrate the close association between sexuality and transformation, the term for both 'shaman' and 'jaguar' is represented by the cognate *yee* (plural, *yeea*), which is related to *yeeri*, meaning 'to copulate' (Reichel-Dolmatoff 1979, pp. 50-3; 1987, pp. 11, 13, 16, 21).

The spiritual and metaphysical aspects of the energies and forces of life, according to the Jívaro, may be tapped by means of hallucinogens. The spiritual realm, this antipodal World, thus entered, is where the knowledge of great cosmic causality can be apprehended. All the events that occur inside the Otherworld are manifestations of the 'true' reality, and exert and impact on the daily, physical aspect of existence. Consequently, the everyday, non-visionary, life is considered 'fake' and 'false.' Within the last few days of its awaited birth, a baby may be given (through the mother) hallucinogens so it can encounter the features of the true reality and hopefully establish contacts with the entities of the 'ancient specter', who may be willing to assist the infant in coping with the immediate hazards of this ordinary life, and prepare it better to avoid the pitfalls scattered along its path. Even older children are not exempt from a similar treatment at the hands of their parents, who may feel the need to re-substantiate, by 'consensual validation,' their own authority and values, as well as those of the community. By experiencing visions of the 'true' reality, the child can obtain glimpses of the root-matrix of his or her traditional (and the only valid) culture and be helped to come to terms with the essence of what it *is* to be a Jívaro. So important to them is the encounter with the spiritual dimension that sometimes they offer a special hallucinogenic admixture to their hunting dogs so the animals, too, may validate their souls by confronting the realities from another plane of existence (Harner 1972, pp. 134-5).

Likewise, we find a kindred situation among practically all Indian tribes of southern California. For them *Datura* has constituted an important plant hallucinogen that has been continually used in solemn religious ceremonies. *D. meteloides* is the only psychotomimetic plant employed by the Coahuilla Indians (in the proximity of the Coachella Valley) to produce a state of narcosis. The Native Americans are fully aware of the toxic properties and unpredictability of this plant. They caution against its uninformed use and admit that occasionally it has been known to cause death. All parts of *Datura* contain powerful psychoactive compounds and different sections of the plant are utilized varyingly, depending on the desired effect to be attained. Called the dream weed, Coahuilla shamans have used *Datura* in conservative doses to prognosticate illness and devise proper remedies. This plant has been crucial in the shaman's performance of his essential functions, including magical flights that form a part of the soul-journeys to the Otherworlds. Its ritual use has been stressed, particularly during puberty ceremonies, called *manet*, which primarily concern boys' initiation rites that focus around drinking *toloache* (datura concoction). During the enactment of the vital rites, and after experiencing all the significant aspects of the visions, the Coahuilla reality and cosmology receive confirmations in the minds of the neophytes. Ultimately, they become capable of assessing 'objectively' and 'empirically' the validity of their people's tradition. Once the re-confirmation is established through these visions, the initiates are locked into the old belief system and into the normative behavior of their culture (Ripinsky-Naxon 1995, pp. 36-38).

Validation constitutes one of the principal keys in the institution of shamanism. In a sense, it can be said that the effectiveness of shamanistic rituals is depended on their validation by myths aimed at explaining the aetiology and the cosmological paradigms associated with them. Culture influences social behavior, and from social needs emerge the dynamics that give impetus to the process of cultural change. Traditional cultures not only define, but also create the roles for the shamans. By reinforcing the established worldview, the shaman validates the age-old purpose and renders renewed vitality and legitimacy to his or her function through the enactment of shamanistic rituals.

Shamanistic Cosmology of the Ancient Maya

To gain the proper conception of the shaman and his visionary worlds, we need to understand the components and structure of the shamanistic universe. The cosmic totality, with the co-existential continuum, is a metaphor – an idiomatic expression of the shaman's cosmological worldview. Such beliefs found material realizations in the epigraphy and iconography of the ancient Maya and reflect the visions that these people of the forest developed of themselves, their history, and the natural environment – in short, the universe about them. Their cosmology reflects a complex interdependence of man and the natural world. Many of these beliefs represent anthropomorphic incarnations of celestial and numerological quantities. For example, the numbers 7, 9, and 13, representing shamanistic cosmological concepts, were 'numerological prime factors' and critical quantities among the Uralo-Altaic and Mesoamerican shamans alike. Cosmological ideas are perhaps the most abstract and least known aspects of prehistoric religion. Shamanism provides one key to reconstructing their general motives and, as in the case of the Maya, their complex and fascinating content. If viewed from this perspective, many of the enigmatic motifs and myths could be elucidated by more satisfactory explanations. Just as importantly, this view allows us to comprehend how such information, once it becomes integrated into the symbolic domains of culture, validates the religious beliefs, rituals, and all other aspects of sacred and secular existence.

The visible sky is the common denominator that uniformly unfolds its vistas to human experience. The early skywatchers often witnessed celestial manifestations that had been produced by similar phenomena all over the globe. The movements, configurations, and behavior of celestial bodies presented essentially the same puzzles in each hemisphere, despite the fact that the heavens were observed from different vantage points. Thus, it is hardly surprising that the sky is commonly credited with being the principal cause underlying the origins of numerous myths and religious traditions that belong to different cultures. A famous Navajo *hatali*, or medicine man, Hosteen Klah, explained this in a story. The primordial First Woman wanted to write down the laws for the First People. The only permanent medium was the sky. Everybody could gaze upward and study the sacred laws.

In its ultimate endeavor as a mode of existential quest for meaning, shamanism developed techniques for addressing the mysteries of the cosmos, including the movements of the celestial bodies, the secrets of magical plants, and the paradox of life and death. The psychodynamic processes activated by the ritual techniques of ecstasy were used to induce visions of the cosmic worlds. Hallucinogenic substances quite frequently played a vital role in such techniques. The structure of the cosmic worlds was reflected in the visionary experiences (Ripinsky-Naxon 1989, p. 222; 1992; 1993, pp. 44, 105-7, 217-8 n. 75). Consequently, shamanistic experiences and syllogistic reasoning promulgated an orderly structure for the universe based on interrelationships between the spiritual and the material. In Western civilization, such a concept found its elaborate expressions in the Pythagorean and Platonic ideas of the cosmos, and centuries later in the enlightened philosophy of Leibniz.

The obsession of the ancient Maya with celestial observations was motivated not by the acquisition of astronomical knowledge for its own sake, but by an urge to probe into the symbolic and religious realm of their existence – in other words, not to observe astronomical processes, but to follow divine phenomena and behavior of the gods (see figure 6.5). Despite the fact that their primary interest focused around temporal events, they were also preoccupied with the entity of space – not physical space, but transcendental. The foundations of religious thought and worldviews of these people reach deeply into a shamanistic past. The existence of shamanistic fonts at the roots of the ancient Maya belief system, although poorly understood as a phenomenon, is no longer a matter of scholarly contention.

Although we are still far from having obtained a clear picture of shamanism and its ontology in ancient Mesoamerica, some important advances have recently been made in this direction. For example, Houston and Stuart (1989) deciphered the reading of Glyph T539 consisting of a face of an *ahau* ('lord') half covered with jaguar skin. This glyph has the phonetic value of *way*, and its root is associated with 'co-essence,' 'dream,' 'sleep,' 'witchcraft,' 'nagual,' 'animal transformation,' and other spirit.' There also can be no doubt that its other cognates include 'anima/animus,' 'sorcerer,' and 'shaman.' Almost at the same time, a young and talented German epigrapher, Nikolai Grube,

135

arrived independently at the same cognitive value for this glyph (Schele & Freidel 1990, p. 45).

A factor that plays a crucial role in the development of the shaman's cosmological concepts is a function of the mythic language and metaphors. The iconography and epigraphy of the ancient Maya reflect, through their extremely rich symbolism, the visionary and cognitive experiences that these forest people formulated for their ethnogenesis, the natural world, and their place in it. The Maya cosmology is an expression of a delicately balanced, yet complex interdependence between man and the natural world, which, at the same time, is also populated by numerous spirits and other supernatural entities. Many of these beings exist as anthropomorphic personifications of celestial quantities and numerological values.

Among the Mesoamerican shaman-priests, the numbers 7, 9, and 13 were numerological prime factors endowed with vital potencies. For the Maya, these numbers represented seven planes of the Middleworld (earth), nine Lords of Xibalbá, and thirteen planes of the Upperworld. The sacred number 584 formed an integral part of Maya religious existence, and in the *Dresden*

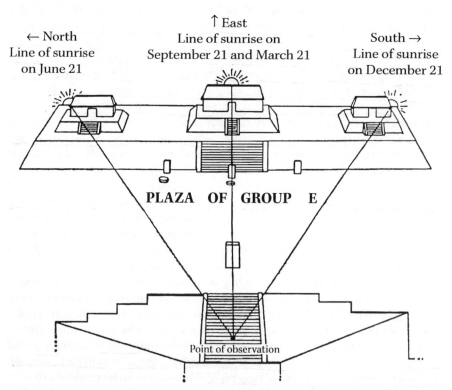

Figure 6.5 Diagram of the Maya astronomical observatory at Uaxactum in Guatemala, showing accurate alignments for sunrise at solstices and equinoxes.

Codex it is tabulated for the synodic period of Venus. There are 236 days between one helical rising and another. These are followed by 90 days before Venus reappears as the Evening Star. Another 250 days must pass until it vanishes in the light of the setting sun. Finally, after 8 more days, Venus has its new helical rising as it appears once more in the sky before the sun. The total number of days add up to 584. Modern calculations for the synodic period of Venus equal 583.92 days, and for a lunar eclipse equal 173.31 days.

Shamanistic and astronomical subjects form the dominant themes on many of the Maya painted ceramic ware and sculptures, in the several books of *Chilam Balam* and the *Popol Vuh*, and in the four Maya codices that survived the European purge. An example of such astro-shamanistic motifs can be seen in the representations of the resurrected radiant form of the Sun, skeletonized each night in its nocturnal abode as it journeyed from west to east (Thompson 1970, p. 181). Skeletonization and dismemberment (cf. the Greek ritual *sparagmós*) constitute transcultural themes that play integral functions in shamanistic initiations. The books of *Chilam Balam* were named after a Maya seer, or a jaguar (*balam*) shaman-priest (*chilan*: 'n' becomes 'm' before 'b').

Skeletonization

A classic, recurrent shamanistic motif is skeletonization. The bone, which symbolizes the fountainhead of life, must have its flesh trimmed off. In shamanistic terms, this condition is analogous with the return to the womb of primordial existence followed by a mystical rebirth in the arcane process of eternal return (see Eliade 1964, p. 63; Ripinsky-Naxon 1993, pp. 76, 82-4). And so the skeletal bones of the initiate await re-assembly into a revivified whole, signifying rebirth from a condition of weakness into a more powerful state. Some discussion of the Mesoamerican archaeological evidence can shed most interesting light on the religious rituals of the ancient Maya that seem to contain characteristic shamanistic themes.

A large dedicatory stela from the North Acropolis of Tikal in Guatemala was discovered in 1895 by Teobert Maler (1911, pp. 62-7, plates 12 & 13) during his exploratory work on behalf of the Peabody Museum. Among the intricate motifs depicted on this monument, known as Stela 1 and now in the Tikal Museum, we can discern various individuals ascending poles (cf. the shaman's pole, the World-Tree, etc.). It is probable that the main figure of the relief represents a priest of high rank, not an actual deity, while the other numerous representations of figures might be regarded as deities and mythological personages pertaining to the Maya Heaven. All the mythological accessories of the relief are puzzling figures. However, the significant detail for us consists of a large human skeleton shown with a string of vertebrae, enclosed inside a king's body, probably that of Stormy Sky (ruled from ca. A.D. 417-457). He is wearing a belt ornamented with supernatural beings and crossed bands. His ankle ornaments contain feather wings. The Tikal emblem glyph forms a headdress on a mask, which is depicted in profile and belongs to a panel supporting the king. For all its rich and intricate symbolism, the iconography of the carving has not been studied sufficiently. I would like to point out some noteworthy motifs depicted in the carving of the stela, which hitherto have gone unmentioned, as well as note their special significance in the light of shamanistic initiation.

The ruler is accompanied by the image of God K, who is visible inside the jaws of a two-headed serpent. This is perhaps a partial reference to Stormy Sky's name-glyphs, God K-Cleft Sky, where God K is shown with a 'smoking axe' in the forehead and the suffix for Cleft Sky. (In conjunction with the figure of Stormy Sky, however, the glyph for God K might have been sufficient to denote this ruler.) The god's leg is transformed into the extended body of the snake, and the reptile's other head becomes the king's foot. In itself, this scene might be allowed to pass for an unexplained piece of esoterica. However, in conjunction with the skeleton of Stormy Sky, we have here an allusion to shamanistic initiation and transformation – death and rebirth. Skeletonization is an integral part of the shaman's development. The shaman is dismembered by the spirits, who remove his flesh and organs. Later the body is re-assembled, and a supernatural object, such as a quartz crystal, is placed in lieu of an organ or a bone. This episode is critical in the shaman's rites of passage. It influences the development of his powers and abilities. Consequently, it is of importance to the entire community. The emergence of a snake as God K's leg is nothing other than the shaman-king's (Stormy Sky?) transformation into his animal counterpart (Ripinsky-Naxon 1993a, p. 51). Incidentally, this also indicates the association of the serpent rain-god with cloudy and stormy sky, or the wet season. Consequently, a possible reference to *Chicchan*, the celestial serpent that causes rainfall, cannot be overlooked.

The astronomical or celestial meaning of this scene cannot be ignored either. A skull is a Maya emblem for Venus. However, as suggested by Coe (1975, p. 92-3), a skull may have been as closely related to the Lowerworld as to death or the death god. It should be kept in mind that the skull was also the personified form of a glyph for *Cimi* – the name-day of the god of death and of the sixth day in the twenty-day month of the Maya calendar count. Venus played a crucial role in the everyday drama of cosmic events, just as it did in the ritual life of all Mesoamerican cultures. It was laden with the religious significance of death and rebirth. The Maya priests watched closely the heavenly firmament for any signs accompanying a demise or (re-)creation in the cosmic structure. Such occurrences were later extended to the gods-on-earth, that is, the human lords. Venus, at the helical rising, represented the powers of the Lowerworld, with their destructive potential force engulfing the earth. Darkness precedes creation. Hence, this event in the heavens represented the cosmic mystery of eternal return, and in some way it symbolized its validity here on earth. *Lamat* is the sign of the lord of the 'great star', that is, the planet Venus. Its symbol is represented by a cross-sected cartouche, with each section displaying a small circle. In personified variants, we find, in its place, the celestial dragon bearing the four Venus circles. Thus, the celestial aspect of Stela 1 only enhances our notion of shamanistic imagery in the Maya cosmology.

Kinich and Chicchan: Time and Space in Maya Cosmology

The Center forms a basic component in the symbolic syntax of shamanistic cosmology. (On its neuropsychological significance, see Naranjo 1973, who experimented clinically with substances used by the South American shamans to induce visions.) It designates the *axis mundi*, or the World-junction where the entrances to the Middle, the Upper, and the Lower worlds can be found. The center, or the Cosmic Mountain, and the spiral (cyclical or helical rather than circular) process of eternal return are all morphological elements integral to the structure of the shaman's universe. The archetypal Cosmic Mountain has been related to Mesoamerican pyramids and is a cross-cultural theme (Ripinsky-Naxon 1993, p. 114).

The spiral – hence, the tunnel and the mandala – is a passageway to the Lowerworld and annihilation, as well as to re-emergence and rebirth through shamanistic initiation. The principle of eternal return appears to be fundamental to the religious lives of ancient and indigenous societies. For the ancient Maya, this principle established that the quality of time is intrinsic to the essence of the deities (León-Portilla 1973, pp. 37-38). The gods were responsible for the cycles and changes in the universe, which also determined the fate of man.

However, space – physical or transcendental – is the abstract vessel into which man organizes this universe of his. He has devised realms to satisfy his spiritual and worldly requirements: the former existing under the exclusive sovereignty of a deity of a spirit; the latter being inhabited by humans, and subjected overtly to their manipulative actions in accordance with the prescribed norms of ritualized behavior. Sacred space does not necessarily imply an upper realm, as envisaged in our own idea of heaven. It refers to an existential concept of extraordinary dimension, as opposed to a mere physical or material domain.

The Maya cosmos contains pronounced shamanistic motifs. It rests on a multi-leveled pyramid, which is placed atop a cosmic monster amidst a primordial sea. Each quadrant is associated with a specific color. The center represents a fifth orientation – a vortex where all the other directions meet. Four supernatural beings uphold the celestial dome, represented by a two-headed dragon. Other astral entities consist of a sky band with celestial symbols, the moon goddess, the sun god, the planet Venus in a skeletonized form, and the Pleiades stars as the tail of a rattlesnake. The cosmic geometry of the archetypal blueprint was underscored by an *axis mundi* that was demarcated by the concept of a four-directional orientation of the cardinal points. Not only did the Maya universe have these orientations, but its four quadrants converged at the center, thus creating a fifth point or direction. All Maya communities, small and large, were sectioned into four quadrants, each corresponding to one direction (Coe 1965, p. 101; León-Portilla 1973, pp. 81-2, 85) – either cardinal, east-west-north-south, or one coinciding with solstices and equinoxes (see figure 6.6).

The cosmic serpent, *Chicchan*, was responsible for rainfall, together with the four ophidians living at the four corners of the world, symbolizing the four-directional axis, or points of cardinal orientations. *Chicchan* was the

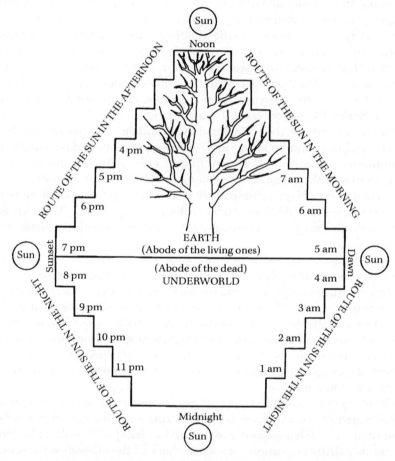

Figure 6.6 Spatial image of the universe, preserved to this day among the Tzotzil Maya in the state of Chiapas, revised from Villa Rojas (1973, p. 141).

140

Figure 6.7   The face of Kinich in the table of the eclipses of the Dresden Codex 56a (León-Portilla 1973, p. 83).

deity of the fifth day in the Maya twenty-day month, and its various glyphic forms are suggestive of the snake. Such a model (*imago mundi*) was a reflection of the three-dimensional universe – an inflection of hexagonal crystal structure and a trueshape of the Maya cosmos – where time was, as León-Portilla (1973, p. 96) phrased it eloquently, the 'primordial reality' that subsumes all, and *Kinich* (sometimes referred to as *Kinh*) was the divine manifestation of time in the all-encompassing universe. By the same token, space was a matrix made up of 'the framework of colors' in which *Kinich* displayed his countenance through the idiom of time (see figure 6.7).

The Maya quality of sacred space encompasses an essential temporal dimension, rendering space and time as coexistent functions of the same continuum. Time can be suspended, may be reversible, and is always repetitive or cyclical. Its coordinates are those of a curved space and, like the interior of a sphere without boundaries, it projects into mythological existence. With the passage of a specific number of years, months, and days, time would become re-aligned on its temporal coordinates, and the same date with identical supernatural attributes would be repeated all over again. The *Wheel of the Katuns*, recorded in the first eleven pages of the *Paris Codex*, as well as by Bishop Diego de Landa and in the various books of *Chilam Balam*, demonstrates that it will take approximately 256 years of 365 days for the same date to repeat itself (see figure 6.8).

For the ancient Maya, and even today, time was a function of the infinite progression of solar cycles and underscored all processes of transition. More importantly, it was a manifestation of the divinity of supernatural beings.

141

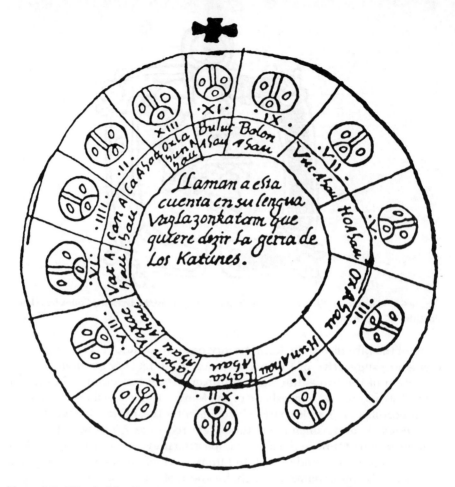

Figure 6.8 Wheel of the *Katuns* according to Diego de Landa (1566)[2]

A*hua*, the twentieth and last day-sign, is the embodiment of the radiant presence of the sun. The journeys of the divine bearers of time resemble, in many ways, the travels of the shaman, especially when they concern the supernatural quality of time. Such instances seem to reflect historico-cultural interconnections. In shamanistic societies, the keeper of the calendar and sacred time is the shaman, whose function as a mythologue is to ascertain that all prescribed rituals are enacted on time. He or she maintains close links with the Otherworlds, to which journeys are undertaken in quest of supernatural knowledge (Ripinsky-Naxon 1993a, p. 54). In fact, the very nature of time was divine (León-Portilla 1973, pp. 33, 35). Every single day was not only represented by a deity, but was an incarnation of supernatural powers (Thompson 1960, p. 69). Moreover, the control of the movement of time through the use of ritual hallucinogens lends a sacred dimension to human existence on earth. Thus, it is apparent that one of the main keys to understanding the Maya cosmology and religion is to be found in their concept of time.

Wacah Chan – The World Tree

A sacred pole, a symbol of the cosmic pillar, or the World-Tree, is the celestial ladder that the shaman ascends into the company of the spirits to reach another cosmic plane, or a star, a river, a bridge, or a 'razor's edge' (e.g. Hultkrantz, in Bäckman and Hultkrantz 1978, pp. 12-14; Eliade 1964, p. 265f.; cf. also Jacob's ladder in the Old Testament). The Finnish hero, Vainamoinen, and his shamanic companions must cross a bridge constructed of piercing knife points and swords to get to the Otherworld, *tuonela*. Similar themes are to be found in Celtic folklore, too. The Muslims believe that a bridge to paradise is suspended over the abyss of hell, and it is as wide as a razor's edge. The better-known motifs comprise Sir Lancelot's death-like trance and visionary experiences, during which he struggles across the mortifying sword-bridge. Such imagery is commonly encountered in the cosmography of a spiritual voyage of the shamanistic type.

In the Maya cosmological iconography, frequent uses are made of the World-Tree motif, called *Wacah Chan* in the Maya glyphs. At Palenque alone, it is found in several places, including the Temple of the Foliated Cross, the Temple of the Cross, the Temple of Inscriptions, and the Temple of the Sun. One example comes from the great tomb of Lord Pacal, discovered by Ruz (1968, pp. 186-7). It is a carved sarcophagus lid depicting a World-Tree together with scenes that take place in another realm of existence (see figure 6.9). Ruz identified it as a maize tree, and is followed by Schele and Freidel (1990, p. 409). But the tree symbolized here is probably the sacred ceiba, surmounted by a quetzal bird, as I suggested some time ago (1993a, p.55). In the Maya religion, the ceiba was strongly identified with the Tree of Life, growing from the center of the earth and visible sometimes inside deep caves.

Birds perched atop World-Trees are well documented for pre-Columbian Mesoamerica, including western Mexico. Furst (1975, p. 53, n.3) reports that the Huichol Indians allude to the souls of unborn children as birds, and their shamans transform children into birds in the chants associated with the Drum and Squash ceremony, as part of the introduction to the peyote ritual. The motif of a bird or birds perched on top of the World-Tree is also widespread in Siberian shamanism. The Goldi, the Dolgan, and the Tungus (Evenks) uphold that the shamans go to the Cosmic Tree to find the souls of children waiting to be born, who sit like birds among its branches. In Yucatan, Belize, and the rest of Peten, formations of stalagmites and stalactites may at times bear striking resemblance to trees. By the same token, caves were regarded by the Maya as sacred precincts. This belief has survived in many communities, together with the notion that the Tree of Life stems from the earth's center.

Tozzer (1907, p. 154) noted quite early that some of the Maya of Yucatan

Figure 6.9 The Maya Lord Pacal of Palenque, buried at the pyramid tomb known as the Temple of Inscriptions.[3]

believed that the ceiba branches, growing from different levels of the tree, formed the levels of each cosmic plane (see figure: 6.10). A ladder made of vines was sometimes used by the souls for moving between the various levels,

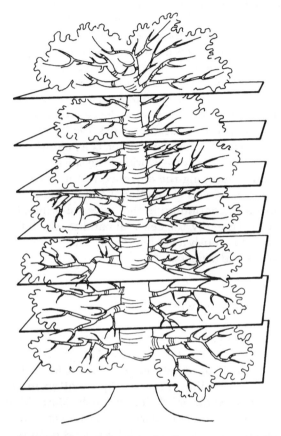

Figure 6. 10 The celestial levels and the sacred ceiba tree among the Maya of Yucatán (Villa Rojas 1973, p. 137).

which were governed by supernatural entities. Interestingly, from a shamanistic perspective, the fourth level contained the Protector or Master of the Animals. The seven tiers of the ceiba tree have cognitive counterparts in South American and Siberian shamanism. Michael Coe (1975, p. 102) rightly questions the long-established tradition, since the days of Seler, which interprets the World-Tree as supporting the sky. He believes, instead, that the World-Tree is growing from the Lowerworld and upholds the earth. Moreover, the identification of the surrounding carved band, containing celestial symbols, simply as a 'sky band' is to miss part of the picture. Coe believes that the band represents specifically 'the night sky,' thus fitting better his notion of the Underworld origins of the World-Tree.

145

I have mentioned already the celestial pole carved on Stele 1 atTikal. Clearly, the theme of the World-Tree recurs in shamanistic contexts all over the world. However, it functions as an actual support for neither the sky nor the earth, but serves as a point of entry into earthly and Otherworldly dimensions of the universe. It grows from an existential cosmic center – an *axis mundi* – which also symbolizes the navel of the Great Mother (the Underworld). The tree emerges from there as a kind of repository of souls. It intersects all the Worlds and domains as it traverses the universe and holds entrances to the Otherworlds at certain sacred sites.

In *The Book of Chilam Balam of Chumayel*, we read of a cosmogonic event: 'On 2-Eb he made the first stairway. It descended from the midst of the heavens, in the midst of the water ...' (Roys 1967, p. 117). In shamanistic imagery, the stairway is the shaman's ladder, or a pole, which he uses to travel between the Upper and the Lowerworld of the spirits – while the bottom of water is the nadir containing the entrance to the Lowerworld. Thus, the World-Tree is a nexus of all the directional and temporal axes. At the same time, it functions as a continuum in the universal principles of duality and polar biunity. Consequently, the celestial band to which Coe (1975, p. 102) refers may be simultaneously a 'sky band' and 'the night sky,' for it represents the Sky in all forms and aspects.

Xibalbá: The Maya Lowerworld

In a shamanistic cosmography, for example, the boundary between this World and the Other is often demarcated by a river. Along its course, one encounters often strange and horrifying creatures. Among the Maya, the *cenotes* – deep natural wells, usually in limestone and quite often in caves – signified entrances to the Underworld, or Xibalbá, in Quiché Maya. Most Maya believed that the entrance to the Lowerworld was in a cave located in the Alta Verapaz. The Maya shaman-priest was responsible for regressing through this entrance all the diseases sent by the Lords of Xibalbá upon mankind. We find explicit incantations listed in the Rituals of the Bacabs for the use by the shaman-priest in reverting visited ailments back through the portals of the Lowerworld (see Roys 1965). When a person died, he or she might end up in any of the nine levels comprising the Underworld. These special cavities became the sites for the performance of sacred rituals. Bearing this in mind, we can gain better insight into the significance of sacrificing humans in the sacred *cenotes*.

The Quiché Maya believed that Xibalbá was the residence of the supernatural beings who were hostile to humans. The descriptions of Xibalbá visited by the Hero-Twins in the *Popol Vuh* are allusions to shamanistic soul-journeys to the Otherworld. In ancient times, according to Fray Tomás Coto (ca. 1690), the word *Xibalbay* had been used to denote the images of demons and spirits of the dead that the natives perceived in their visions. Such visions, among others, were induced by the sacred hallucinogenic mushroom, to which Coto refers by its Cakchiquel Maya name as *xibalbaj okox*, meaning 'mushroom of the (gods of the?) underworld' (Xibalbá = 'Underworld,' 'hell'; *okox* = 'mushroom'). He also asserts that this mushroom was known also as *k'aizalah okox*, that is, a mushroom that causes one to lose judgment. Despite a strong belief in the immortality of the soul, which characterizes Maya culture, the accounts of Bishop Diego de Landa (1566) indicate that these people possessed a strong fear of death that was evidenced as a dominant cultural preoccupation. Perhaps the fear was directed toward the hostile creatures of the Underworld, rather than merely death. This feature differs from the 'stoic fatalism' encountered in other Central American cultures.

Thus, cosmographic knowledge of the spirit world became a dire necessity to prevent annihilation. The soul had to undergo a perilous journey through the nine levels and four directions of the Maya Underworld. This Lowerworld had a counterpart in the world of humans: it resembled the earth and was populated with all kinds of creatures and plants. With the setting sun, *Xibalbá* rotated on its axis to become the nocturnal celestial dome over the earth. In a more perceptive reinterpretation of some of the texts and iconography bearing on the Classic Maya conceptions of the Otherworld, Schele and Freidel (1990, p. 425 n.4) affirmed my belief that *Xibalbá* actually means the Otherworld as perceived through shamanistic visions.

The sacred books of the *Popol Vuh* (see Tedlock 1985) can be compared to many northern European epics containing accounts of the ordeals symbolic of shamanistic initiations and the hero-shaman's triumphs over supernatural evil or death. The astral nature of the legend of *Popol Vuh* is indicated at the beginning with the first set of brothers, 1 Hunahpu and 7 Hunahpu. It has long been known that 1 Hunahpu corresponds to the lowland Maya *tzolkin* day 1 Ahua. *Tzolkin* is the 260-day 'short-count' calendar. Its astronomical basis has not been determined, but it is obviously neither lunar nor solar. A colleague of mine, John W. Burgess, an astronomer formerly with the Fernbank Science Center in Atlanta, has argued plausibly that it represents an astronomical cycle based on the ecliptic of the planet Venus. This period marks the beginning of the Venus calendar, with the helical rising of the Morning Star. In a complementary position, '7 Hunahpu' stands for the Evening Star (Coe 1975, p. 90).

With the passage of time, the brothers are destroyed by the Lords of Xibalbá. However, the head of 1 Hunahpu (i.e. the helical Venus), as it hangs on a calabash tree, manages to impregnate the daughter of one of the lords by spitting on her hand. The girl gives birth to the Hero-Twins, Hunahpu and Xbalanque. As the Twins grow older, they are impelled to embark upon a perilous soul-journey – one of the characteristic traits of shamanism – filled with all kinds of ordeals, agons, and immolations. The myth describes events that represent their voyage as an obvious transition through shamanistic initiation, consisting of symbolic death by dismemberment of these two ordinary men, and their eventual rebirth as magicians bestowed with powerful secret knowledge. The spittle, which had impregnated their mother, is considered in both Hemispheres to be the locus of the most vital shamanic potencies and is often identified with liquefied quartz crystal – a shaman's most valuable power object.

The story reverberates with accounts of shamanistic initiations, complete with narratives of soul-journeys to the Lowerworld and ordeals connected with the rites of passage. These include the characteristic steps, or a shaman's ladder (symbolic of the cosmic tree); the crossings of mountain passes, ravines, and rivers of blood and degeneration; axial directionalities and demarcations of the cosmic worlds; as well as dismemberment, which symbolizes shamanistic initiation and rebirth. When 1 Death and 7 Death, lords of the Lowerworld and pernicious adversaries of the Hero-Twins, asked the brothers to dismember them in hope of attaining renewal through the process of eternal return, the two crafty lords expedited their own demise at the hands of revitalized youth by making such a request.

In one of the trials, described in the *Popol Vuh* as taking place in the House of Knives, we have an obvious counterpart to a 'shaman's crossing of the abyss of the life-death continuum, on a bridge no wider than a knife's edge, to re-establish the natural balance in the universe by making the proper sacrificial restitutions' (Ripinsky-Naxon 1993, pp. 92-4). The knife's or sword's edge is a characteristic motif encountered in the extraordinary dimension of shamanic state of consciousness; as may be expected, it plays a powerful role in many old religions, including Celtic and Eskimo shamanism, as well as Hinduism. At long last, the Hero-Twins become deified as celestial personages. Hunahpu is identified with the Hunter Venus (although deified as the Moon in some interpretations), and Xbalanque is equated with the Jaguar Sun. Kinich's journeys to the Lowerworld represent nocturnal time and the night voyage of the sun from west to east; at such times, he is the lord of the Underworld, and his animal counterpart is the jaguar. As Carlson (1990, p. 98) observed:

> Astronomically, Venus (Hunahpu) behaves like a brother to the sun (Xbalanque), either rising before it at dawn or setting after it at dusk. The complete cycle takes 584 days.
>
> The other twin, the sun, rises each day at a different point on the landscape and so, from solstice to solstice, apparently travels back and forth along the horizon. By astronomical coincidence, five 584-day cycles of Venus equal eight 365-day years. The Mesoamericans constructed an eight-year almanac based upon the interlocking Venus-sun cycles.

Xbalanque also becomes the Great Shaman associated with the realm of the dead, at least among the southern Pokomán (Fuentes y Guzmán 1932, I, p. 266). It is he who, in his shamanic role as a psychopomp, guides the souls of the deceased Pokomán overlords to their final destination. One of the principal functions of the shaman is to act as an intermediary between this and the Otherworld. Thus, Michael Coe (1975) has observed correctly 'that in some way they [the Hero-Twins] were the supernatural, mitigating force between the living and the dead, at least as far as the hereditary nobility was concerned' (op. cit., p. 91).

Ritual Hallucinogens and the Maya

The function of the shaman or the shaman-priest is impregnated with culturally defined meanings – meanings that, in turn, seek and find validation in the shamanistic experience underscoring native epistemology. the shamanistic experience itself is facilitated by a mode of ecstatic techniques in which hallucinogenic substances have more often than not played an integral part. The ancient Maya culture and its surviving tradition have preserved a considerable legacy that gives witness to the enduring existence of a shamanic heritage amidst these people. The iconography of Maya art, ranging from the periods of the Early and Preclassic to the post-Conquest, contains a wide representation of biodiversity, including mushrooms, toads, water lilies, and tobacco. The significance of these motifs lies in the fact that they probably refer to the religious status of these objects, owing to the psychoactive properties of the alkaloids intrinsic to them. These substances produce hallucinogenic visions by modifying the biochemistry of the brain and functions of the nervous system. The effects of cultural affirmation, in combination with the psychological predisposition of the individual, help structure and pattern the imageries formed in the preternatural reality of shamanic states of consciousness. As a result, drug-induced visionary experiences conducted in a prescribed and traditional mode will, in turn, validate both the cultural norms and worldviews of a community (Kensinger 1973; Dobkin de Rios 1972, 1996; Ripinsky-Naxon 1989, 1995).

As early as 1961, and quite possibly influenced by Wasson's work with psilocybin mushrooms in Mexico, de Borhegyi (1961, 1963, 1965) suggested that hallucinogenic mushrooms had been known and used in religious ceremonies by the ancient Maya. He documented this claim with many finds of pre-Columbian mushroom stones and mushroom pottery, covering the time-span from the Preclassic onward. De Borhegyi's perceptive observations on the ritual associations of his finds lent support to his assertions. Mushrooms are mentioned in the Maya texts of the *Popol Vuh* and the *Annals of the Cakchiquels*.

Re-evaluations of old, as well as new, archaeological evidence points to the fact that trance-induced experiences were widespread in Classical Maya times, at least, among the elite and the upper sphere of common folk. It is also highly probable that women took part in trances and saw, as Schele and Freidel (1990, p. 266) phrased it, 'vision serpents.' Many of the graffiti in Tikal,

149

depicted on the interior of structures, seem to be products of visions experienced by individuals (Haviland & de Laguna Haviland 1995). One of these structures (6F-27), known as Temple VI, displays a large number of graffiti, and it is worthwhile to note that, on the basis of glyphic evidence alone, Schele (1990, p. 34) believes that the building was a *waybil*, a term that can be loosely rendered as a 'trance house' or a 'shaman's house' (see above for discussion of the glyph *way*).

At Palenque, the maize deity is depicted in conjunction with the vine-like parts of the water lily, and one of the nine Lords of Xibalbá is shown in its context. I believe that this aquatic plant symbolizes the Otherworld, despite the fact that Rands (1953, 1955), who conducted iconographic comparisons, associated the water lily motif with death. *Imix* is the first day of the month in the Maya twenty-day count. This day belongs to the earth-monster (the Great Mother), the source of all things. It is symbolized by the water lily, the fountainhead of all life. The cosmic monster, impersonated by the phantasmagorical Earth-crocodile, was one of the earliest images conceived by the Maya to symbolize the spatial form of the earth. Dobkin de Rios (1974, 1996) suggested, as early as 1971, that the water lily might produce psychotropic effects, or altered states of consciousness. Diaz (1976) confirmed that, indeed, this plant contains psychoactive alkaloids. Emboden and Dobkin de Rios (1981) published a joint article on the plant's significance among the Maya, while Emboden (1981, 1982, 1983), inspired by the findings, published additional papers on the ritual significance of the water lily not only among the Maya, but in other cultures, as well, such as the ancient Egyptian. It should be kept in mind that the lotus flower is a member of the waterlilly family.

An analysis of the ethnobotanical significance of the Maya pictorial glyphs in the *Dresden Codex*, undertaken by Emboden (1983), offers a telling insight into the floristic diversity that formed an integral part of the secular and religious life of the Maya. In addition to various food plants, such as maize, a plethora of medicinal and ritual plants is depicted, with a high percentage of psychoactive plants among them. One species, depicted with particular frequency, is the regional white water lily, *Nymphaea ampla* DC., with the psychoactive alkaloids aporphine, nupharine, and quinolizidine entering into the phytochemistry of its rhizomes.

Figure 6. 11 Jaguar with water lily in headdress, Dresden 8a (Thompson 1960, fig. 12/12).

A selection of a few examples from the main body of the codex offers a good indication as to its nature. The section T9 of the divinatory Almanac 8, in the *Dresden Codex*, depicts a death god wearing a water lily pendant as part of his elaborate headdress. In another section of the same Almanac (op. cit., p. 4a, T1), we see a rather unusual deity not to be found elsewhere in this corpus, represented as a toad, holding a snake, with its headdress ornamented by the water lily emblem. The association of water lily and toad probably stems from the similar psychopharmacological

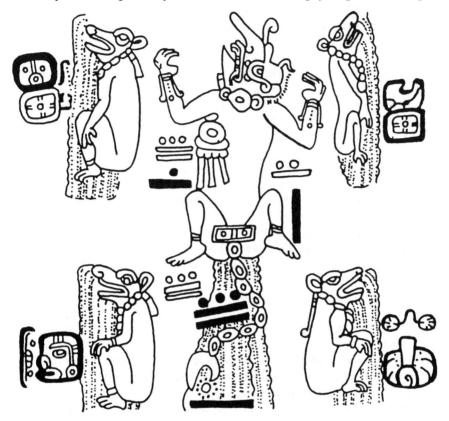

Figure 6.12 In the center, Chac, the god of rain; in the four extremes, the *uoob* (frogs), companions of Chac, with the glyphs of the cosmic directions, Madrid Codex 31a (León-Portilla 1973, p. 67).

effects of the indoline alkaloids bufotenine, secreted by the *Bufo* toad, and nupharine and aporphine, derived from the rhizomes of the water lily (Emboden 1983, p. 91).

In a still different section of this work (Codex p. 8a, T14), we have a jaguar with a water lily emerging from the frontal part of its head (see figure 6.11). The indoline bufotenine secreted through the skin of the *Bufo* toad contains potent alkaloids capable of inducing trance and altered states of consciousness. Curiously enough, the toad stands in a peculiar relationship to the important Maya deity Chac (see figure 6.12). The toad is Chac's messenger and a guest, and it plays a role in the rain ceremonies, probably as

151

a signifier of the coming rainfall. The prototype of Chac may be a late manifestation of the universal *Great Spirit.*

There exists little doubt that the ancient Maya possessed extensive knowledge of hallucinogenic plants and used these substances intensively, if only for ritualistic purposes. This claim can be supported not only by the archaeological evidence, but also by the contents of the surviving codices. In a discussion on the ethnobotanical nature of the *Dresden Codex*, we read:

> The frontal head dress of this figure [Almanac 11, p. 13a, T2] is a bilabiate flower suggesting *Salvia divinorum* Epl. and Jat., a hallucinogenic member of the mint family cultivated in riparian habitats to-day by the Mazatecs and possibly corresponding to *pipilzinzintli* of the ancient Nahuas.... Likewise, the water lily, *Nymphaea ampla* on the back side of the head dress reinforces the contention that we are dealing with a multiplicity of narcotic plant elements ...
>
> It is worthy of note that from his back [God D, Almanac 13, p. 15a, T1] a peduncle and bud of the hallucinogenic *Nymphaea ampla* ascends....
>
> A diving death god [T2] has cordate leaved vegetation replacing his right foot suggesting the leaves of both *Turbina corymbosa* (L.) Raf. and *Ipomoea violacea* L. Both plants bear seeds containing amides of lysergic acid and are hallucinogenic. The relationship of this to the creation story is recapitulated in Almanac 23 ... (Emboden 1983, pp. 93-4).

The majority of shamans throughout the world, and not just among the Maya, depend on the use of some kind of psychoactive substance in their repertoire. This ethnographic fact represents a genuine aspect of shamanism. Hallucinogenic experiences during shamanistic seances constitute the key religious expression for such a society. The critical importance of the shaman's worldview in the development of cosmo-religious metaphors and symbolic syntax cannot be fully understood without giving serious consideration to the role played in this process by hallucinogenic substances. The vision-inducing alkaloids prompt enhanced consciousness, while the development of shamanism gave impetus to the systematization of the universe into a functional and meaningful model. Such perceptions more often than not reflect the recognizable imagery derived from psychotropic experiences.

Maya Cosmological Paradigms

One of the more intriguing elements in Maya cosmology is the notion that the universe – with all humanity and the world in which it dwelt – had been born in the visionary experiences perceived of the gods. Time was an all-pervasive cosmic entity. Its cyclical nature was viewed as an implicit cause – a vortex – and as an apparent matrix of all manifestations ordinary and supernatural, which occurred in the universe. To understand the nature and function of time was to be able to mitigate or divert misfortunes and to benefit from benign forecasts. Consequently, preoccupation with time as a universal property permeated every aspect of life – down to the smallest and most mundane. The Maya cosmos was also infused with many elements that are recognized as characteristic of classic shamanism. Undoubtedly, some traits have survived until the present, if only in a syncretic guise. For example, the contemporary Ixil Maya, in western Guatemala, earnestly consult their close equivalent of a shaman. Among the many questions that the Ixil put before this ritual specialist are those pertaining to the *nagual*. More specifically, they attempt to discover the nature of the animal helper or animal familiar that will belong to a child born on a given day (Villa Rojas 1973, p. 157).

As has been noted, the theme of transformation is a dominant feature in shamanistic belief systems. The ecstatic rapture transforms the individual into a god, and in this state of ecstasy the essential knowledge of the divine can be attained. The ancient Maya performed rituals of blood offering. They also employed techniques of shamanistic trance to induce visions, through which the spiritual essence of the gods and their ancestors was transmuted into 'material' existence in the Middleworld. The Primordial Monster shed its blood of rain as a counterpart to the holy sacrifices on earth (Ripinsky-Naxon 1993a, p. 59).

The prevailing notion in the worldview held by the Maya, in the past and today, has been 'the opaque nature of human access to reality,' as Gary Gossen (1996, p. 531) phrased it compellingly. It constitutes a key idea for the understanding of the Maya world and existence. The opaqueness can be compared to a haze formed by breath on the mirror. The reflections of objects in the looking glass can be seen, but unclearly and obliterated by condensation. However, the Maya opaqueness of reality is not to be compared to Plato's shadows on a cave wall representing a degraded version of ideal forms. Instead,

> Perceived reality in Maya thought derives from generative forces that are *not* fixed ideal forms; these causal forces are multiple, complex, constantly in flux, usually invisible, and interactive among themselves. Furthermore, these forces reside, for the most part, outside the body and individual consciousness (Gossen 1996, p. 532).

Throughout history, the basic principles of Maya ethos have reflected the transitory, if not dubious, nature of reality, where nothing is what it appears to be except when it can be perceived from very close. Therefore, all things – perceptions and experiences – contain unknown or uncertain elements that remain outside the very reality that affects them.

Dennis Tedlock (1993) addresses the important concept of opaque reality within the context of Maya mythic tradition. The Popol Vuh informs that the demise of the original 'motherfathers' (human precursors, Titan-like beings) and the emergence of modern humans (Maya vigesimal beings) was connected to the loss of vision.

'Their visions came all at once. Perfectly they saw, perfectly they knew everything under the sky, whenever they looked.' ... Their limits, then, were those of the world itself (Tedlock op. cit., p. 3).

However, the Maya gods were quite displeased with the fact that they and the human precursors possessed the same capacity for vision, which allowed the latter to share in the knowledge of the gods, making them apparent equals. The hubris made the gods angry. They devised a plan to cause the downfall of these beings, thus, setting off a chain of events that proved critical to the development of humanity:

And when they changed the nature of their works, their designs, it was enough that the eyes be marred by the Heart of Sky. They were blinded as the face of a mirror is breathed upon. Their eyes were weakened. Now it was only when they looked nearby that things were clear.

And such was the loss of the means of understanding, along with the means of knowing everything, by the four humans. The root was implanted (Tedlock 1985, pp. 167).

Survivals of these old beliefs exist today in various forms, not least, shamanism. They are integral to interpreting the stucture of reality and the processes underlying its matrix. Such a cultural worldview creates a need for ideologues – be it shamans, priests, or secular leaders, whose claims to visionary clarity establish them as interpreters and custodians in whose hands rests the blueprint for the community's survival.

Through a complex religion and an intricate political organization, the Maya succeeded in transforming themselves from agrarian village communities into a mighty civilization that endured over a millennium. Chronology and astrology for the Maya comprised a means of divining the future. To make prophesies and augur events – functions held by the *chilans* – was a serious preoccupation among them, bordering almost on obsession. At the same time, these techniques became effective means of organizing political power in their society.

What makes the Maya community model unique, however, is that they alone seem to have hit upon a permutating time count as a kind of automatic device to circulate power among kin groups of the primitive state (Coe 1965, p. 112).

Theirs was a religion that defined existence and the cosmic process. Cosmogony and entropy were seen as co-existent, and existence was regarded as a continuum between life and death. They formulated answers to such existential questions as the nature of the gods, the purpose of human life, and the meaning of the human condition. The ideas formed around these issues were not merely based on their conceptions of the supernatural world, or focused around the divine enigma of time, but also expressed deeply-rooted shamanistic concepts. Objects in the universe have vital essence – an inner soul (*ch'ulel*). It is a common belief among the Maya today that truly important relationships in life are not those between people, or people and objects, but between the inner soul of a person and the inner soul of an object. A similar notion in the West was expressed in the philosophy of Leibniz.

The Maya principle of polar biunity finds, in many ways, an intellectual resonance in Niels Bohr's 'principle of correspondence' in which a single entity can be both matter (a particle) and pure energy (a wave); its nature is determined by its behavior at a given moment of observation. The observation of such physical behavior is subject to laws, formulated by Werner Heisenberg in his Uncertainty Principle, that are an inescapable property of the universe. One may wonder about the real differences between Western views on the structure and behavior of the physical universe and the dogmas formulated by the ancient Maya on the varied nature of their gods, the corresponding realities, and the several levels of existence in their universe. These constructs give support to the assumption that such cosmological systems are not, in essence, incompatible descriptions of the world.

Discussion

From time to time, a voice is heard challenging shamanism as a religion on the grounds that it lacks a body of scriptures and a priestly hierarchy, in contrast to the recognized world religions. Such claims, however, cannot divest genuine shamanism of its ritualism, spiritualism, magico-mythic elements, and eschatology - all the essential ingredients of a *bona fide* religious complex. Its transcultural parameters delineate the second most, if not the most, enduring ritual tradition in human history. Undeniably, certain differences in shamanistic techniques and practices can sometimes, but not always, be attributed to the syncretism with another religion co-existing along in that particular culture. Other differences result from the diversity of cultural contexts and correspond to those encountered among different peoples with different religious practices.

Myths become the effective cultural expressions for religious and ethical codes in native and traditional cultures. They are of great significance to shamanistic rituals and ideology. Anyone who has ever studied the phenomenon of shamanism realizes immediately the keynote function that myths perform in the shaman's repertoire. Many of the shamanistic ceremonies worldwide are validated by myths attempting to explain the creations of such rites, as well as of cosmic paradigms. These myths often rationalize the enactment of rituals in terms of cultural materialism or social pragmatism. The essence of social existence is centered around mythic imagery, which lends to life an existential dimension. Pure, rational thought is no more an objective reality than the myths from whence such a concept is derived. Myths make up, in part, the fundamental responses to the basic human need for meaning. This need is an inescapable condition of human existence, pervading all areas of interactions: from techno-mechanical and sexual to highly symbolic and creative. The quest for the existential metaphor, in the mythico-religious realm, conditioned human societies along the lines that can submit to interpretations in terms of a cognitive approach – a paradigm – germinal to a theoretical model. The attempts to understand the worldviews and daily dramas of aboriginal cultures must take into account the roles of the diverse factors exerting an impetus on the developmental process.

To ensure survival, man learns and devises cognitive meanings. These can be found in the parallel extensions formed by the antipodal worlds and available through the diverse techniques utilized by the shamans. It is the shaman's task to organize and impart coherence to the inveterate journey of existential quest, thus affording ideological purpose and ecological possibilities to the human condition. Shamanistic states of consciousness are not regarded as extraordinary occurrences, neither are these alternate states viewed as separate realities. It is all part of a larger monistic whole (Ripinsky-Naxon 1992, p. 43).

A person does not exist only in a physical world, he lives also in a world of symbols. The components of such a world are language, myth, art, and religion. They are different threads from which is woven a symbolic net – a closely knit web of human experience. All human progress in the areas of thought and experience causes this web to become stronger and more refined. A human being is already incapable of becoming directly dependent on reality; he cannot stand up to face it directly. In so far as human symbolic activities appear to be progressing, the personal physical reality seems to recede. Instead of being involved with phenomena and objects in themselves, he constantly, in a sense, maintains a dialogue with himself. Man has become so dependent on linguistic forms, artistic pictures, mythical symbols, and religious rituals that he is incapable of seeing or experiencing anything without these abstract tools. His position remains the same in the theoretical and practical domains. Even in the latter sphere alone, a person does not exist solely in the world of unmitigating facts, nor, for that matter, does one live exclusively according to one's direct desires and needs. One rather exists among imagined feelings, fears, and hopes, among delusions and disappointments, among illusions and fantasies.

156

Reason is a narrow and inadequate term that cannot grasp the cultural forms of human life in all their richness and diversity. Religious thought does not always stand in unmitigated opposition to rational or philosophical thought. The mysteries of faith cannot be fathomed by reason alone. All these forms, however, are symbolic. As a result, instead of defining Man as *animal rationale*, he should be defined as *animal symbolicum*. This way, as Ernst Cassirer (1946, 1955) rightly suggested, we can underscore this special human characteristic and understand the role of symbolism in the course of cultural development and civilization. Culture and society constitute the world of symbolic forms.

Irrespective of how one views the process of culture growth, it is obvious that religion is a fundamental 'monadic' institution in the cultures of all peoples. The expressions of religious systems constitute the characteristic metaphors that make up the symbolic language and cognitive foodstuff of individual psychology and cultural ideology. The primary sociocultural aim of mystery rituals is to arouse great mystical sensations. These may be separated into empathy (a 'recognition of the shared, finite measure of humanity') and rapture (frenzy, ecstasy, terror, numen). In certain societies, these experiences can be induced by ritual drama, enacted according to a special formula. Such performances may eventually transform into a social metaphor which can serve as a substitute for the actual mystical experience formerly attainable through a spiritual ecstasy, be it shamanistic or some other form of a *kathartic* process that satisfies the condition for a kind of metaphysical prototype of human existence. After all, religious metaphors are created to remind man of his spiritual transcendence, so that, paradoxically, through this experience, he may no longer need such metaphors. Ultimately, shamanism is an important and dynamic cultural form that facilitates an ecological appreciation of the natural environment, as well as a psycho-epistemological understanding of the universe.

Notes

1. Plotinus, *Enneads*, I.vi.[1] 9.
2. 'The passing of each *katun* should be read clockwise (20 X 360 days = 7,200). The *katuns* receive their calendrical designation depending on the name of the last day of the same, which is always an *Ahau*, accompanied by a numerical between 1 and 13. Only until after 256 years of 365 days, approximately, will the same date be repeated; that is to say, an *Ahau* day with the same number as the termination of a *katun*' (León-Portilla 1973, p. 9).
3. Framed by a skyband with celestial symbols, he descends with the setting Sun in the west, entering the jaws of the Earth Monster. Pacal will rise again as the new Sun in the east in the form of a dawning World-Tree.

References

Anisimov, Arkadiy F. (1963), 'Cosmological Concepts of the Peoples of the North,' trans. Lilian Ackerman and Barbara Krader, in Henry N. Michael (ed.), *Studies in Siberian Shamanism*, pp. 157-229, Anthropology of the North: Translations from Russian Sources No. 4, University of Toronto Press: Toronto.

Bäckman, Louise and Hultkrantz, Åke (1978), *Studies in Lapp Shamanism*, Stockholm Studies in Comparative Religion, Vol. 16, Almqvist & Wiksell: Stockholm.

Barbeau, Marius (1958), *Medicine-Men on the North Pacific Coast*, National Museum of Canada Bulletin No. 152, Department of Northern Affairs and National Resources: Ottawa.

Borhegyi, Stephan F. de (1965), 'Archaeological Synthesis of the Guatemalan Highlands.' in Robert Wauchope (ed.), *Handbook of Middle American Indians*, Vol. 2, pp. 3-58, University of Texas Press: Austin.

— (1963), 'Pre-Columbian Pottery Mushrooms from Mesoamerica,' *American Antiquity*, Vol. 28, No. 3, pp. 328-38.

— (1961), 'Miniature Mushroom Stones from Guatemala,' *American Antiquity*, Vol. 26, No. 4, pp. 498-504.

Carlson, John B. (1990), 'America's Ancient Skywatchers,' *National Geographic*, Vol. 177, No. 3, March, pp. 76-107.

Cassirer, Ernst (1955), *The Philosophy of Symbolic Forms, Vol. 2: Mythical Thought*, trans. Ralph Manheim, Yale University Press: New Haven.

— (1946), *Language and Myth*, trans. Susanne K. Langer, Harper & Brothers: New York.

Coe, Michael D. (1975), 'Death and the Ancient Maya,' in Elizabeth P. Benson (ed.), *Death and the Afterlife in Pre-Columbian America*, pp. 87-104, Dumbarton Oaks Research Library and Collections: Washington.

— (1965), 'A Model of Ancient Community Structure in the Maya Lowlands,' *Southwestern Journal of Anthropology*, Vol. 21, No. 2, Summer, pp. 97-114.

Coto, Fray Tomás de (1983), *Thesavrvs Verborv: Vocabulario de la Lengua Cakchiquel v[el] Guatemalteca*, René Acuña (ed.), Universidad Nacional Autónomia de México: México.

Díaz, José L. (1976), 'Etnofarmacologia de Algunos Psicotrópicos Vegetales de México,' in José L. Diaz (ed.), *Etnofarmacologia de Plantes Alucinógenas Latinoamericanas*, Centro Mexicano de Estudios en Farmacodependéncia: México.

Dobkin de Rios, Marlene (1996), *Hallucinogens: Cross-Cultural Perspectives*, Waveland Press: Prospect Heights.

— (1974), 'The Influence of Psychotropic Flora and Fauna on Maya Religion,' *Current Anthropology*, Vol. 15, No. 2, pp. 147-64.

— (1972), *Visionary Vine: Psychedelic Healing in the Peruvian Amazon*, Chandler Publishing Co: San Francisco.

Eliade, Mircea (1964), *Shamanism: Archaic Techniques of Ecstasy*, trans. Willard R. Trask, Bollingen Series LXXVI, Bollingen Foundation: New York.

Emboden, William A. (1983), 'The Ethnobotany of the Dresden Codex with Especial Reference to the Narcotic *Nymphaea ampla*,' *Botanical Museum Leaflets*, Vol. 29, No. 2, Spring, pp. 87-132 (plus 2 additional pages inserted after binding).

— (1982), 'The Mushroom and the Water Lily: Literary and Pictorial Evidence for *Nymphaea* as a Ritual Psychotogen in Mesoamerica,' *Journal of Ethnopharmacology*, Vol. 5, No. 2, January, pp. 139-48.

— (1981), 'Transcultural Use of Narcotic Water Lilies in Ancient Egyptian and Maya Drug Ritual,' *Journal of Ethnopharmacology*, Vol. 3, No. 1, January, pp. 39-83.

Emboden, William A. and Dobkin de Rios, Marlene (1981), 'Mayan-Egyptian Uses of Water Lilies (*Nymphaceae*) in Shamanic Ritual Drug Use,' in George G. Meyer, Kenneth Blum, and John G. Cull (eds), *Folk Medicine and Herbal Healing*, pp. 275-86, Charles C. Thomas: Springfield.

Fuentes y Guzmán, Francisco Antonio de (1862), *Recordación Florida: Discurso Historial y Demostracion Natural, Material, Militar y Politico del Reino de Goathemala*, 3 Vols, Sociedad de Geografía e Historia: Guatemala City.

Furst, Peter T. (1975), 'House of Darkness and House of Light: Sacred Functions of West Mexican Funerary Art,' in Elizabeth P. Benson (ed.), *Death and the Afterlife in Pre-Columbian America*, pp. 33-68, Dumbarton Oaks Research Library and Collections: Washington.

Gossen, Gary H. (1996), 'Maya Zapatistas Move to the Ancient Future,' *American Anthropologist*, Vol. 98, No. 3, pp. 528-38.

Hamayon, Roberte N. (1993), "Are 'Trance,' 'Ecstasy,' and Similar Concepts Appropriate in the Study of Shamanism?" *Shaman*, Vol. 1, No. 2, Autumn, pp. 3-25.

Harner, Michael J. (1972), *The Jívaro: People of the Sacred Waterfalls*, Doubleday: Garden City.

Haviland, William A. and de Laguna Haviland, Anita (1995), 'Glimpses of the Supernatural: Altered State of Consciousness and the Graffiti of Tikal, Guatemala,' *Latin American Antiquity*, Vol. 6, No. 4, pp. 295-309.

Houston, Stephen and Stuart, David (1989), "The *Way* Glyph: Evidence for 'Co-essences' among the Classic Maya," *Research Reports on Ancient Maya Writing*, No. 30, Center for Maya Research: Washington.

Kensinger, Kenneth M. (1973), '*Banisteriopsis* Usage Among the Peruvian Cashinahua,' in Michael J. Harner (ed.), *Hallucinogens and Shamanism*, pp. 9-14, Oxford University Press: New York.

Landa, Diego de (1566), *Relación de las Cosas de Yucatán*

Langdon, E. Jean Matteson (1992), 'Shamanism and Anthropology,' in E. Jean M. Langdon and Gerhard Baer (eds), *Portals of Power: Shamanism in South America*, pp. 1-21, University of New Mexico Press: Albuquerque.

León-Portilla, Miguel (1973), *Time and Reality in the Thought of the Maya*, trans. Charles L. Boilés and Fernando Horcasitas, Beacon Press: Boston.

Lévi-Strauss, Claude (1963), 'The Effectiveness of Symbols,' in Claude Lévi-Strauss, *Structural Anthropology*, pp. 186-205, trans. Claire Jacobson, Basic Books: New York.

Maler, Teobert (1911), 'Explorations in the Department of Peten, Guatemala – Tikal: Report of Explorations for the Museum,' in *Memoirs of the Peabody Museum of American Archaeology and Ethnology*, Harvard University, Vol. 5, No. 1, pp. 1-91, plates 1-28, Peabody Museum: Cambridge.

Naranjo, Claudio (1973), *The Healing Journey: New Approaches to Consciousness*, Pantheon: New York.

Plotinus (1964), 'Beauty,' in Elmer O'Brien (trans.), *The Essential Plotinus*, pp. 33-43, Mentor Books: New York.

Rands, Robert L. (1955), 'Some Manifestations of Water in Mesoamerican Art,' in *Bureau of American Ethnology*, Bulletin 157, pp. 265-393, Smithsonian Institution: Washington.

— (1953), 'The Water Lily in Maya Art: A Complex of Alleged Asiatic Origin,' in *Bureau of American Ethnology*, Bulletin 151, pp. 75-153, Smithsonian Institution: Washington.

Reichel-Dolmatoff, Gérardo (1990), Written personal communication, 20 December 1990.

— (1987), *Shamanism and Art of the Eastern Tukanoan Indians, Colombian Northwest Amazon*, Institute of Religious Iconography, State University of Groningen, E. J. Brill: Leiden.

— (1981), 'Things of Beauty Replete with Meaning – Metals and Crystals in Colombian Indian Cosmology,' in *Sweat of the Sun. Tears of the Moon: Gold and Emerald Treasures of Colombia*, pp. 17-33, Natural History Museum Alliance of Los Angeles County: Los Angeles.

— (1979), 'Some Source Materials on Desana Shamanistic Initiation,' *Antropológica*, Vol. 51, pp. 27-61.

— (1971), *Amazonian Cosmos: The Sexual and Religious Symbolism of the Tukano Indians*, The University of Chicago Press: Chicago.

Ripinsky-Naxon, Michael (1997), *Sexuality, Shamanism, and Transformation*, Series Ethnomedicine and the Study of Consciousness, Verlag für Wissenschaft und Bildung: Berlin.

— (1996), 'Evolution, Cognition, and the Origins of Shamanism,' *Yearbook for Ethnomedicine and the Study of Consciousness*, Vol. 5, in press.

— (1995), 'Psychoactivity and Shamanic States of Consciousness,' *Yearbook for Ethnomedicine and the Study of Consciousness*, Vol. 4, pp. 35-43.

— (1993a), 'Maya Cosmovision and Shamanistic Symbolism,' *Journal of Prehistoric Religion*, Vol. 7, pp. 49-61.

— (1993), *The Nature of Shamanism: Substance and Function of a Religious Metaphor*, State University of New York Press: Albany.

— (1992), 'Shamanism: Religion or Rite?,' *Journal of Prehistoric Religion*, Vol.

6, pp. 37-44.

— (1989), 'Hallucinogens, Shamanism, and the Cultural Process: Symbolic Archaeology and Dialectics,' *Anthropos*, Vol. 84, pp. 219-24.

Roys, Ralph L. (1967), *The Book of Chilam Balam of Chumayel*, University of Oklahoma Press: Norman.

— ed. and trans. (1965), *Ritual of the Bacabs*, University of Oklahoma Press: Norman.

Ruz Lhuillier, Alberto (1968), *Costumbres funerarias de los antiguos Mayas*, Universidad Nacional Autónoma de México: México.

Schele, Linda (1990), *Proceedings of the Maya Hieroglyphic Workshop, March 1–11, 1990, University of Texas at Austin*, University of Texas: Austin.

Schele, Linda and Freidel, David (1990), *A Forest of Kings: The Untold Story of the Ancient Maya*, William Morrow: New York.

Schultes, Richard and Bright, Alec (1981), 'Ancient Gold Pectorals from Colombia: Mushroom Effigies?' in *Sweat of the Sun, Tears of the Moon: Gold and Emerald Treasures of Colombia*, pp. 37-43, Natural History Museum Alliance of Los Angeles County: Los Angeles.

Tedlock, Dennis (1993), *Breath on the Mirror: Mythic Voices and Visions of the Living Maya*, HarperCollins: San Francisco.

— trans. (1985), *Popol Vuh. The Mayan Book of the Dawn of Life*, Simon & Schuster: New York.

Thompson, J. Eric S. (1970), *Maya History and Religion*, University of Oklahoma Press: Norman.

— (1960), *Maya Hieroglyphic Writing: An Introduction*, University of Oklahoma Press: Norman.

Tozzer, Alfred M. (1907), *A Comparative Study of the Mayas and the Lacandones*, Macmillan: New York.

Vasilevich, Glafira M. (1963), 'Early Concepts About the Universe Among the Evenks (Materials),' trans. Mrs. Rainey, in Henry N. Michael (ed.), *Studies in Siberian Shamanism*, pp. 46-83, Anthropology of the North: Translations from Russian Sources No. 4, University of Toronto Press: Toronto.

Villa Rojas, Alfonso (1973), 'The Concepts of Space and Time Among the Contemporary Maya,' in Miguel León-Portilla, *Time and Reality in the Thought of the Maya*, pp. 113-59, trans. Charles L. Boilés and Fernando Horcasitas, Beacon Press: Boston.

7 The Meaning of Ecstasy in Shamanism

Åke Hultkrantz

In recent years, leading representatives of shamanology have questioned the basic ecstatic structure of shamanism. This article, which reassesses the ecstatic elements in shamanism, concludes that if we want to retain the concept of shamanism as a scholarly instrument we must continue to stress its ecstatic character. To that end, a particular discussion focuses on the meaning of ecstasy in shamanism.

In the history of ideas shamanism has been viewed through the magnifying glasses of four different disciplines: psychology, historical ethnology, history and psychology of religion, and social anthropology. Each of these disciplines has moved shamanological research in a new direction. This has been particularly the case with respect to the key role that ecstatic phenomena play in shamanism, and in recent years, that role has been diminished or completely abandoned. This is, in the present writer's view, an unfortunate development if we want to retain the concept of shamanism as a meaningful element in the analysis of early ideologies.[1]

Some authors wish to do away with shamanism as a scientific tool altogether. For instance, the American writer, Robert Spencer, denounces shamanism as a specific category and characterizes it as 'a potentially random phenomenon' in the cultural world (Spencer 1968).[2] A leading anthropologist, Clifford Geertz, deplores that

> the individuality of religious traditions has so often been dissolved into such desiccated types as 'animism', 'animatism', 'totemism', 'shamanism', 'ancestor worship', and all the other insipid categories by means of which ethnographers of religion devitalize their data (Geertz 1966, p. 39).

Such immature declarations denigrate the complex underpinnings of shamanism, which serves as a mediator between the social group and the gods, spirits, and beings of the other world. Furthermore, that mediation is implemented by and through an ecstatic experience. It is my task here to prove the validity of this last statement, and thereby to pay special attention to shamanism in North America, an area where ecstasy appears to be rather weak, particularly in comparison with the ecstasy of the Siberian shaman (Dixon 1908, p. 9).

The Appreciation of Ecstasy in Shamanism

Let us begin by investigating how ecstasy has been evaluated in the professional writing on shamanism. The first presentations of shamanism were mostly descriptive, and described dramatic séances in the northern parts of the Russian Empire.[3] At this time (eighteenth to nineteenth centuries), and up to the 1900s, shamanism was understood as the religion of northern Eurasia (MacCulloch 1961, p. 446). As a unique phenomenon, shamanism was taken up from a psychological perspective by many European scholars who debated whether the shaman was psychically sound, whether shamanic ecstasy was genuine, and similar problems. Marie Antoinette Czaplicka paved the way for this exploration, and was followed by Russian scholars such as Vladimir Bogoras, Dimitri Zelenin, and Sergei Shirikogoroff, German authors like Hans Findeisen, Georg Nioradze, and T. Konrad Oesterreich, and French authors like Lucien Lévy-Bruhl, and Marcelle Bouteiller, all of whom emphasized the psychic state of shamans. In terms of its compelling interest to the scholarly world, this subject was second only to the fascinating phenomenon of the shaman as such. More recent writings in the history and psychology of religion have also addressed shamanic ecstasy. Among these are the works of Åke Ohlmarks, Mircea Eliade, and Ernst Arbman. Eliade's (1964) contribution was path-breaking; most scholars engaged in analyses of shamanism refer to him. For all of these scholars shamanism stands and falls with ecstasy, or religious trance, as Arbman also calls it (Arbman 1963-1970).

Until the 1950s, ethnology was predominantly either historical and phenomenological (classifying) or, as in the Soviet Union, evolutionistic. Typical exponents of ethnological shamanology include the Austrians Wilhelm Schmidt, Martin Gusinde, and Matthias Hermanns, the Germans Andreas Lommel and Ulla Johansen, the Estonians Ivar Paulson and Gustav Ränk, the Hungarians Laszlo Vajda, Mihály Hoppál, and Vilmos Diószegi (the last predominantly influenced by Soviet scholars), and the Russians A. F. Anisimov, S. I. Vainstein, and V. N. Basilov. It is characteristic that all of these writers have presupposed ecstasy as a natural psychic disposition in the shamans.

This common understanding of the role of ecstasy in shamanism was slowly overcome when social anthropology appeared on the scene. Indeed, even in the early North American anthropology there was little concern with shamanic trance states. In an early paper on shamanism in North America, Roland Dixon (1908) reported that the shaman is more or less a type of vision seeker of the common American Indian kind, although particularly directed in his profession, the cure of his fellow human beings. Dixon defines shamans as

> that motley class of persons, found in every savage community, who are supposed to have closer relations with the supernatural than other men, and who, according as they use the advantages of their position in one way or another, are the progenitors alike of the physician and the sorcerer, the prophet, the teacher, and the priest (op. cit., p. 1).

However, besides mentioning that 'the shaman goes into a trance,' Dixon is not particularly interested in the nature of this trance.

The same general attitude toward shamanism is reflected in the writings of A. L. Kroeber, one of the founders of American anthropology. For him, the shaman is mainly a healer with an honored and respected status, and is 'associated' with a spirit (Kroeber 1948, pp. 298-9). In our personal discussions, Kroeber described the shaman primarily as a religious leader. Edwin M. Loeb expressed a more positive feeling for the inner world of the American shaman, but erroneously characterized shamanic possession (particularly on the Northwest Coast) as an 'inspirational' state (Loeb 1929, p. 275). In their ethnographical tribal overviews, more recent authors observe occurrences of ecstatic shamanism, but in general they do not expend much energy on ecstatic phenomena. There are notable exceptions, however, particularly among psychiatrically trained anthropologists such as Georges Devereux, Bryce Boyer, and Wolfgang Jilek. But these modern scientists can scarcely be said to have emanated from traditional American anthropology.

Modern social anthropology, with its roots in French sociologism and structuralism and British empiricism, has largely taken over the cultural and social anthropological scene in recent years. Society is in the foreground, not culture, and certainly not religion. Ritual is an important word, and Victor Turner is the dominant name in ritual analysis, while Ioan Lewis has been ranked as one of the leading scholars in shamanic research. It should be noted, however, that Lewis deals primarily with spirit possession, not shamanism, although his tendency to regard Siberian shamanism as a case of possession is not entirely correct (cf. Lewis 1971, pp. 50-1).

Roles, Rituals, and Ecstasy

The emphasis that social anthropologists put on ritualism in shamanism is an important one that has not been sufficiently investigated. Some recent contributions in this field are particularly significant: Lucile Charles' worldwide exemplifications of shamanic drama (Charles 1953) and Lauri Honko's and Anna-Leena Siikala's discussions of the shaman's ritual role-taking. Although these authors are American and Finnish folklorists, they testify to the scope of social-anthropological influence. Whereas Honko (1969, p. 33) tends to reduce the import of ecstasy as a distinguishing mark of shamanism, Siikala sees the shaman's ritual interaction between this world and the other world as 'fundamentally an ecstatic role-taking technique' (Siikala 1978, p. 28). In other words, Honko emphasizes the social role-changing of the shaman, while Siikala seeks to show how 'role changes or the shaman's role-taking technique link up with his ecstatic behaviour' (Siikala 1978, p. 29). Both investigations are invaluable, but Siikala's is more relevant to our discourse on the role of ecstasy.

This example shows how ritual analysis can be coordinated with ecstatic analysis. While this is less often the case where social-anthropological methods are more rigorously applied today, such coordination of ritual and ecstatic analyses was evident in the beginning, as earlier works on shamanism in France indicate. It is well known that Marcelle Boutellier, in her book comparing American shamanism and French folk medicine, paid attention to dreams and ecstasy (Boutellier 1950, pp. 119-26), and that Mircea Eliade first published his grand oeuvre on ecstatic shamanism in Paris (Eliade 1951).[4] In this connection we could also mention that fine student of South American shamanism, Michel Perrin (1992). Nevertheless, later French publications on shamanism generally give the impression that the psychic state of the shaman is less important than the social drama of the séance. This is, for instance, the case with the works of Roberte Hamayon, an outstanding expert on Siberian shamanism.

Mme. Hamayon has written one of the monumental works on Siberian shamanism (Hamayon 1990), based on her own field investigations in Siberia and her studies of Buryat shamanic literature. A cluster of special studies has emerged from this research. Among her many valuable observations is her emphasis on the mutual relations between the spirits and man (the shaman's marriage with the daughter of the game-giving spirit, the parallelism between the human's feeding on game animals and the animal master's feeding on human flesh and blood). Hamayon stresses the partnership between man and animal; indeed, she diminishes the supernatural factors and focuses on the social tasks and bonds of the shaman. Thus,

> being similar to man's soul in essence and on a par with men as alliance and exchange partners, spirits are not transcendent, ... they are feared but not worshipped (Hamayon n.d., p. 4).[5]

As to the shaman, his exercise of power is controlled by the community, and if he does not achieve the right results he is dismissed by the community (op. cit., p. 6). This is a consequent social-anthropological approach: the investigation of the interior experiences of the shaman is depreciated in favor of sociological analyses.

In effect, Hamayon attacks the religious interpretation of shamanism. In her study of the ritualization of shamanism she writes about observers of shamanism in Siberia by noting,

> s'ils ont tous perçu le phénomène chamanique comme religieux, tous sont restés perplexes face au comportement du chamane en séance, et certains l'ont mis sur le compte de la pathologie (Hamayon 1989, p. 149).[6]

To this one might say, of course not everything pertaining to the shamanic complex is religious, but the rites of shamanism are dependent on the beliefs and ideas of the religious experience (see below). Hamayon does not see shamanism from this angle, however. She retorts, how can one consider an action as being religious which is characterized by

> une conduite qui n 'a rien de codifié, mais offre au contraire l'apparence de la folie?[7]

She adds that shamanism does not present any of the usual supports of a religion, a dogma, a temple, cultic objects common to a collectivity of people (op. cit., pp. 149-50). Her own solution is that shamanism offers a 'pragmatic' ritual, symbolically related to the action of hunting. (A discussion of that 'solution' is beyond the scope of this paper.)

In a recent article, Hamayon declared that shamanism is not, as preceding scholars have asserted, meaningfully explained as founded on experiences made in 'ecstasy' or 'trance' (Hamayon 1993, cf. also Hamayon 1990, pp. 29ff.). This is a startling point of view considering the overwhelming evidence of ecstatic shamanism from around the world, not least from Siberia.[8] We remember, for instance, how Eliade saw the kernel of shamanism in 'archaic techniques of ecstasy,' and how Findeisen, from a psychological and phenomenological point of view considered the spiritistic trance or ecstasy to be the constitutive basis of shamanism (Findeisen 1957, p. 8; 1960). On the contrary, says Hamayon, any approach to shamanism through the study of trance or ecstasy[9] is 'an obstacle to the anthropological analysis of shamanism,' 'is irrelevant,' and 'impedes anthropological analysis of the shaman's behaviour' (Hamayon 1993, pp. 4, 6, 18). Instead, she finds a conceptual continuity in the shaman's ritual behavior that portrays his or her contact with the spirits, 'a functional behavior that follows a prescribed pattern' (op. cit., p. 3). We notice here a reductionistic tendency to exclude all operations that involve an approach other than the strictly social-anthropological.[10] To my understanding this means that a more holistic scholarly approach is sacrificed on the altar of the demands of a method.

Further, Hamayon also tries to disqualify trance as an analytical object.

In her opinion, there are no native terms homologous to 'trance,' which as she points out is Latin for 'to die, to go beyond, to pass from one state to another' (op. cit., p. 7). I am afraid she is quite mistaken. My investigation shows that the American shaman's trance state is conceived as, and is called death (Hultkrantz 1953, pp. 280-2).[11] It is thus not true that native tongues only interpret trance as a 'ritual episode' without reference to 'a specific physical or psychic state.' Hamayon is certainly right when she concentrates on the relationships between the shaman and the spirits as a major theme in people's discussions about the shamanistic art, but this does not exclude their awareness that the shaman's trance is likened to death, indeed, it is death. Hamayon considers that the characterization of shamanism as trance appeared in the great Western religions in order to denigrate, in the eyes of a transcendent religion like Christianity, the notion that man and spirits are equals (Hamayon 1993, pp. 17ff.). However, I disagree with her use of 'transcendent.' Spirits are both transcendent and immanent in American Indian beliefs. Even in Christianity the two may coincide, as in mysticism, for instance, where the soul of man and the spirit of God may coalesce.

My position is thus clear: Ecstasy is a necessary part of the shaman's psychic equipment. Moreover, it is the precondition for all shamanic ritual actions. There are, certainly, shamanic ritual actions where the ecstatic element is not palpable, such as in the Spirit Canoe curing ceremony among the Coast Salish Indians. The sources on this ritual, which involves visualizing a journey to the spirit land of several shamans, do not provide reliable clues about the presence of ecstasy. Still, there are details to suggest that this was the case (Hultkrantz 1992, p. 69), just as the Siberian shaman climbing the world tree obviously presupposes an ecstatic trance. Ohlmarks (1939, pp. 122ff.) calls this shamanism imitative, and believes it goes back to an original fully-fledged trance. As noted earlier, Siikala embraces a more cautious attitude with a preference for a parallelism between ecstatic absorption and role-taking.

At any rate, shamanism and shamanic rituals cannot be understood without the ecstatic experience of the shaman in mind. If shamanism is to be retained as a concept in the international debate – and, considering the homogeneity of the shamanic institutions over wide areas of the globe, it is hard to see that it should be abandoned – then the ecstasy of the shaman should be reckoned as an inalienable part of shamanism, indeed, as the overture of the shamanic séance, the shamanic ritual, the myths and legends surrounding shamanism. Implications of this position will be discussed in the following section.

The Meaning of Ecstasy in Shamanism

If Professor Hamayon and this author cannot agree on the import of ecstasy in shamanism, we are nonetheless both inclined to find a dichotomy in the world interpretation of most peoples between the ordinary, natural world and the other, supernatural' world, or, as Mme. Hamayon formulates it, *nature* and *surnature* (Hultkrantz 1983, Hamayon 1990). The difference between us is that Professor Hamayon and I do not draw the same conclusions from this dualism. This is apparent in our evaluations of shamanism which to her is a role play and drama in social surroundings more than a supernaturally sanctioned complex of beliefs, rituals, and sacred narratives (myths and legends). The latter interpretation is my own, but many other investigators share it with me. I do not assert that the shamanic complex in all details should be relegated to the supernatural sphere, but I do contend that its motivation and force have a supernatural origin, according to the belief in the shamanic circles.[12]

Since the sanction for shamanic beliefs and rituals is supposed to be bestowed in a supernatural experience, we are now within the confines of religion. Religion gives the impetus to the entire shamanic scenario. This has been underlined by many of the classic authors on shamanism, as well as by recent authors (Closs 1960; Harner 1980, p. 21; Ripinsky-Naxon 1992, pp. 38, 42). In an earlier paper, I have also voiced a similar opinion (Hultkrantz 1988). In that connection I also declared that not everything about shamanism is religion:

> There is also the element of human care, the shamanic personality, profane existence as a part-time shaman, the construction of drums and other auxiliary instruments, the role-playing of the shaman, his social position and sexual life, the poetry of shamanism, and so on (op. cit., p. 37).

Still, the driving motor of shamanism is, beside the social needs, the shaman's contact with the spirits. This contact is realized through experiences that are anormal, transferred to another world, the world of gods, spirits, and ghosts. No sound being meets these supernaturals in the natural world. Only trance, dreams, and coma open the door to that mystical world.

It is the shaman's privilege to be able to initiate a journey to the other world, or to call on the spirits for help and information. In order to reach this other world the shaman has recourse to trance. Two types of occasions require a trance: the time of the initial calling when the helping spirits appear to the shaman in visions, and during the shamanistic séance when curing and divination demand communication with the powers of the other world.

In other writings I have pointed out that if we want to find a boundary line between the shaman and the medicine man (the common term for an aboriginal doctor and magician in North America among both scholars and the public at large), the occurrence of ecstasy is diagnostic (Hultkrantz 1985). The ordinary medicine man may experience an ecstatic calling, as he does in

North America, but his curing séance is not typically of the ecstatic kind (Hultkrantz 1989, 1992). The typical shaman, on the other hand, is an ecstatic on both accounts. Of course, the ecstasy or trance is a relative concept, since we can observe different degrees of trance. Thus, the mere visits of supernatural beings in a curing procedure may take place in a light trance, whereas the shamanic expeditions to the other world or to remote places of the ordinary world are usually enacted in a deep trance.[13] However there are certainly exceptions where imitative shamanism and shamanic role-taking occur. Still, it is difficult to draw an absolute line between trance and role-taking, and role-taking often imperceptibly changes to trance (Siikala 1978, pp. 61ff., 330-41).

As Hamayon and others have insisted, the shamanistic séance certainly mirrors the social situation and the popular demands of those taking part in the séance. However, no séance would occur without the main figure, the trained practitioner in ecstasy, who not only plays the first role, but is in control of the communication with the spiritual world. Contact with the spiritual world can only be attained in ecstasy or trance.

Seen at its deepest, the communication with this other world is the source of health, harmony, and power – all those qualities the audience of the shamanic session wish to achieve. The shaman opens this channel to the wonderful supernatural beings. The ecstasy realized with the aid of guardian spirits transports the shaman from his mundane surroundings to the supernatural world. That is the meaning of ecstasy or trance, and makes it inalienable to shamanic action. No account of the shamanic ritual is satisfactory if the ecstatic framework is left out.

Notes

An earlier version of this essay was printed in *Shaman*, Vol. 5, No. 1, Spring 1997, pp. 35-46. I would like to thank the Editors of *Shaman* for their kindness in allowing me to re-publish this article.

1. On my definition of shamanism as an ecstatic complex, see Hultkrantz (1973, 1978, 1993).
2. Cf. my criticism of Spencer's point of view in Hultkrantz (1977), pp. 87-8.
3. Cf. for example W. L. Sieroszewski's (1902) descriptions of Yakut shaman performances, and V. M. Mikhailovskii's (1895) work.
4. As a Rumanian emigré, Eliade was, of course, only temporarily in France.
5. Cf. my criticism of her use of the concept of transcendence below.
6. 'if they all have perceived the shamanic phenomena as being religious, they were all puzzled at the strange behavior of the shaman in trance, and some of them understood it as a form of pathology' (trans. Å. H.). To this may be added that no understanding scholarly observer today thinks

that the shaman's behavior is struck by madness, nor does he expect that a religion with shamanism necessarily should have a temple and a dogma. Many tribal religions lack these accessories.

7. 'a behavior which has nothing orderly, but on the contrary gives an appearance of craziness' (trans. Å. H.).
8. There is now an excellent collection of shamanic pictures published by Mihály Hoppál (1994) that shows ecstatic shamans and shamans with the ecstatic instrument par préference, the drum.
9. Hamayon makes a distinction between the trance and ecstasy (on grounds I cannot endorse) and reserves the 'term' trance for the shaman's possible inner state.
10. Cf. Hamayon (1993), p. 7: Trance 'does not belong to the system of representations which is the ultimate subject matter of the anthropological analysis.' See also op. cit., p. 20.
11. Although I have not perused the terms for trance in Arctic Eurasia I have occasionally noted that some languages place trance on an equal footing with death. My colleague, Professor Louise Bäckman, herself a Saami told me that the Saami word for dying, *jaamedh*, is included in the word for going numb, *jaamelgidh*, 'die a little.' Cf. also Bäckman and Hultkrantz 1978, pp. 98, 101-2.
12. Cf. the discussion of the basis of mystical phenomena in Arbman 1963, vol.1, pp. 433ff.
13. For a more detailed treatment of this subject, see Hultkrantz (1975), Bäckman and Hultkrantz (1978, pp. 94-109). Both these references concern the Saami. There are similar cases among North American Indians, but I have not as yet made a thorough analysis of the material, except among Shoshoni Indians. See however Hultkrantz (1992, pp. 158-68).

Bibliography

Arbman, Ernst (1963-1970), *Ecstasy or Religious Trance,* 3 volumes, Svenska Bokförlaget: Stockholm.
Bouteiller, Marcelle (1950), *Chamanisme et guérison magique.* Presses Universitaires de France: Paris.
Bäckman, Louise and Hultkrantz, Åke (1978), *Studies in Lapp Shamanism.* Stockholm Studies in Comparative Religion, Vol. 16. Almqvist & Wiksell: Stockholm.
Charles, Lucile H. (1953), 'Drama in Shaman Exorcism,' *Journal of American Folklore,* Vol. 66, No. 260, April - June, pp. 95-122.
Closs, Alois (1960), 'Das Religiöse in Schamanismus,' *Kairos,* Vol. 2, pp. 29-38.
Dixon, Roland B. (1908), 'Some Aspects of the American Shaman,' *Journal of American Folk-Lore,* Vol. 21, No. 80, pp. 1-12.

Eliade, Mircea (1964), *Shamanism: Archaic Techniques of Ecstasy*, trans. Willard R. Trask, Bollingen Series LXXVI, Bollingen Foundation: New York.

— (1951), *Le Chamanisme et les techniques archaïques de l'extase*, Librairie Payot: Paris.

Findeisen, Hans (1960), 'Das Schamanentum als spiritistische Religion,' *Ethnos*, Vol. 25, Nos. 3-4, pp. 192-213.

— (1957), *Schamanentum*, W. Kohlhammer Verlag: Stuttgart.

Geertz, Clifford (1966), 'Religion as a Cultural System,' in Michael Banton (ed.), *Anthropological Approaches to the Study of Religion*, pp. 1-46, Tavistock Publications: London.

Hamayon, Roberte N. (1993), "Are 'Trance,' 'Ecstasy,' and Similar Concepts Appropriate in the Study of Shamanism?" Vol. 1, No. 2, Autumn, pp. 3-25.

— (1990), *La Chasse à l'âme: Esquisse d'une théorie du chamanisme sibérien*, Société d'ethnologie: Nanterre.

— (1989), 'Pragmatisme et ritualisation dans le chamanisme,' in Anne-Marie Blondeau and Kristofer Schipper (eds), *Essais sur le rituel II*, pp. 149-69, Peeters: Louvain-Paris.

— (n.d.), *Shamanism in Siberia: From Partnership in Supernature to Counter-Power in Society*, 14 pages.

Harner, Michael (1980), *The Way of the Shaman*, Harper & Row: San Francisco.

Honko, Lauri (1969), 'Role-taking of the Shaman,' *Temenos*, Vol. 4, pp. 26-55.

Hoppál, Mihály (1994), *Schamanen und Schamanismus*, Pattloch: Augsburg.

Hultkrantz, Åke (1993), 'Introductory Remarks on the Study of Shamanism,' *Shaman*, Vol. 1, No. 1, Spring, pp. 3-14.

— (1992), *Shamanic Healing and Ritual Drama: Health and Medicine in Native North American Religious Traditions*, Crossroad: New York.

— (1989), 'Health, Religion, and Medicine in Native North American Traditions,' in Lawrence E. Sullivan (ed.), *Healing and Restoring: Health and Medicine in the World's Religious Traditions*, pp. 327-358, Macmillan: New York.

— (1988), 'Shamanism: A Religious Phenomenon?,' in Gary Doore (ed.), pp. 33-41, *Shaman's Path*, Shambhala: Boston and London.

— (1985), 'The Shaman and the Medicine-Man,' *Social Science & Medicine*, Vol. 20, No. 5, pp. 511-5.

— (1983), 'The Concept of the Supernatural in Primal Religion,' *History of Religions*, Vol. 22, No. 3, February, pp. 231-53.

— (1978), 'Ecological and Phenomenological Aspects of Shamanism,' in Vilmos Diószegi & Mihály Hoppál (eds), *Shamanism in Siberia*, pp. 27-58, Akademiai Kiadó: Budapest.

— (1977), 'History of Religions in Anthropological Waters: Some Reflections Against the Background of American Data,' *Temenos*, Vol. 13, pp. 81-97.

— (1975), 'Shamanistic Experience and Religious Ideology: Levels of Religious Cognition in the Lapp Shamanistic Trance,' in *History of Religions: Proceedings of the Thirteenth Congress*, pp. 113-4 , Leicester.

— (1973), 'A Definition of Shamanism', *Temenos*, Vol. 9, pp. 25-37.

— (1953), *Conceptions of the Soul among North American Indians*, Monograph Series 1, The Ethnographical Museum of Sweden: Stockholm.

Kroeber, Alfred L. (1948), *Anthropology, Revised edition*, Harcourt, Brace and Company: New York.

Lewis, Ioan M. (1971), *Ecstatic Religion: An Anthropological Study of Spirit Possession and Shamanism*, Penguin Books: Harmondsworth.

Loeb, Edwin M. (1929), 'Tribal Initiations and Secret Societies', *University of California Publications in American Archaeology and Ethnology*, Vol. 25, No. 3, pp. 249-88.

MacCulloch, John A. (1961), 'Shamanism', in James Hastings (ed.), *Encyclopaedia of Religion and Ethics*, Vol. XI, pp. 441-6, Charles Scribner's Sons: New York.

Mikhailovskii, Viktor M. (1895), 'Shamanism in Siberia and European Russia', trans. Oliver Wardrop, *Journal of the Anthropological Institute of Great Britain and Ireland*, Vol. 24, pp. 62-100, 126-58.

Ohlmarks, Åke (1939), *Studien zum Problem des Schamanismus*, Lund & Copenhagen: Gleerup and Munksgaard.

Perrin, Michel (1992), *Les praticiens du rêve, un example de chamanisme*, Presses universitaires de France: Paris.

Ripinsky-Naxon, Michael (1992), 'Shamanism: Religion or Rite?', *Journal of Prehistoric Religion*, Vol. VI, pp. 37-44.

Sieroszewski, Wenceslas (1902), 'Du chamanisme d'après les croyances des Yakoutes', *Revue de l'Histoire des Religions*, Vol. 46, pp. 204-33, 299-338.

Siikala, Anna-Leena (1978), *The Rite Technique of the Siberian Shaman*, Folklore Fellows Communications 220, Academia Scientiarum Fennica: Helsinki.

Spencer, Robert F. (1968), 'Review of Studies in Shamanism, Carl-Martin Edsman (ed.)', *American Anthropologist*, Vol. 70, No. 2, April, pp. 396-7.

8 'Ecstasy' or the West-Dreamt Siberian Shaman

Roberte N. Hamayon

A common view of shamanism, both within the field of anthropology and in other disciplines, has tied it closely to the practice of entering states of 'trance' and 'ecstasy' (see, for example, Hultkrantz, this issue). While it is not comfortable to go against a common view, repeated fieldwork conducted since the late sixties among the Mongols and their Siberian relatives, the Buryats, and a thorough examination of approaches to shamanism based on that research have led me to challenge that belief. My challenge was first expressed as a question: 'Are "trance," "ecstasy," and similar concepts appropriate in the study of shamanism?' (Hamayon 1993). My answer can be found in the title of a later, enlarged version of that article: 'Pour en finir avec la 'transe' et l'extase' dans l'étude du chamanisme' (1995). This sentence, 'To put an end to the use of "trance" and "ecstasy" in the study of shamanism,' also served as a subtitle to a lecture delivered in the framework of the Jordan Lectures at the SOAS in London in November, 1995 (manuscript in preparation). I take the liberty to refer to these papers here for examples, more extensive bibliography, and detailed argumentation.

For the sake of clarity, before considering the points specifically discussed by Åke Hultkrantz (namely, anthropology as an approach to shamanism), I shall first recapitulate those points that are either not discussed or are touched on only briefly, and shall make a few additional remarks. For convenience, I shall more particularly refer to 'trance' as I did in my previous papers, although in doing so, I have in mind the 'ecstatic' terminology as a whole. In this regard, it is useful to recall the subtle distinction elaborated by Gilbert Rouget (1985) who claims that spirit-possession and shamanism both are instances of trance, however, they do not display the characteristics of ecstasy.[1] Nevertheless, most authors, including Hultkrantz, use the terms almost 'alternatingly, for they refer to the same state of mind' (1992, pp. 18-9), although Hultkrantz does differentiate between them, considering 'trance' to be 'medical' and 'ecstasy' to be 'theological.' More generally, the confusion between these two notions is maintained by the use of one and the same adjective, 'ecstatic,' in both cases. Through the discussion of 'trance,' I shall first question the accuracy of the 'ecstatic' terminology, then the presuppositions underlying its use. Finally, I shall assert that the features of the shaman's behavior alluded to by using these terms fall within the purview of an anthropological approach.

Trance: A Word with Uncertain Meanings

What is referred to by sentences like 'the shaman is in trance' is anything but clear. Detailed descriptions of shamans in such states are rather scarce. Most of the time, 'trance' is only stated as such and the reader is left to imagining precisely what the shaman does or how he or she behaves. Some scholars explicitly apply 'trance' to a physical behavior, others to a psychic state, and still others to both. In addition, 'trance' is usually considered to be a culturally defined pattern of behavior.

When detailed physical depictions are provided, 'trance' appears to be highly variable, depending on the specific society, the particular rites within the society, the individual shamans involved, and even the precise occurrences of performance by that shaman. It covers a full range of modes of behavior that go from convulsions to lethargy, from shaking or jumping to lying motionless, from utter excitement to dead faint. All parts of the body are likely to be involved in the 'trance' behavior, from the tongue to the toes, together or independently. However, occurrences of 'trance with no visible manifestation' are also reported, in which cases we would like to know what is the root for calling them 'trance.' More generally, my question would be: what is the use of this all-embracing word, given that all moves, features, or aspects of the shaman's behavior could be described by specific terms, particularly since each is carefully distinguished from the others in native languages and reflect different symbolic meanings (see below)?

Characterization of 'trance' as a specific psychic state or state of mind is no less troublesome. One problem is that the state in question is defined (when it is, in fact, defined) in terms that oscillate between poles (from reduction or loss of consciousness, for a majority of scholars, to focused awareness for some of them [see Bahn 1997, p. 63]). Of greater concern, however, is that most often the existence of this state is asserted or presumed on the basis of a widely agreed upon assumption that it should be so, with no explicit indication about the grounds for supporting it, i.e., about the conditions of observation or the means of evaluation, and merely relying on the nature of the initial information. In other words, most often the reality of 'trance' (or 'ecstasy') as a specific interior state is taken for granted by virtue of the usual expectation, despite a lack of any specific empirical data. This raises two series of problems.

Before exploring these problems, I wish to make it clear that I am in no way denying the existence of 'states of mind'! I am, however, arguing against the way this question is dealt within in the literature about shamanism, and I am arguing, too, against the assumption that it is a necessarily relevant question to the study of shamanism in 'traditional' or 'tribal' societies.

The first series of questions concerns how we actually know *about* someone's 'trance' as a psychic state. Do we know about it from his or her physical appearance and behavior? Do we learn about it through the shaman's words? Or do we know about it through records, and if so, in what languages? How do we know about the state of mind or internal experience of shamans of past centuries or in far away countries? On what grounds are we incited to think that each and every shaman should automatically reach such a state when performing? On what grounds can an inference of 'ecstasy' be justified, such as suggested by Flaherty from a depiction by Falk, where mere mention is made, on the one hand, of ritual gestures and utensils (costume, drum) and on the other hand, of symbolic language and representations (gods, devils, talking with them and their supposed reactions), and where nothing at all is said about the shaman's state?

> With regard to shamanic ecstasy, Falk stressed the importance of drumming: 'The kam, who goes around dressed very foolishly, understands how to drum so that the gods appear to him and answer his questions, grant or deny his requests – but also so that the devils cannot endure his drumming and take leave' (Flaherty 1992, p. 69).[2]

There is even no clear answer to the mere question: Who decides, and on what grounds, whether someone is or is not 'in trance'? In fact, in the absence of any kind of explicit methodology, it is most often the scholar's subjectivity that happens to decide. But does an assertion ever replace an analysis and a demonstration? Clearly, if the statement of 'trance' is neither demonstrable nor falsifiable as required of scientific concepts (to follow Karl Popper), what kind of concept is it?

This question is all the more crucial since the alleged state of mind is not associated with a physical mode of behavior that would make it palpable. Very much to the point here is the thorough investigation of the notion of belief conducted by Rodney Needham (1972). Starting from a general interest in the empirical grounds of cultural concepts and associated states of mind, he more specifically scrutinizes the reality of an inner state associated with the notion of belief, taken for granted by so many field observers. After fruitlessly looking for behavioral signs of the presumed state of mind, he makes the point that:

> It is a notorious matter of common experience, after all, that the conventional externals of religious belief do not entail a real adherence

to the doctrines that they are supposed to acknowledge. Genuflections at the altar, prostration on a prayer met [sic], and bloody sacrifice tell us equally little about the internal states of those who perform these public actions. No rite shows by its performance that the participants do or do not hold a certain attitude towards – 'believe' – the ideological premises of what they do.... there are no sure signs that the protestation or enactment of a belief is accompanied by any special any characteristic state of mind. Even when we are convinced that a person genuinely believes what he says he believes, our conviction is not based on objective evidence of a distinct inner state. If it were possible for us ever to have this knowledge, then all the social dissimulation would not matter, for in that case there would be a true archetype which the dissemblers artfully affected; but this is not so, and all we actually have are *assertions of belief* [my emphasis, R. H.] and the acts and postures which may conventionally accompany them. If these culturally formulated tokens of belief are taken away, or discounted, does anything remain? (op. cit., pp. 100-1).

Finally, Needham concludes that

the phenomenon of belief consists in no more than the custom of making statements about belief.... 'We are ... analyzing ... the use of a word'[3] ... [more generally,] the states of mind ... can be conceived only through the categories of language' (op. cit., pp. 131, 137).

On one hand, this conclusion is closely akin to the current opinion about mystics: all that we know about mystical experiences is what the mystics themselves say or write of them – starting with the comment that these experiences are 'ineffable,' both indescribable and incommunicable. On the other hand, this stresses the importance of native terms to studies of shamanic 'trance,' and this also renders doubtful any such study in the absence of native reports, i.e., assertions of 'trance' in Western languages.

The second series of questions concerns the grounds for the above-mentioned expectation of 'trance' as a necessary component in the shaman's behavior. It appears that a good many references of such *a priori* assumptions turn to Mircea Eliade's definition, a point to which I shall return below.

First, it is noteworthy that statements of 'trance' as a psychic state or state of mind mainly emanate from specialists of social sciences and humanities (from theologians and psychoanalysts to specialists in the performing arts). On the other hand, this question has generally been disregarded by 'hard-nosed' psychological and medical communities. It is relevant here that the latter produce only *case studies* and do not draw general conclusions on such matters as states of mind. (There is no need to point out here that the so-called 'psychological experiments' conducted nowadays within the framework of neo-shamanist groups on people who are patients, trainees, or followers in these groups are scientifically unacceptable: such a pre-selection clearly distorts the results of any experiment.) Moreover, the obvious involvement of the sociocultural context is commonly asserted as a reason for the medical profession's disconnection from this realm. More generally, the question of the context at issue here is to be examined from two different, though interrelated, points of view – historical and epistemological.

A Three-Step History of Approaches to the Shaman's Behavior

During their three-century history, studies in shamanism have focused on the shaman's behavior, though there has been a shift from religious to psychological interpretations over the course of time, and finally, a merging of both. Schematically, and at the risk of oversimplifying, I rank these interpretations in three steps.

Devilization. In early works, due to Russian orthodox missionaries, the shaman's figure is taken to be religious, although aimed at serving the devil instead of God, which accounts for the shaman's 'wild' behavior. Both restless and animal-like, this behavior was mainly seen as opposed to Christian reverential attitudes. I call this obviously ideological view the *'devilization'* of shamanism based on its intended purpose of favoring the spread of Christianity. At this stage, it was understood that the shaman communicated with supernatural entities whose basic conceptualization was that they were opposed to civilization such as represented by the Russian Empire: the shaman's spirits were seen as wild, primitive, related to a hunting way of life and tribal organization instead of being an agricultural and state-controlled society. Therefore they were considered to be subversive, evil, 'black.' This was the view resulting from the watchword of the Russian Empire: 'one God in the sky and one Tsar on the earth.' Interestingly, native societies of Siberia continued to define themselves as 'peoples with shamans' in contrast to 'peoples with God,' such as Russians and Jews, which reveals a meaningful difference in the focus of their respective relation to the world.

Medicalization. During the course of the nineteenth century, there were shifts in scholarly concerns due to the influence of the Enlightenment philosophers and the concurrent changes in traditional societies brought about by colonization. In these societies, shamanism was often the main answer to changes and subsequent troubles. Henceforth, healing tended to become prominent in shamanic practice and ordinary (i.e., non-shaman) individuals increasingly resorted to 'shamanizing' as a call for help to spirits. Among scholars, this resulted in a view of shamanic behavior as psychopathological and of shamanic practice as therapeutical. At the turn of the century, this view was reinforced by psychoanalysis and it has prevailed since that time, inspiring, among other things, comparisons between the shaman's 'trance' and illnesses like hysteria. I apply the label 'medicalization' to this view, which has been so heavily permeated by Western ideology.

Objections of all kinds have developed against this medicalized view over the last three decades. For one thing, the assumption that the shaman's personality is pathological has been abandoned. Further, it has been acknowledged that, in spite of its actual importance, healing cannot be considered the basic foundation on which rests the entire set of shamanic representations, institutions, and practices. Besides, healing sometimes appears to be merely a mask put on traditional customs, since these are better tolerated by colonial and modernizing powers when aimed at healing – a well-known feature that paved the road toward incorporating therapeutic aspects into rituals that were not basically meant for healing (Olivier de Sardan 1994). As a matter of fact, the periodical shamanic rituals in Siberia are on the whole aimed at reasserting the exchange relationships with the surrounding world the community lives on. In addition to reinforcing tribal values and identity, reasserting the exchange is considered to also have positive effects such as good luck, good weather, good health, which can be separately emphasized.

In short, according to these two approaches, resorting to the mode of behavior called 'trance' reveals some kind of inferiority: if viewed as a religious culture, it means being savage, or, if pertaining to an individual, it means being ill.

Idealization. The third trend can be called the '*idealization*' of shamanism. Although this trend has a number of previous external roots (see for instance Flaherty 1992), it is tightly bound to the name of Mircea Eliade, who wrote the first – and still the only – general book on shamanism. This trend started as a reaction against previous deprecations and tried to reconcile religion and psychology into a common approach. In assuming that the shaman's 'trance' or 'ecstasy' expressed 'the religious experience in the rough,' Eliade (1951) succeeded in rehabilitating shamanism, and he spread a deliberately mystical view of the shaman that subsequently became extremely popular.

This is neither the place nor the time to criticize Eliade's book. Nevertheless, I wish to underscore that it is currently used as a reference, even though its approach and definitions cannot be said to be scientifically demonstrated (not only had he not been in the field, but he also used only second or third hand sources and did not know native languages). As early as 1953, Eveline Lot-Falck made the point that this book was not reliable as a source on shamanism. Since the actuality of 'trance' or 'ecstasy' is at stake here, and although I am sorry to probably disappoint Åke Hultkrantz, I cannot refrain from reporting my surprise in discovering the sentence added by Eliade to a description whose initial reference is to a text in Russian by the Buryat Khangalov. The text describes the ritual episode of climbing trees during the ceremony for investing a candidate as a shaman. Following after the shaman, a number of young men also climb the trees. 'In climbing, all of them fall in ecstasy,'[4] Eliade adds on page 109 of the 1968 French edition. This is a particularly unfortunate invention, for all Buryats and observers of Buryat rites stress that everybody's care is *not to fall from the tree*, which would be a very bad omen, a token that the spirits do not support the candidate. This appears all the more unfortunate when we learn from Åke Hultkrantz that 'ecstasy [in North America] is considered to appear rather weak compared with Siberia,' if Siberia, mainly known in the West from Eliade's book, is 'where the ecstatic definition comes from.'

Incidentally, the modern-day successors of shamans in urbanized Siberia confine themselves to such practices as speaking with their patients, laying on of hands, massaging, etc.; clearly references and concerns have changed. However, they do not call themselves shamans, but *ekstrasens*, a term borrowed from the Russian, or various other names. Moreover, ordinary people consider that what maintains shamanism in their contemporary situation is their periodical festivals with dances and songs: their claim is 'shamanism without a shaman,' conveying a general idea of 'a harmonious relationship with surrounding nature' (Hamayon 1992, p. 71). A definition based on the shaman's behavior is helpless to account for such a variety of shamanism.

Determinist Presuppositions

As a result of the merged religious and psychological approaches, the notion of 'trance' has been reinforced as simultaneously covering the above-mentioned levels of references. Thus, through the multifarious uses of 'trance,' a link is implicitly made among a physical behavior, a state of mind, and a cultural behavior; that is, a link between mind and body, on the one hand, and nature and culture on the other hand.[5] Whether an instance of correlation or of causality, this link presupposes a determinist standpoint that would probably seem unacceptable to a majority of scholars who nevertheless use this vocabulary with the three implied levels of content. The problems arising out of this implicit link and its underlying presuppositions, from both epistemological and ideological points of view, are too obvious to need further comment or development here. Not to mention the role imparted to 'social dissimulation,' as suggested by Needham in the above quotation: a mutual implication between a given pattern of behavior and a given state of mind would make social life merely impossible! The very possibility of 'social dissimulation' is something indispensable.

'Moving legs' or Realities and Representations

What is referred to by the 'ecstatic' terminology can be divided into three categories in the languages of those shamanist societies of Siberia belonging to the Altaic family, which I have personally studied. Similar categories can be found in some other areas that I have investigated in a comparative perspective. The first two categories are designations of and symbolic representations about the shaman's ritual behavior; the third consists of representations about the process of becoming a shaman.

Imitative Movements. In Siberia, the vocabulary of shamanic ritual action essentially refers to bodily movements. The Tungus root, *sam(a)-*, where the term 'shaman' comes from, primarily means 'moving legs' and applies to shamanic dancing (together with singing) in ritual context (Tsintsius 1975-1977). Words standing for shaman and shamanic activity in other Siberian languages have similar etymologies. Thus the Yakut word for 'shaman,' *oyuun*, is formed from the root *oy-*, meaning 'to jump, to leap; to play,' widely used in Turkic central Asia for certain kinds of ritual performances. Among the verbs meaning 'to shamanize' in Buryat are *mürgekhe*, 'to simultaneously gore (with horns) and stomp (with forefeet)' (as do horned ruminants) and *khatarkha*, 'to trot' (as reindeer). A number of terms also refer to manners of singing, crying, or shouting, which derives from the model of some types of wild mammals and birds. On the whole, most roots belong to the animal vocabulary and designate movements and physical attitudes characteristic of animals, especially during the mating season. As a matter of fact, the shaman's movements and gestures during ritual performance are patterned on animal models. This is consistent with, among other things, the traditional costume, which is made of animal skins.

Social-like Relationships. During ritual performance, the shaman is supposed to get in touch with spirits. In the hunting societies of the Siberian forest, he is invested by his community primarily to meet game-giving spirits, that is, the spirits believed to animate the wild animals that support human life. The fact that these spirits are conceived of as having an animal shape accounts for the shaman's animal-like behavior and attire. He is supposed to 'marry a wife' among them to rightfully obtain promises of game from her. He therefore adapts, the better to seduce her. Finally, he has to repay the spirits for the promised quarry: he lies on his back, as if he were dead, symbolically offering them his own flesh and blood, like a quarry. It is a token that the principle of exchange is respected: in the hunter's worldview, animal spirits feed on humans in the same way that humans feed on game animals. The shaman may also be in charge of relations with other spirits (mainly derived from souls of dead humans) and of rituals aimed at other ends (such as favoring the weather, moving to the next nomadic camp, or helping to fight against enemies or epidemics, etc.). In all cases, the proclaimed aim of the ritual performance is negotiation with the spirits who, either animal or human, are conceived of as *partners* of humans. Negotiations with souls of the dead are the most explicit of all representations evoked in this paragraph.[6] Representations about animal spirits are deduced not only from features of performance and costume, but more importantly, from comments about rituals by native peoples, whether shaman or non-shaman. However, one topic is resolutely concealed: the shaman's spirit-wife, who is supposed to punish him by death if he reveals anything about her.[7] Such secrecy applies to whatever concerns game in hunting societies.

From all of this it becomes clear that relations with spirits are conceived of on the model of human relationships: exchange, negotiation, revenge, reward, and so on. Some types of relations, such as those that give the shaman his legitimacy as a shaman are expressed in the shape of metaphorical kinship relations with spirits: marriage with an animal spirit, descent from a shaman spirit-ancestor, and the like. Such expressions make anthropological approaches and, more particularly, methods derived from kinship analyses, most relevant to the study of shamanism.

Selecting Trials. As for the process of becoming a shaman, it appears to contrast with the ritual behavior of the shaman as such. As a rule, the candidate is supposed to be 'elected' by a spirit in a 'dream.' Then, he is expected to go through a series of experiences that allow him to become more and more familiar with the world of spirits. Thus he runs away into the forest, refrains from eating meat, produces animal-like sounds, and does everything that can make him look strange and possibly ill to his relatives; his attitude may go from extreme taciturnity to extreme excitement. These patterns of behavior are highly conventional, and so is their interpretation within his family circle as a sign of his starting relations with spirits. Precisely, they are conceived of as proofs that his soul is in touch with the spirits, in their world – or, still more precisely, with those soul-like spirits of the forest animals.[8] Indeed, the reason is that, in the context of the hunting societies referred to, the 'electing' spirit is an animal spirit – the one that symbolically will be 'married' by the shaman and will consequently bestow on him the legitimacy of that role. Thus, the symbolic contents of this process account for its specific behavioral features. Significantly, this behavior stops when the shaman is ritually invested. It is not a part of his subsequent activity. On the whole, one *prepares* for a shaman's function by demonstrating certain *attitudes informally in private contexts*, whereas one *practices* by *performing* dances and songs *ritually in public circumstances*. However, in both cases, one is supposed to come into contact with spirits.

Comment

When analyzing the three categories above, I never felt a need to resort to the 'ecstatic' terminology. Nothing (no feature of the shaman's behavior, no representation of spirits) required such words, no mystic concern ever emerged. This was so, as well, when talking with people in the field. In spite of communist oppression, people did speak freely about their past and also about their present, on the condition that it was referred to as 'the past.' Besides, although religious practices were forbidden, popular interest in occultism, parapsychology, and mysticism never waned in Russia and was tacitly tolerated. More basically, all features of shamanic behavior and representations were convincingly accounted for by the above-mentioned concrete kind of comments. Both the conception of spirits and the care for maintaining relations with them reflected the genuine concern of symbolically acting upon the world. This renders doubtful whatever assumption about the shaman's 'living an interior experience' as central in his 'attaining the spiritual world.' At least, there is no evidence of any kind to support such an assumption. On the contrary, stating that entering into contact with spirits is aimed at obtaining game – which is the most crucial concern for hunting societies – is not only claimed by these societies but also confirmed by a series of practices. Thus, many features underscore that ritual performances are *collective* affairs.[9] As an example, at the end of every ritual, the participants must express their agreement upon the performance (which is often done under the guise of divination) as a way to get involved in the efficacy expected from the ritual.

For all these reasons, I have suggested in my previous papers that the shaman's ritual mode of behavior is, first of all, the expression of the role prescribed for his function. He has been invested by his community, and his community expects him to perform in this way, which is considered to be both the proof of his being in touch with spirits and the means for obtaining something from them. Of course, one cannot cynically play one's own role. However, this applies to all social roles and is not to be made into an element of definition in the case of 'trance.' In that case, would not 'trance' characterize the rock-singer as well as the shaman? Moreover, whatever the ;interior states' of individual performers of any social role, they cannot provide an explanation of the pattern of behavior prescribed for it. No social role can be accounted for by the psychological underpinnings of those who play it.

Conclusion

Several points are to be underscored here, and they may highlight the contribution of anthropology to the study of shamanism.

First, the idea of a 'contact' between the shaman's 'soul' and the 'spirits' may be conveyed by certain states (such as dreaming), gestures (such as jumping), manners of shouting, etc., depending on circumstances. Conversely, several modes of behavior may convey a similar idea. This is an incentive to take careful account of the context of a given pattern and the conventional character of the relation between an idea and its expressions. This is also an incentive to question the very notion of *symbolic representation*.

In this regard it is critical to note that representations only *represent*; that is to say, they make present what is not – and cannot be – really present, as for instance, a 'spirit,' which can only symbolically be made present. Although they may have the force of reality for those who adhere to them; therefore they are likely to have social effects such that they may induce behaviors, practices, and feelings. Nevertheless, a figurine or a possessed person 'is' a spirit in the same way that a host 'is' the flesh of Christ, that is, *symbolically*. In still the same way, reporting a dream about a spiritual wife-to-be 'is' a sign of spiritual election. Holding to such symbolic representations does not make them stop being mere ideas. This point is related to the above discussion of the notion of belief. Representations are to be considered *per se*, with no inference from representation to belief and from belief to reality.[10]

Further, representations are a privileged object of anthropological analysis as constituents of internally consistent symbolic systems that, as a rule, are widely shared in a traditional society and command its institutions and practices. Therefore, as topics of our studies, symbolic systems, which are socially operative, cannot be substituted by actual psychic and physical states or inner feelings, which are basically individual.

The last point suggests a further comment. In my opinion, making 'ecstasy' or the 'inner feeling of the believer' the basis of a religious definition of shamanism amounts to reducing religion to spirituality, and following in that vein, somehow reducing culture to the individual. Now, specific cultural conditions are necessary for 'individual inner experiences' to be socially acknowledged and set up as an ideological 'framework.' It is also a matter of culture that the concern and interest for individual spirituality is currently increasing in the West. Would it not be worthwhile to search for their roots, which, of course, go back far beyond the relatively recent trend of 'idealization' of shamanism pointed out above?

Notes

I would like to thank Professor Wautischer for inviting this reply to Professor Hultkrantz' critical reaction to my contest of the 'ecstatic' terminology in the study of shamanism. I am grateful to him for this opportunity to provide my perspective.

1. Rouget identifies ecstasy and trance as 'opposite poles of a continuum.' Rouget lists the opposing attributes for Ecstasy/Trance as follows: immobility/movement, silence/noise, solitude/in company, no crisis/crisis, sensory deprivation/sensory overstimulation, recollection/amnesia, hallucinations/no hallucinations (op. cit., p. 11).

2. Quoted in Falck (1785-1786, Vol. 2, p. 560).
3. Needham is quoting here Wittgenstein (1958, sec. 383).
4. 'En grimpant, ils tombent tous en extase' (trans. R. H.).
5. Two problems related to this implicit link are dealt with in my previous papers: the problem of the induction of trance and that of its authenticity versus simulation. I also refer to previous papers for a discussion about the approach developed by Gilbert Rouget (1985), Luc de Heusch (1981, especially 'Possession and Shamanism,' pp. 151-64, and 'The Madness of the Gods and the Reason of Men,' pp. 165-95), and others: they consider 'trance' to be both a 'natural propensity' (therefore universal) and a culturally-defined mode of organizing, socializing, and ritualizing this natural propensity (which is not observed in every kind of society and religion and is therefore specific to some cultures).
6. To my knowledge, the best reports of such negotiations are those noted by Khudiakov (1969) during his exile among the Yakuts in the late 1860s.
7. This is the reason why such relations have been rarely mentioned in literature about shamanism, although examples from many societies all over the world can be provided. More generally, metaphors of 'marriage' and 'alliance' applied to relationships with supernatural beings are found in many religions, including the world religions. Let us only remind of 'the Alliance' in the Holy Bible, of such female mystics as Saint Theresa of Avila who thought of Christ as 'her Husband,' and so on.
8. The spirits that animate animals are viewed in the same way that the soul of man animates his body; however, we are accustomed to say 'soul' for man and 'spirits' for animals. What matters is that they are similar in essence and have an equal status.
9. For this and other reasons, I agree with the following statement by Åke Hultkrantz found in his Lecture on Shamanism, delivered at the Institute of Ethnology in Vienna in 1973: 'the shaman is most definitely a *social functionary*' [my emphasis, R. H.]; this idea – whether in the same or in slightly different terms – is found in several of his other works as well (see for instance Hultkrantz 1978).
10. By the way, native peoples are much more cautious than many Western scholars suppose: their attitude is rather of the type, 'I do not know for sure, but maybe...; if there is a chance that the ritual works, I do not want to miss it; or, if I do not practice, there is a risk that things will get worse.'

References

Bahn, Paul G. (1997), 'Membrane and Numb Brain: A Close Look at a Recent Claim for Shamanism in Palaeolithic Art, Review of Les chamanes de la préhistoire: Transe et magie dans les grottes ornées, by J. Clottes and D. Lewis-Williams, 1996, Le Seuil, Paris, 119 pages, 114 illustrations, F 249.00,

ISBN 2-02-028902-4,' in *Rock Art Research*, Vol. 14, No. 1, pp. 62-8.

Eliade, Mircea (1968), *Le Chamanisme et les techniques archaïques de l'extase*, Librairie Payot: Paris.

Falck, Johan P. (1785-1786), *Herrn Johann Peter Falk ... Beyträge zur Topographischen Kenntniss des Rußischen Reichs*, 2 vols., Kayserliche Akademie der Wissenschaften: St. Pertersburg.

Flaherty, Gloria (1992), *Shamanism and the Eighteenth Century*, Princeton University Press: Princeton.

Hamayon, Roberte N. (1995), 'Pour en finir avec la "transe" et l'"extase" dans l'étude du chamanisme,' *Études Mongoles et Sibériennes*, Vol. 26, pp. 155-90.

— (1993), 'Are "Trance," "Ecstasy," and Similar Concepts Appropriate in the Study of Shamanism?' *Shaman*, Vol. 1, No. 2, Autumn, pp. 3-25.

— (1992), 'Stakes of the Game: Life and Death in Siberian Shamanism,' trans. Thomas Epstein, *Diogenes*, Vol. 158, Summer, pp. 69-85.

— (1990), *La Chasse à l'âme: Esquisse d'une théorie du chamanisme sibérien*, Société d'ethnologie: Nanterre.

Heusch, Luc de (1981), *Why Marry Her?, Society and Symbolic Structures*, trans. Janet Lloyd, Cambridge University Press: Cambridge.

Hultkrantz, Åke (1992), *Shamanic Healing and Ritual Drama: Health and Medicine in Native North American Religious Traditions*, Crossroad: New York.

— (1978), 'Ecological and Phenomenological Aspects of Shamanism,' in Vilmos Diószegi and Mihály Hoppál (eds), *Shamanism in Siberia*, pp. 27-58, Akademiai Kiadó: Budapest.

Khudiakov, Ivan A. (1969), *Kratkoe opisanie Verkhoianskogo okruga*, Akademiia Nauka: Leningrad.

Lot-Falck, Evelyne (1952), 'Compte-rendu de M. Eliade *Le Chamanisme et les techniques archaïques de l'extase*,' *Diogène*, Vol. 1, pp. 128-34.

Needham, Rodney (1972), *Belief, Language, and Experience*, The University of Chicago Press: Chicago.

Rouget, Gilbert (1985), *Music and Trance: A Theory of the Relations between Music and Possession*, trans. Gilbert Rouget and Brunhilde Biebuyck, The University of Chicago Press: Chicago.

Olivier de Sardan, Jean-Pierre (1994), 'Possession, affliction et foile: Les ruses de la thérapisation,' *L'Homme*, Vol. XXXIV, No. 131, Juillet - Septembre, pp. 7-27.

Tsintsius, Vera I. (1975-1977), *Sravnitelnyi slovar tunguso-manchzhurskikh iazykov: Materialy k etimologicheskomu slovariu*, Akademiia Nauka: Leningrad.

Wittgenstein, Ludwig (1958), *Philosophical Investigations*, trans. G. Elizabeth M. Anscombe, Blackwell: Oxford.

Rejoinder

Åke Hultkrantz

In her critical paper Professor Hamayon presents a good survey of her position on some central problems in the study of shamanism, and particularly on her interpretation of the role of trance or ecstasy. While I think that many of her ideas are very reasonable, for instance her overview of the phases of shamanic research, and her plea for the import of studying the role-play of shamans in a ritual context, I do not share her viewpoints on the role of trance or ecstasy. Due to the lack of time and space I will only briefly rebut some of Professor Hamayon's charges.

First, her remarks refer to a very limited area of the extension of shamanism, the Buryats and Mongols of Southeastern Siberia and Mongolia. This is no doubt an important area of shamanism, but this is not the exclusive area for shamanic research. A treatise on shamanism needs to have a broader perspective that also includes the Americas, Middle Asia, Southeastern Asia, and Polynesia, where shamanism flourishes or has flourished in different forms. We have to define a core of shamanism that joins together the different manifestations that occur in various parts of the world. It is impossible to proceed from the idea that the specific, historically developed cultural forms appearing in Buryat shamanism provide us with a norm for what shamanism represents. Thus, such features as the shaman's spirit-wife, of his offering to the spirits of his own flesh and blood, are Buryat traits that we do not find among peoples outside Siberia and Central Asia.

Moreover, the question can be posed as to whether the shamanism, as experienced by Roberte Hamayon, is performed in the same way today as it was in pre-Soviet times. However this is a problem that I leave to her as the specialist in this area.

Professor Hamayon would probably say that the core of shamanism should be the ritual role-play in the public shamanistic performance. She fights for a social-anthropological interpretation of shamanism. It is difficult however to find a satisfactory meaning of shamanism with this program. In setting aside the religious import of shamanism, Dr. Hamayon misses the very clue to shamanism: that appeal is made to the supernatural powers to aid man. A direct contact with these powers is established through a special mediator, an inspired man or woman. The contact is usually realized in ecstasy (trance).

Second, Professor Hamayon dismisses ecstasy as an important factor. She even does away with the concept of ecstasy in shamanism, and she declares that the séances she has witnessed did not expose any trance states; the performances contained a ritual play, not psychic change. And if they occurred, who could be able to state their presence? Referring to Needham, she questions our ability to read the shaman's state of mind. On top of that, she attacks my identification of trance and ecstasy. To begin with this last problem, I do not accept Rouget's claim, apparently shared by Hamayon, that ecstasy and trance are opposing poles on a continuum of alternative consciousness. In this matter I have followed Professor Ernst Arbman who wrote the basic work on ecstasy – a tome that appeared in three volumes and contains descriptions and analyses of ecstasy from different eras and different places. It is a pity that this work, because it was not written by an Englishman, Frenchman, or American, has not received the attention it so well deserves. Arbman discusses the connection between trance and ecstasy, and he finds that there is, in our terminology, no difference between them. I think his statement has a more solid basis than Rouget's arbitrary judgment. It is curious that the investigations of near-death visions, now accepted as actual experiences, could be referred to by medical doctors as examples of ecstasy, not of trance, even though in Rouget's opinion trance is not supposed to give evidence of hallucinations whereas ecstasy is. These doctors have always adhered to the use of trance, not to ecstasy.

According to our records, ever since the first reports of Siberian shamanism, of all shamanistic phenomena ecstasy has, by far, attracted the most attention. I simply do not understand how Professor Hamayon could question its presence in shamanism, particularly since there are hundreds of reliable accounts of shamans in trance, both in the old literature and in field reports from more recent times. I have myself witnessed shamans overcome by ecstasy. While the mild varieties of ecstasy may be difficult to register, the deeper kind can be disclosed by their physiological effects (which are sometimes similar to attacks of hysteria and schizophrenia): tonic cramps, convulsions, breath cessation (apnoea), catatonic states (all stuporous) like hyperkinesia and lethargic stupors. The shaman's journey to the other world, and his/her fight with the ghosts of the dead, are often reflected in these states. In pauses during their performance, or after their return to normal consciousness, shamans can relate the things that had happened during the trance. In many areas, in particular South America, the drinking of intoxicant plant juices may impair the shaman for some time in an artificial ecstasy experiencing colorful visions.[1]

Hamayon questions how it is possible to know the psychic states of a shaman in trance. This is, of course, a problem, particularly where the physical manifestations are weak or do not present an indirect testimony, and the shaman – or his/her human mouthpiece – do not give evidence. In those cases, however, we mostly have other indications in the cultural tradition. There are traditions of how the first shaman acted, and how they paved the way to the other world, or summoned their helping spirits. There are tales, as well, of how other shamans in later generations have experienced their sojourn in the other world.

Madame Hamayon's standpoint seems to be that trance cannot be defined, and consequently should be omitted from the description of the shamanic

189

seance. I consider this to be a strange attitude, and certainly not necessary. Moreover, several written works have explored the physiological foundations of religious ecstasy, and modern social-anthropological investigations of ecstatic shamanic states combine them with temporary physiological changes (Heinze 1990). Trance comprises a series of physiological and psychological phenomena whose common denominator is, to quote Arbman, 'the total suggestive absorption of the personality and the entire inner conscious life in the object of belief' (Arbman 1963, p. XVI).

It is apparently Roberte Hamayon's intention to ignore the most distinctive feature in shamanism in order to press the shamanism into the ritual frames of social anthropology. In fact, however, social anthropology is so much more than ritual analyses. It is contrary to empirical findings to deprive a shamanistic trance of its apparent meaning for the shaman in an anthropological analysis just for the sake of the anthropological model that has been used.

Professor Hamayon's paper raises many other points that could be argued here, but will remain uncontested due to the lack of time and space. In closing, however, let me say that I respect Mircea Eliade's work as a pioneer achievement, although like most scholarly works it, too, has mistakes. My own occupation with shamanism goes back to the 1940's, that is, some years before Eliade's book (in French) appeared.[2] It is surprising that shortly after Eliade's publication, which concerned itself with ecstasy as the password to shamanism, there arises a theory that disclaims its importance to shamanism. What next?

Notes

1. A disciple of mine, Dr. Luis Edouardo Luna, has, in several works described his extremely violent experiences of consumption of the vine ayahuasca in South America.
2. This means that I did not learn Siberian shamanism from Eliade, if this is what Hamayon thinks. I have an unpublished book manuscript on Siberian shamanism – in particular Samoyedic and Tungusian – which only partly follows Eliade.

References

Arbman, Ernst (1963), *Ecstasy or Religious Trance in the Experience of the Ecstatics and from the Psychological Point of View*, Vol. I, Stockholm: Svenska Bokförlaget.
Heinze, Ruth-Inge (1990), *Shamans of the 20th Century*, Irvington: New York.

Part Five
Converging Knowledge in Cultural Diversity

9   Myths and Morals
Images of Conduct, Character, and Personhood in the Native American Tradition

Nina Rosenstand

Introduction

'Stories with morals,' an ancient literary device, offer shortcuts for presenting, understanding, and discussing moral problems (cf. Rosenstand 1997a). From an historical perspective, the first examples of these shortcuts to moral wisdom are surely tribal myths.

Until recently, there was little new research by philosophers into the connection between myth and philosophy. The most frequently cited author remained Friedrich Schelling, with an occasional mention of Northrop Frye and Joseph Campbell. Now several works are available in a genre that is becoming known as 'Philosophy of Myth.' These include Hübner's *Die Wahrheit Des Mythos* (The Truth of Myth), Detienne's *The Creation of Mythology*, Kolakowski's *The Presence of Myth*, and Daniel's *Myth and Modern Philosophy*. The predominant philosophical interest in mythology seems to be ontological, while very little work is being done to link the study of myth with the philosophical discipline of ethics. I find this surprising because, while the ontological connections between myth and philosophy are deep and intriguing, the most obvious connections between myth and philosophy are in the area of ethics. In this essay I will focus on ethics as it may be represented by Native American tribal mythology; and I will draw parallels to discussions within the modern traditions of Western philosophy.[1]

Tribal Myth As Social Ethics

When cultural anthropology embarked on its trend of functionalism early this century, with Bronislaw Malinowski as its key proponent, some attention was paid to the normative aspect of tribal myths, the social do's and don'ts embedded in the narratives. Myths were viewed exclusively as charters for the culture in question, outlining why certain social structures had to be in place, and providing a warrant for the local power structure: the myth of origin set people and things in their proper place, and that was how everything ought to remain. Myths, according to functionalism, had no other purpose, and the meaning of individual stories could be reduced to their social messages. To functionalism, myths are social vehicles for the how and why of the social order.

This viewpoint is considered outdated by many scholars, but we should be careful not to abandon it altogether. Myth has many other functions, but being a vehicle for normative rules is most definitely one of its most enduring. Perhaps we should focus less on the aspect of 'power structure,' though, and more on the normative function of traditional myths as vehicles for transmitting community values.

Myth as a social and moral charter corresponds, to some degree, to elements of modern social ethics as the arena where policies are determined; in the tribal setting, policies are generally not disputed (unless, as some anthropologists have commented, there is a power struggle within the tribe; in which case we see the emergence of different myths of origin, or different interpretations of existing myths). By contrast, in modern social ethics we thrive on disputes; we argue about abortion, euthanasia, the death penalty, affirmative action, and countless other subjects.

We don't look to any founding stories for support if we hold a mostly secular view of social policies. Nevertheless, the founding stories are often there if we care to look for them: the American Revolution, the civil rights movement, the assassinations of the Kennedys, the triumphs and tragedies of the space program, and other historical events involving sacrifices of heroic ancestors. Such stories are told to new generations not just for their informative content, but more importantly to create and maintain cultural identity; and as times change, the stories are revised and rewritten. Two examples come to mind: since the early 1990s, the story of Columbus has been generally told to school children in a way much different from the way it had previously been told; and the story of Custer at the Little Big Horn has come full circle these days among historians (mostly of European descent) from the tale of a 'heroic Custer' to one of 'Custer the villain' and, more currently, to that of a 'rehabilitated Custer.'

As an aside, this is, of course, why it is so interesting in these times to watch the American cultural identity expand with stories deriving from the multicultural American traditions. New founding stories are being added to the mainstream narratives of cultural identity, and it is still an unresolved question whether these stories are to become a shared foundation for everyone, or will remain stories told by separate groups to themselves about their own heritage. Given that most children delight in listening to stories from around the world, and that telling stories to children may be the best way to begin the process of teaching cultural traditions, it seems likely that creating a shared foundation of stories from many cultural backgrounds holds great promise for developing mutual understanding.

One of the cultural identities that makes up that shared foundation is the Native American tradition. In a class I taught some years ago, we used a collection of American Indian myths, and one of my students told me that each night she would read a story from this book to her four-year-old son, who would thus grow up knowing about the Hero Twins and Coyote the Trickster as well as he knew the fairy tales of the European tradition. Of course, it didn't make him an Indian, and it wasn't supposed to; but, as my student related, it did expand the cultural horizons of her entire family. This became evident, she remarked, when the boy requested that she carve their Hallowe'en Jack-o'-lantern not in the traditional one-face style, but with four faces honoring the four directions of the Indian tradition!

In tribal societies, the myths about how society got started, how humans were created, and how the food elements were given to the people are all a part of their system of social and political philosophy, made concrete through the telling of the founding story, the 'How and Why' story. The social gender structure, for example, may be determined by the roles of the culture heroes; in a Cherokee myth the figure of Grandmother Spider brings a piece of the sun back in a homemade clay pot, and this sets a standard for women's work, which is to include pottery. Similarly, the myths about weaving lay the ground work for the practice of weaving as a social function.

A well-known Native American story with several variations is the Lakota Sioux myth of White Buffalo Woman, as told by the Sioux 'holy man,' John Fire Lame Deer:

> One summer so long ago that nobody knows how long, the Oceti-Shakowin, the seven sacred council fires of the Lakota Oyate, the nation, came together and camped. The sun shone all the time, but there was no game and the people were starving. Every day they sent scouts to look for game, but the scouts found nothing.... Early one morning the chief sent two of his young men to hunt for game. They went on foot, because at that time the Sioux didn't yet have horses. They searched everywhere but could find nothing. Seeing a high hill, they decided to climb it in order to look over the whole country. Halfway up, they saw something coming toward them from far off, but the figure was floating instead of walking. From this they knew that the person was *wakan*, holy.
> ... This *wakan* stranger was Ptesan-Wi, White Buffalo Woman. In her hands she carried a large bundle and a fan of sage leaves. She wore her blue-black hair loose except for a strand at the left side, which was tied up with buffalo fur. Her eyes shone dark and sparkling with great power in them.... "Good things I am bringing, something holy to your

195

nation. A message I carry for your people from the buffalo nation. Go back to the camp and tell the people to prepare for my arrival. Tell your chief to put up a medicine lodge with twenty-four poles. Let it be made holy for my coming" (Erdoes & Ortiz 1984, pp. 48-9).

On her arrival in camp, White Buffalo Woman now instructed the chief how to build an altar. She opened her bundle and took out a pipe, and proceeded to teach the people the right way to fill it, smoke it, and offer the right kind of prayer.

> "With this holy pipe," she said, "you will walk like a living prayer. With your feet resting upon the earth and the pipestem reaching into the sky, your body forms a living bridge between the Sacred Beneath and the Sacred Adobe. Wakan Tanka smiles upon us, because now we are as one: earth, sky, all living things, the two-legged, the four-legged, the winged ones, the trees, the grasses. Together with the people, they are all related, one family. The pipe holds them all together."
> ... The White Buffalo Woman then spoke to the women, telling them that it was the work of their hands and the fruit of their bodies which kept the people alive. "You are from the mother earth," she told them. "What you are doing is as great as what the warriors do."
> And therefore the sacred pipe is also something that binds men and women together in a circle of love. It is the one holy object in the making of which both men and women have a hand (op. cit., p. 50).

Then White Buffalo Woman told the people how to cook corn and meat the proper way, and she prepared to leave, promising that she would return once in every generation cycle:

> The people saw her walking off in the same direction from which she had come, outlined against the red ball of the setting sun. As she went, she stopped and rolled over four times. The first time, she turned into a black buffalo; the second into a brown one; the third into a red one; and finally, the fourth time she rolled over, she turned into a white female buffalo calf. A white female buffalo is the most sacred thing you could ever encounter.... As soon as she had vanished, buffalo in great herds appeared, allowing themselves to be killed so that the people might survive. And from that day on, our relations, the buffalo, furnished the people with everything they needed – meat for their food, skins for their clothes and tipis, bones for their many tools (op. cit., p. 52).

This story must have been a morale booster for Lakota women as well as a promise of the future for all the people. Similar stories tell of half-human, half-animal men and women who create links between the human and animal worlds, for the purpose of benefiting humans. In these narratives we have elements of the social ethics of functionalism, outlining the social structure of the tribe, its role in the world, and the importance of rituals. But we also have an emphasis on individual character: generosity, steadfastness, and loyalty, often combined with an element of self sacrifice.

Individual Virtue Ethics in American Indian Mythology

Beyond these elements of social structure, tribal lore contains moral elements of equal or greater importance. The major theme of much tribal mythology worldwide is the battle between good and evil, which surely embraces a social function, as when the powers of society are seen as 'good' and their enemies are seen as 'bad.' But this classic battle plays an even deeper role by signifying the very structure of meaning in the tribal universe as well as the battle fought in the hearts of individuals trying to do the right thing. In Native American mythology, however, the battleground is often more subtle than a mere standoff pitting the forces of light against the forces of darkness. Most often, bad things happen not because of the evil intentions of malevolent powers, but because of ignorance or bungling; evil powers are not often associated with a founding battle for human souls, but rather are associated with individual humans through their powers of witchcraft. Stories of origin more often revolve around the concept of the good creator/creatrix whose powers are limited and the trickster – usually Coyote – who tries to wreak havoc. But Coyote is neither inherently evil nor representative of any powers of darkness; with his tricks he often initiates a useful development in the order of things. Thus, the American Indian tradition does not have as obvious a dichotomy between good and evil as we find in some other traditions. This does not, however, preclude an individual moral element. On the contrary, the dichotomy is more varied, as is evident from some typical themes: loyalty versus disloyalty, trust versus distrust, or strength versus weakness.

While the social ethic of the tribal story is correctly described by classic functionalism as static – it is supposed to remain the way it has always been – we can describe the individual ethic as dynamic, oriented toward the shaping of a person's character. The ethics of tribal Indian myth has much in common with what is known in philosophy as 'virtue ethics,' which deals with the question of character, of *how to be*, rather than 'ethics of conduct,' which addresses the question of *what to do*. As the style explored by Plato and Aristotle, virtue ethics is the oldest form of moral theory in Western philosophy; and today it is having a remarkable comeback. Ethics of conduct is the most common modern form of Western ethics, focusing on rules of behavior, usually justified by an appeal to reason. American Indian mythology contains clear evidence not only of the fundamental social ethics examined above, but also of virtue ethics and ethics of conduct.

197

American Indian mythology abounds with quest stories – quest for fire; for food; for love; for lost brothers, sisters, husbands, wives, or children; for medicine; for direction – and they all involve trials. These stories speak to the individual on a personal level: it is an element that many know from European fairy tales where the two older brothers or sisters give up the quest, but the younger brother or sister, having the virtues of steadfastness, loyalty, and tenacity – not to mention intelligence – succeeds and brings home the treasure. Those who set out but failed usually lose not only their reputation, but also their life, or at least their identity. In the Native American traditions, those persons are generally transformed into animals or landscape features. These didactic stories are obviously not only for entertainment of for laying down the rules of the social structure, but also serve as spirit guides for the individual, as their counterparts do in other cultures.

Virtue ethics are also involved in the stories where the supernatural descends on the tribe and teaches the people the essentials of some life sustaining practice. The White Buffalo Woman is such a story (although it actually has all three elements: social structure, virtue, and conduct). Another one is the Cochiti story of Salt Woman:

In the days when nobody used salt, old Salt Woman and her grandson were very poor and went begging for food from house to house in the village of Cochiti. But even though people were busy cooking for a feast, nobody gave them anything. So when the two came to a place outside the pueblo where the children played, Salt Woman showed them a great magic crystal, and they flocked to her. Using her magic, she turned the children into chaparral jays because their parents wouldn't give her or her son anything to eat. The birds flew off, never to return to their homes. But when Salt Woman and her grandson came to the village of Santo Domingo, they were well fed, and as a reward she left the people a piece of her flesh and told them to use it in their cooking, admonishing them not to laugh or sing or fool around, but to be quiet and clean. So she went south to Salt Lake and settled there.[2]

This unforgiving story does more than just inform about the origin of salt; it also teaches the virtue of generosity, warns about the dangers arising from the vice of indifference (as a parallel to the story of the Pied Piper), and lets all prospective cooks know that cooking is a serious business.

Traces of Ethics of Conduct in American Indian Mythology

In modern ethical theory battle lines are sometimes drawn between virtue ethics (the development of character) and ethics of conduct (the do's and don'ts). Some philosophers argue that one is more important than the other.[3] Others argue that there is no need to choose – we need both to become complete, morally mature persons. In tribal Indian mythology, even with its clear emphasis on the element of character building, rules of conduct are often quite explicit. In the story of White Buffalo Woman, the tribe is taught how to carry out the sacred rituals:

> She told him what she wanted done. In the center of the tipi they were to put up an *owanka wakan*, a sacred altar, made of red earth, with a buffalo skull and a three-stick rack for a holy thing she was bringing. They did what she directed, and she traced a design with her finger on the smoothed earth of the altar. She showed them how to do all this, then circled the lodge again sunwise. Halting before the chief, she now opened the bundle. The holy thing it contained was the *chanunpa*, the sacred pipe. She held it out to the people and let them look at it. She was grasping the stem with her right hand and the bowl with her left, and thus the pipe has been held ever since (op. cit., p. 49).

Many of these stories contain role models for character building as well as rules of moral conduct particular to the tribe; and for those scholars of ethics who are looking for the argument, the justification of the rule, it is usually there, too: the myth generally contains not only what rules to follow and how to be, but also the rationale for why the rules need to be followed. White Buffalo Woman explains why it is important to show respect toward the sacred pipe:

> You will use it to keep the soul of a dead person, because through it you can talk to Wakan Tanka, the Great Mystery Spirit. The day a human dies is always a sacred day. The day when the soul is released to the Great Spirit is another.... Remember, this pipe is very sacred. Respect it and it will take you to the end of the road (op. cit., pp. 51-2).

Because the rules and rituals laid down by the origin myths are usually explained and appear to the listener as mostly reasonable these stories are sometimes referred to as 'How and Why' stories. It is thus evident that Native American myths have an ethical tradition that goes well beyond the limited explanation of functionalism: not only do they provide a social charter, but they are also vehicles for transmitting tribal values, virtue ethics, and ethics of conduct.

Who Is a Person? – Western and American Indian Thinking

One approach by which we may achieve understanding of the moral values of a culture is by looking at how that culture defines a person. As a Western concept, the idea of personhood has changed considerably over the centuries, and still remains in flux. The Australian philosopher Peter Singer talks about the 'Expanding Circle' (1981) of our moral universe from the intimate beginnings of tribal loyalties to the twentieth century concept of global human rights. Most often credit is given to Immanuel Kant for creating a philosophical framework for the idea that human beings (or at least rational beings) should not be treated merely as a means to an end, but always as an end in themselves. This is an inclusive concept that, ideally, accepts the personhood of all human beings regardless of race, gender, and other characteristics; and as such, it has become an important contribution to the development of the concept of human rights. In spite of criticism from twentieth century readers concerning Kant's own reluctance to include women and the unfortunate gray area into which nonrational humans fall, at least in Kant's early version of his ethics, his idea that everyone with rational capabilities deserves respect and fair treatment still has immense influence. And who knows? If the day comes when a computer declares that it thinks, therefore it is, then we have a ready-made policy of rights for Artificial Intelligence within reach, thanks to Kant's insistence on respect for all rational beings. However, the area that continues to generate criticism of Kant's moral theory is the denial of rights to animals, nonrational beings; Kant was never willing to consider them as anything but a means to an end. For Kant, if you are not a person, then you are a thing; and a thing receives its value only from being appreciated by a person. It has no value in itself and can be disposed of without concern. Kant does advise against cruelty to animals, but not for the sake of the animals themselves; the rationale is that if one is cruel to an animal, cruelty to a human being can't be far off.

The moral tradition that offers itself as an alternative to Kant's ethics is utilitarianism. It holds that anyone who can suffer is a member of the moral universe and should be taken into consideration, and that we ought to maximize happiness and minimize unhappiness for as many as possible. The utilitarian Jeremy Bentham, prescribing what future followers of his theory ought to ask themselves in terms of whose pain and pleasure should be taken into consideration, stated that the truly important question is not whether one can talk or reason, but whether one can suffer. One generation later, John Stuart Mill expanded the principle of utility to apply to what he called 'the whole sentient creation.' However, while the utilitarian tradition certainly has a built-in requirement to take animal suffering seriously, it does not offer much more help to the critic who wishes to expand the concepts of rights and personhood beyond the human realm. Classical utilitarians are interested in the capacity for suffering, not necessarily in personhood, and they are not at all interested in the concept of rights because the idea of intrinsic rights is not part of the utilitarian legacy. A utilitarian may accept the idea of rights as social constructs invented for the sake of the common good, but not the idea of natural rights that are valuable in themselves regardless of consequences. Because the classical utilitarian must seek to create as much happiness for as many as possible, we find that the price paid for the happiness of the many may be the unhappiness of the few; and no rights can protect them from misery if their misery is outweighed by the overall good consequences for the majority.

For this reason, some critics of Kant who are interested in expanding the rights concept, instead of opting for utilitarianism, suggest changing Kant's strict interpretation of what constitutes a person (which would be someone who is capable of thinking in universal terms and capable of taking responsibility for his or her actions). There are two ways in which we might change the concept of a person without abandoning the Kantian ideal of persons having rights: one is suggested by some researchers of animal intelligence who point out that many animals have much higher capacities for rational thinking than Kant could ever have envisioned; in other words, a redefinition of the concept of rationality would include certain animals as persons with rights. Another way is to create a subcategory of rights called 'partial rights' to recognize that while most animals, in all probability, will not reach the level of even rudimentary human rational thinking, there is still no reason to label them as 'things'; they might be given rights in proportion to their emotional and rational intelligence (and, as a logical step, also their capacity for suffering).

A third alternative to the Kantian restriction of the concept of personhood for humans only is occasionally sought in other cultures – in particular, the Native American tradition. So, how does this tradition regard the concept of personhood?

In the Dîné (Navajo) origin myth, First Man and First Woman are putting the universe in order, continually harassed by Coyote, who interferes with their plans. Animals are given their names and their tasks, and some don't take kindly to their new lot. The myth tells us that

> Up to this time all beings were people and could remove their coat forms at will; but because of wrongdoing they were made to keep their coats; and they were made to keep to their kind and to live among themselves in different parts of the earth (O'Bryan 1993, p. 34).

This myth, an interesting reversal of the Christian myth of the Fall, with the animals as the sinners, shows that there is no fundamental conceptual difference between humans and animals in Native American mythology. The Okanogan origin myth tells of the Ancients, people of the world, who were people, yet also animals; they are no longer around, because they were too selfish and stupid and couldn't tell the difference between legitimate prey animals, like the deer, and real human beings, so Coyote was sent to kill them off (Erdoes & Ortiz 1984, p. 14). The White River Sioux tell of the old days before Columbus when

> we were even closer to the animals than we are now. Many people could understand the animal languages; they could talk to a bird, gossip with

a butterfly. Animals could change themselves into people, and people into animals (op. cit., p. 5).

To the American environmentalist J. Baird Callicott (1982), the predominant view shared by tribal Indians toward nature may serve as an alternative to the traditional Western approach. Callicott find this view more 'civilized' than the view brought to the continent by Europeans and their traditions based on Greek and Judeo-Christian metaphysics (as well as Cartesian philosophy). Callicott states:

> The Ojibwa, the Sioux, and if we may safely generalize, most American Indians, lived in a world which was peopled not only by human persons, but by persons and personalities associated with all natural phenomena. In one's practical dealings in such a world it is necessary to one's well-being and that of one's family to maintain good social relations not only with proximate human persons, one's immediate tribal neighbors, but also with the nonhuman persons abounding in the immediate environment. For example, Hallowell reports that among the Ojibwa "when bears were sought out in their dens in the spring they were addressed, asked to come out so that they could be killed, and an apology was offered to them."[4] ... Now a most significant conceptual connection obtains in all cultures between the concept of a person, on the one hand, and certain behavioral restraints, on the other. Toward persons it is necessary, whether for genuine ethical or purely prudential reasons, to act in a careful and circumspect manner (op. cit., p. 305).

Several elements of this excerpt deserve comment. For one thing, these nonhuman persons are not just the bears, but also the rocks sheltering their cave and the trees surrounding it, a radical expansion of the concept of personhood envisioned by very few of those who are looking for a broader concept. Also interesting is that the recognition of bears as persons does not entail that they have any right not to be interfered with or killed, but means they are entitled to an apology – in other words, treated as powerful inhabitants of an environment in which people have to keep living in the foreseeable future.

How does this concept of personhood compare with the modern Western view of basic rights for all humans? The Kantian idea of respect for all persons is inherent in the American Indian view of what constitutes our 'moral community,' but the idea of rights seems not to be directly – or even indirectly – expressed. When we look beyond mediators such as Callicott to the Native American tribal sources themselves, we find a world view dominated not by abstract issues of laws and rights, but by very concrete survival concerns.[5] For those who hope that Native Americans might teach other Americans about equal rights for all living beings, the actual story may be disappointing;

202

I personally find it more fascinating because it points to the Native American tradition as being a response to immediate human concerns. Looking for abstract discussions of rights issues may well be misunderstanding the whole endeavor of tribal myth. A book by Ernest Bulow, *Navajo Taboos*, testifies to the concrete nature of tribal ethics.[6] Bulow notes that the rules and admonishments should be seen not as signs of an irrational and superstitious people, but as part of an ancient cultural identity.

> The bear taboos all share a common motif, that if a human being mimics a wild animal he will become like that animal. In the case of bears the taboo is more potent because of the humanlike resemblance and because bears are one of the were-animals associated with witchcraft ... (op.cit., pp. 95-6).

In this excerpt, containing typical samples from the book, there is only one example of animals having protection because of who they are and not because of humans' own safety concerns: the horned toads are 'grandfathers.'[7]

Table 9.1
Some Navajo taboos

Advise	Explanation
Don't make fun of a bear.	It will make you sick.
Don't step on a bear's waste.	It will bother you – you'll act like a bear.
Don't step on rocks turned over by a bear.	Bears will chase you.
Don't say "Shush" (bear) in the mountains.	Bears will come to you.
Don't kill horned toads.	They are grandfathers – guardians of arrowheads – You'll get a stomach ache – swell up – have a heart attack.
Don't run over a snake in your car.	You'll have a bad life.
Don't kill grasshoppers.	It will give you a nosebleed.
Don't shoot an arrow at a snake.	It will go crooked – hit something else – be spoiled.

Source: Bulow 1991, pp. 79-96

Of course the taboos may be much older than the ad hoc explanations and may truly reflect an attitude of respect for personhood in itself; but for the modern Navajo interpretations, it is the prudential advice that is important. Callicott's view of the Native American approach to the environment as displaying a universal respect for natural entities as persons should thus be tempered with a qualification: to readers within the Western political tradition, the term 'person' generally implies abstract concerns for rights and responsibilities, but this is not necessarily the sense in which the American Indian tradition uses the concept.

Conclusion: A Synthesis?

In advocating the American Indian approach to the environment, Callicott does not suggest that non-Indians simply copy the Native American traditional way of life, because that life reflects a world view that is not relevant for most people anymore (such as self-interested taboos and rules for the hunt). However, the American Indian attitude toward the environment as inhabited by persons may be regarded by modern Westerners as an ideal, an expanded form of communitarianism from which one may take lessons. In Callicott's words,

> The implicit overall metaphysic of American Indian cultures locates human beings in a larger *social*, as well as physical, environment. People belong not only to a human community, but to a community of all nature as well. Existence in this larger community, just as existence in a family and tribal context, place people in an environment in which reciprocal responsibilities and mutual obligations are taken for granted and assumed without question or reflection (1982, p. 306).

This American Indian communitarianism may not have what some people were hoping to find, a new and improved concept of rights for animals; what it does do is make possible a new interpretation of what living in an environment entails: respecting one's natural neighborhood as one would members of one's cultural and social world.

In conclusion, there is much evidence of a strong moral conviction in the myths of the Native American traditions. We see evidence of social ethics, a belief in maintaining a proper kind of social structure; we see evidence of belief in character building, and we are introduced to certain codes of conduct. In addition, the implicit value system displays a concern for the moral community stretching far beyond what the Western mind generally recognizes as a community. If we are looking for a value system that recognizes nonhumans as persons, then American Indian tribal lore does seem to provide an option.[8] But if we are looking for a concept of rights to go with the expanded idea of personhood, we will have to look elsewhere, for it does not have a clear presence in Native American traditional thinking. What we might choose to do is to explore the possibility of an intercultural, pluralistic synthesis between the Kantian idea of rights for persons and the Native American willingness to consider nonhumans as persons, as members of one's moral community.

Notes

An earlier version of this essay under the title 'Ethics in Tribal Mythology' was presented at the 70th Annual Meeting of the American Philosophical Association (Pacific Division) in Seattle, Washington, 3-6 April 1996. Copyright © 1997, Dr. Nina Rosenstand.

1. I tend to use both expressions: Native American and American Indian. Native American, because this is a term that seems to be firmly established in the scientific community as well as in popular culture, and American Indian because it is traditionally used by many scholars. Personally, I have come to the conclusion that I find the term American Indian the more suitable of the two, because, as a spokesperson for the Dîné (Navajo) tribe has said, everyone born in this country is a Native American. Since I don't share that privilege, being a European, I find the argument quite compelling. Current alternatives are Original Americans, First Americans, and the Canadian term First Nations. According to discussions among American Indian groups on the Internet, many prefer to refer to themselves as simply 'Indians.'
2. Adopted and re-told from Erdoes and Ortiz (1984, p. 61).
3. It is interesting to note that in current politics the dichotomy often appears as a question of 'character' versus 'issues.'
4. Hallowell (1960, p. 35).
5. See also Rosenstand (1997, passim).
6. Bulow is an Anglo American; he has lived most of his life in close contact with Native Americans and has a background as a teacher on the Navajo reservation. The taboos are collected from interviews with young Navajos all over the Navajo Nation.
7. In the Hero Twins story, Horny Toad is the helper of a culture hero, giving him his horny spines to use for deadly arrows.
8. While the American Indian approach of granting personhood to all elements of one's immediate environment will seem extreme to most people raised in the Western tradition, many individuals in the Western world may already have crossed over the threshold of an interspecies personhood concept, whether they realize it or not. They may not be animal activists, but they live in a household that includes one or several pets. Not all pet owners regard their pets as members of the family, but a great many do. The well being of the family animal companion is important to the family, not because the pet is considered a working animal, or a toy – in other words a tool, to be used merely as a means to an end – but because the pet is considered an intrinsically valuable member of the household. While critics may call this a sentimental anthropomorphizing of an animal, it is a living reality for numerous families and single persons. So in this everyday way, in a setting that is familiar to a multitude of people, the idea of one's pet as some kind of person may well be where the expansion of our Western concept of personhood into an interspecies application has its small but significant beginning.

References

Bulow, Ernest L. (1991), *Navajo Taboos*, Gallup: Buffalo Medicine Books.

Callicott, J. Baird (1982), 'Traditional American Indian and Western European Attitudes Toward Nature: An Overview,' *Environmental Ethics*, Vol. 4, No. 4, Winter, pp. 293-318.

Daniel, Stephen H. (1990), *Myth and Modern Philosophy*, Temple University Press: Temple.

Detienne, Marcel (1986), *The Creation of Mythology*, trans. Margaret Cook, University of Chicago Press: Chicago.

Erdoes, Richard and Ortiz, Alfonso eds (1984), *American Indian Myths and Legends*, Pantheon Books: New York.

Hallowell, A. Irving (1960), 'Ojibwa Ontology, Behavior, and World View,' in Stanley Diamond (ed.), *Culture in History: Essays in Honor of Paul Radin*, pp. 19-52, Columbia University Press: New York.

Hübner, Kurt (1985), *Die Wahrheit des Mythos*, Beck: München.

Kolakowski, Leszek (1989), *The Presence of Myth*, trans. Adam Czerniawski, University of Chicago Press: Chicago.

Marriott, Alice and Rachlin, Carol K. eds (1968), *American Indian Mythology*, Mentor: New York.

O'Bryan, Aileen (1993), *Navaho Indian Myths*, Dover Publications: New York. Reprint of *The Dîné: Origin Myths of the Navaho Indians*, 1956, Bureau of American Ethnology, Bulletin 163, Smithsonian Institution: Washington.

Rosenstand, Nina (1997a), *The Moral of the Story: An Introduction to Ethics*, Mayfield Publishing Company: Mountain View.

— (1997), 'Everyone Needs a Stone: Alternative Views of Nature,' in Christine Pierce and Donald VanDeVeer (eds), *The Environmental Ethics and Policy Book*, pp. 59-68, Wadsworth Publishing Company: Belmont.

Singer, Peter (1981), *The Expanding Circle*, Farrar, Straus and Giroux: New York.

10 Some 'Shamanistic' Affinities of Western Culture

'Donner un sens plus pur aux mots de la tribu'

Robert M. Torrance

Few words in recent decades have had a more prestigious cachet or been more charged with mystically charismatic aura than 'shamanism,' but have also been so inaccurately used in the popular jargon. Its putative values of personal spiritual vision and intimate communion with other living things are often removed from the tribal context in which they belong and globally opposed to the materialistic technology, impersonal rationality, and arrogant anthropocentrism characteristic of Western culture. From its beginnings in ancient Greece ('man is the measure of all things') and Judaea ('let us make man in our image' to 'have dominion ... over every living thing that moveth upon the earth') down to the self-alienated, self-destructive, postcolonialist and postmodernist present, which has brutally or heedlessly annihilated all but a precarious remnant of tribal cultures by the afflictions it has loosed upon the world, Western civilization stands accused of betraying a planetary heritage traceable back to the cavedwellers of the Paleolithic – a heritage of primal wholeness starkly antithetical (as spiritual practices of the I Ching, Tao, and Zen are likewise held to be) to everything the blindly acquisitive West has been and has become.

Such generalizations rely on conceptions of shamanism so elastic (not to say meaningless) as to encompass almost any tribal practice viewed from without as transcendently spiritual, and thus opposed to the coldly rationalistic logic and empirical science definitive of Western thought. Once uprooted from its tribal matrix and inserted, along with UFOs and out-of-body experiences, into the hodgepodge of New Age spiritualism, shamanism can easily be opposed to everything that smacks of mere reason or, indeed, fact. Yet the very amorphousness of the term does suggest a half truth. The extensive scholarship of the last century and more – from the detailed accounts of Bogoras, Jochelson, and Shirikogoroff in Siberia, Rasmussen in the American Arctic, and others from nearly every continent, to the comprehensive studies of Harva and Eliade, Paulson and Hultkrantz – make it clear that shamanistic practices have never constituted a self-contained religious system untouched by other practices (cf. Torrance 1994, p. 139). Possession and inspiration, vision and ecstatic flight, individually variant and communally fixed ritual, exorcism and sacrifice, treatment of disease caused by soul loss and by external objects, have commingled variously in different tribal traditions, none of which can be made canonical for others. The legitimate plasticity of the concept thus gives plausible cover to its inordinate popular extensions.

Shamanism and Modern Poetry: Rothenberg and Snyder

More fundamentally, the affinities between 'shamanistic' vision and Western rationality (insofar as either of these dubious constructs can be meaningfully discussed as a unity) are at least as significant as the contrasts often glibly affirmed. Among recent appropriations of a presumptive shamanistic tradition none have been more fruitful than those made by American poets such as Jerome Rothenberg and Gary Snyder, whose roots go back to the 'Beats' and their successors in the decades after World War II. Rothenberg – by his experience among the Seneca and his translations of Navajo and other songs, his editing (with Dennis Tedlock) of the journal *Alcheringa* and the 'alternative' anthologies *Technicians of the Sacred, Shaking the Pumpkins*, and (with Diane Rothenberg) *Symposium of the Whole*, and his energetic promotion of a modern 'ethnopoetics' with close affinities to the oral poetry of tribal peoples – has passionately striven

> to maintain and shore up what comes to us as a larger human memory, and to preserve as far as possible ... the real, continuous and localized cultures, the diversity that still exists in the world: to thwart by all means the other process toward a homogenization of cultures into a single monoculture (1981, p. 221).

And Snyder, by his lifelong interest in anthropology – his undergraduate thesis of 1951 was published as *He Who Hunted Birds in His Father's Village*, and he has continued to think anthropology 'probably the most intellectually exciting field in the universities' (1980, p. 58) – and by his firsthand experiences of tribal cultures from California to Australia (complementing his rigorous study of Zen Buddhism in Japan), likewise speaks with impressive authority. Shamanism, for these writers, is far more than the global shibboleth for primitive spirituality that it can easily become.

For Rothenberg, the 'truly intercontinental culture' of the Upper Paleolithic was the source of the '*mainstream* of poetry' through much of subsequent human history (1981, p. 31) – a varied mainstream of many channels, continually engendering diversity and change by its local rootedness and its oral nature, from which the monolithic 'great tradition' of Western poetry and thought has lamentably diverged. 'Increasingly, the model, the prototype of the poet has become the "shaman",' he writes (op. cit., p. 133): 'the solitary, inspired religious functionary of the late paleolithic,' among whose cardinal attributes (linking him with innovators of our own time in a millennial succession) are his emphasis on 'stand-up performance,' on the visionary and ecstatic, and on the communal, all of which have been slighted in the West through long bondage to a stultifyingly canonical written tradition. 'The act of the shaman – and of his poetry –' Rothenberg continues (op. cit., p. 134), 'is like a public act of madness.... It shows itself as a release of alternative possibilities' systematically denied in the West, except by aberrant outsiders such as Blake or Rimbaud. The 'central image of shamanism & of all primitive thought' is 'the intuition of a connected & fluid universe,' and this is what the openness and incessant experimentation of these rare Western dissidents – and of their American counterparts, such as Whitman, Olson, and Zukofsky – have repeatedly revitalized, despite conservative backsliding by those, like T. S. Eliot and even Ezra Pound and William Carlos Williams, who 'pulled back into traditional & institutional securities' (1981, p. 101), thus betraying not only modernism but the shamanistic mainstream itself.

For Snyder, who has called himself 'a practicing Buddhist, or Buddhist-shamanist, perhaps' (1980, p. 33), experience of 'the interdependencies of things, the complex webs and networks by which everything moves' (op. cit., p. 35), is central to both shamanistic poetry and his own. He himself experienced since early childhood 'an immediate, intuitive, deep sympathy with the natural world' such as he later found in both shamanism and Mahāyāna Buddhism (op. cit., p. 92), and he considers it his 'small contribution' to have extended Marxist dialectic from the working class 'to animals, plants: indeed, to the whole of life' (ibid., p. 130). Like Rothenberg, he identifies himself with

> the tradition that runs without break from Paleo-Siberian Shamanism and Magdalenian cave-painting; through megaliths and Mysteries, astronomers, ritualists, alchemists and Albigensians; gnostics and vagantes, right down to Golden Gate Park ... [a] Great Subculture ... opposed for very fundamental reasons to the Civilization Establishment ... [and constituting the *tribe* of all who keep] affectionate company with the sky, winds, clouds, trees, waters, animals, and grasses (Snyder 1969, pp. 115-6).

'The Shaman-poet is simply the man whose mind reaches easily out into all manners of shapes and other lives, and gives songs to dreams' (1969, p. 122),

209

and the public poetry reading 'is a kind of communion' that 'is close to the ancient function of the shaman' (1980, p. 5).

Much might be vigorously contested in such assertions. What can be confidently said about the supposed shamanism of the Paleolithic is absolutely nothing; a postulated tradition running 'without break' from Lascaux to Golden Gate Park is, to put it mildly, in advance of the evidence; the view of tribal societies as notably open and diverse is distinctly an outsider's idealization;[1] the tendency to lump shamanistic cultures together with the civilizations of the East is highly dubious; and affirmation of a companionable *communitas* uniting a countercultural tribe 'exploring the Ways of Zen, Vajrayāna, Yoga, Shamanism, Psychedelics,' and what not in the contemporary West (Snyder 1969, p. 114) overlooks the egocentric self-indulgence that often overshadowed the utopian rhetoric, communal hopes, and cosmic dreams of a generation that touted drug culture and sexual revolution while morphing from hippie to yuppie. Yet Snyder knows

> that a lot of people who use the language of shamanism and write poems that look sort of natural and wild, invoking this and that, have no experience whatever of what they write. They have never actually seen the glint in the eye of an eagle or the way a lizard's ribs quake when he does pushups, or the way a trout turns and flicks, or how a bear backs up (1980, p. 155).

And these are the very qualities of precise observation that give authenticity to his own poetry. Questionable though some of their sweeping contentions may be, he and Rothenberg have greatly enriched our understanding of an imagined shamanism's appeal by the connections they have posited between 'primitive' and contemporary poetic practices and ways of thought – a subject on which poets may have at least as much to tell us as anthropologists.

Neither of these poets engages in blanket condemnation of Western as opposed to Eastern or tribal societies, yet a fundamental antithesis is never far from the surface. Snyder's poetry is embedded (Torrance 1991) not only in the Eastern and shamanistic practices he often cites, but in those of the West from antiquity onward. He freely criticizes the deficiencies of non-Western cultures – 'The Far Eastern love of nature has become fear of nature' (1969, pp. 119-20) – and acknowledges

> the Western discovery that ... societies are human, and not divine, or natural, creations – that we actually have the capacity of making choices in regard to our social systems (Snyder 1980, p. 101).

But he holds that modern Western civilization is 'an aberrant ... outlaw ... on the planet' (Snyder et al 1977, p. 5), all of its culture is 'off the track' (Snyder 1980, p. 94), and '*real* values are someplace else' (op. cit., p. 109); that 'I don't like Western culture' (1974, p. 106); and that 'nothing in our whole occidental tradition' prepares us to understand the transhuman 'interconnectedness of life' characteristic of Eastern and shamanistic cultures (1995, p. 209). Rothenberg, too, while affirming the contributions of Western science, persistently contrasts shamanistic innovation with Western conformity.

It is this frequently asserted dichotomy that careful examination of the rich complexity of Western thought, in particular of its epistemology, in comparison with those of tribal cultures, calls into question. For if the exclusiveness of the Judaeo-Christian (and Muslim) tradition in contrast to the tolerant diversity of 'Asian religion, and the whole world of folk religion, animism, and shamanism,' is among the main charges, along with depredation of nature, leveled by Snyder (1990, p. 42; 1995, p. 187) and others against the West, reductive reliance on analytical rationality and impersonal experimentation as partial and ultimately destructive ways of knowing the world is equally central. (Such accusations, directed especially against science, go back to a much earlier generation of poets: to Wordsworth's 'We murder to dissect,' and Keats's complaint, in *Lamia*, that cold philosophy's 'dull catalogue of common things' must 'Conquer all mysteries by rule and line,' and thus 'Empty the haunted air').

Reason and Vision in the Western Tradition

Rationality and objectivity are of course rightly viewed as distinctive of much Western philosophical thought. 'There are three chief versions of this ideal of impersonal and explicit knowledge with which we must reckon,' Marjorie Grene writes, 'in the philosophies of Plato, Aristotle, and Descartes':

> For all three knowledge is final, impersonal and certain. But what makes Platonic certainty possible is the eternity, the superior, intrinsic reality, of its transcendent object, itself by itself, apart from relativity, contradiction, or decay. This is certainty beyond, even against, the world. What makes Aristotelian certainty possible is the secure natures of kinds of things within the real world itself, and ultimately the eternity of the world itself; it is certainty within the world. Cartesian certainty, finally, relies neither on a really real beyond the world, nor on rootedness in the structure of the world itself. It is the pure, intrinsic certainty of the knowing intellect itself, needing no support beyond the luminous self-evidence of its own act of understanding (1974, p. 17).

These three views – tempered by the British empiricists who responded to Descartes, and by Kant, who attempted a synthesis of what could and could not be known by the human mind – might fairly be called the central tradition of Western rationalism: a tradition surely alien, in its stress on final objective certainty, to the shamanistic quest for personal visionary knowledge.

211

But though this be our central tradition – one responsible not only for destruction of cultural and biological diversity but for much that has vastly enriched human life – it has never been the only, nor always the dominant, one. From the myths of Hesiod and the mysteries of Eleusis to the worship of Isis and the crucified Christ, the mysticism of St. Francis of Assisi and St. Teresa of Avila to that of Jakob Böhme and Emmanuel Swedenborg, the blue flower of Novalis to the Golden Dawn of W. B. Yeats, pursuit of visionary knowledge, often in defiance of an impoverished analytical reason, has never been long neglected in the West, and has often surfaced as a persistent magical or occult, kabbalistic or hermetic, tradition no less significant for the history of Western thought – as Frances Yates (1964) and others have emphasized for the Renaissance – than the rationalism it frequently complements. Blake and Rimbaud were not, perhaps, such outsiders after all. (Nor, as St. Francis should remind us, was the Judaeo-Christian tradition consistently anti-natural; as my selections in *Encompassing Nature* make clear, by their defense against Gnostic dualism of the world as God's creation, the early Christian Fathers, like the Hebrew Psalms and the Song of Solomon, celebrated nature as intrinsically good.) All this should go without saying, but needs to be said: the stale dichotomy of rational West and mystical East is still parroted with distressing frequency.

Still more significantly, the rationalist tradition, before its Cartesian recension, was seldom categorically opposed as a way of knowing the world to vision or revelation: the rational and the mystical have less often been separate channels than mingling currents. The synergy of these dynamically interacting components of Western thought negates any facile antithesis between personally variable shamanistic vision and mechanically objective scientific reason. The criteria most often adduced as characteristic of shamanism include the ecstatically transformative personal quest for visionary knowledge, the sensation of unity with other inhabitants of a divinely living natural world, and the shaman's role, through soul-flight re-enacted in public performance, in binding together the tribe (in which he nonetheless remains an outsider) by mediating between this world and others beyond it. None of these has long been entirely a stranger to Western consciousness, even within the central philosophical tradition misleadingly, because incompletely, labeled rationalist.

The Presocratics

Nowhere are affinities of Western thought with the visionary transcendence ascribed to shamanism more striking than in its beginnings – in those Presocratic *physiologoi*, or natural philosophers, to whom such modern thinkers as Nietzsche and Heidegger have been attracted as others have been to 'primitive' poetry and art. The very concept of *physis*, or 'nature,' probably derived from a root for 'growth,' and signified for the earliest Milesian thinkers a *process* of incessant change by which the divinely living and autonomously ordered *kósmos* is continually coming-to-be and passing-away. (Belief in a universe both living and divine would continue through Plato, Aristotle – who in *Parva Naturalia* 463b calls nature if not divine, *theía*, infused with divinity, *daimónia* – and the Stoics into the Middle Ages and Renaissance). No fragments of Thales, and only one sentence of Anaximander, survive, but according to ancient accounts, Thales held that from transformations of water all things were composed and, as Aristotle reports (*On the Soul* 411a), that 'all things are full of gods.' For Anaximander, no material substance, but rather 'the Boundless,' was the substratum of all, and he speculated that the first living creatures were born in moisture, and that man was originally similar to a fish.

To no thinker has change been more central than the cryptic Heraclitus, of whom Diogenes Laërtius (IX.3) reports that, 'becoming a misanthrope and withdrawing from society, he dwelt in the mountains eating grass and plants.' Like the often cryptic and antisocial tribal shaman, Heraclitus believes, Bruno Snell writes,

> that he partakes of divine knowledge, that his comprehension of the role of the deity in the world transcends the opinions held by the mass of the people (1953, p. 145).

Yet to Heraclitus we owe the philosophical use of *lógos*, from which 'logic' and (through Roman translation as *ratio*) 'reason' derive. For him, the *lógos* signified the proportion underlying the disparate phenomena of a universe in constant flux and providing a measure (*metron*) common to all – one as enigmatically difficult to understand as the logos or discourse of Heraclitus himself. 'One must follow what is common' to all, he writes (DK 2); 'but although the logos is common, most people live as though they had a private understanding.'[2] The metamorphoses of the logos would be many; it is the Logos that in the beginning, for the most mystical of the Evangelists, was God (John 1:1). Tangled are the roots from which Western 'rationalism' has grown.

With such cultic near-divinity did Pythagoras and his followers surround him that virtually nothing certain can be said of him. But mathematics, for his school as for Platonists, entailed visionary insight into the mysteries of a universe continually transformed through metempsychosis, a universe of numbers in which movement of the planetary spheres made music audible to the elect; and Cornford surmises that Pythagoras himself may have

> regarded the mathematical discoveries that came to him in moments of intensely concentrated thought as revelations 'seen' when his spirit had thrown off the trammels of the flesh and visited the unseen world (1952, p. 57).

Both *philosophía* and *theoria* seem to be of Pythagorean origin. Like *lógos*, *sophía* ('wisdom') would take many forms, both philosophical and religious, till Justinian, a thousand years later, erected a great church in her name; and *theoría*, from the same root as 'theater,' indicated not intellectual abstraction but vision. (Indeed, the Greek root *eido*¯, 'know,' is cognate with Latin *video*, 'see.')

Still more intriguing, since he so clearly combines rationality and vision, is Parmenides. In 'The Way of Truth,' the main section of his poem *On Nature* (of which substantial fragments survive), he demonstrates by uncompromising deductive logic that the indivisibility of the One makes multiplicity and movement impossible and therefore illusory – matters of opinion, not truth. Cornford observes,

> He is the first philosopher to offer rigid logical proof instead of making dogmatic announcements.... The procedure is *a priori*, and the conclusions contradict all sensible experience (1952, pp. 117-8).

Yet his epistemology is purely visionary, recalling 'the heaven-journey of the *shaman*'s ritual drama.' In his Proem (DK 1), Parmenides, a 'knowing man,' ascends in a chariot drawn by 'wise steeds' to the gates of Night and Day, which the daughters of the Sun persuade Justice to open, admitting him to the presence of an unnamed goddess who promises to teach him all things, 'both the unshaken heart of rounded Truth [*alētheia*] and men's opinions [*dóxai*].'

Empedocles, for E. R. Dodds, similarly

> represents not a new but a very old type of personality, the shaman who combines the still undifferentiated functions of magician and naturalist, poet and philosopher, preacher, healer, and public counsellor (1951, p. 146),

a type for whom mythos and logos are complementary. Dodds proposes 'a tentative line of spiritual descent which starts in Scythia' – whose sweat baths and ecstatic soothsaying as described by Herodotus (IV.67-75) remarkably resemble those of shamanistic peoples observed more than 2,300 years later – then

> crosses the Hellespont into Asiatic Greece, is perhaps combined with some remnants of Minoan tradition surviving in Crete, emigrates to the Far West with Pythagoras, and has its last outstanding representative in the Sicilian Empedocles. These men diffused the belief in a detachable soul or self, which by suitable techniques can be withdrawn from the body even during life, a self which is older than the body and will outlast it (Dodds 1951, pp. 146-7).

To such beliefs, prominent in mystery religions of Demeter and Dionysus and in 'Orphic' cosmologies, Empedocles gave expression especially in the

Purifications, where he portrays himself as a wonderworker 'no longer / human, but honored as a deathless god' (DK 112). By his Pythagorean prohibition of animal sacrifice and affirmation of a metempsychosis connecting human, animal, and plant in a cycle of continuous rebirth – 'Already I have been boy, girl, and bush, / bird, and dumb fish cavorting in the sea' (DK 117) – he claims the prophetic authority of divinely inspired vision and promotes the legendary self-image that would culminate in the tale of his final leap into Mount Aetna.

Poetic inspiration had been invoked by earlier poets, notably in the *Theogony*'s account of Muses who 'one day taught Hesiod glorious song while he was shepherding his lambs under holy Helicon.' Divine possession, and its shattering consequences, were frequent themes of Greek tragedy, in which visionary prophets such as Tiresias played central roles; and in both the satyr plays that accompanied tragic trilogies and the choruses of many Old Comedies, such as Aristophanes' *Birds* and *Frogs*, figures uniting animal and human appeared. But although Aristotle (*Metaphysics* 984b) acknowledged Hesiod as a predecessor of the natural philosophers, it was these who had made the momentous crossing from mythos to logos without leaving that earlier mode of knowing behind. And if the Presocratics were still half poets, writing in verse or elliptically poetic prose, Socrates (who wrote nothing) might be called the true founder of Greek rationalism: for as Aristotle remarks (*Metaphysics* 987b), he turned away from the natural world to seek the universal in ethical matters, and was the first to scrutinize definitions; he thus developed a dialectic to which all later Western philosophy was in debt. Yet Socrates too had his voice, which he always obeyed (even if it spoke only to dissuade, not to exhort him), and his moments of inspired possession, such as Alcibiades reports in the *Symposium*. And by accepting the verdict of the Athenian tribunal that condemns him to death, and refusing, in the *Crito*, to escape by defying the Laws of the city to which he inseparably belongs, he affirms, like the shamanistic outsider, an indissoluble bond between the dissident gadfly and his resentfully dependent tribespeople.

Plato, Aristotle, and After

All Western philosophy has seemed a footnote to Plato partly because his thought interwove so many strands, both 'visionary' and 'rational,' from his predecessors. Plato, as Dodds hypothesizes,

> in effect cross-fertilised the tradition of Greek rationalism with magico-religious ideas whose remoter origins belong to the northern shamanistic culture (1951, p. 209).

He was deeply affected by Heraclitus; as Aristotle comments

having in his youth first become familiar with Cratylus and with the Heraclitean doctrines (that all sensible things are ever in a state of flux and there is no knowledge about them), these views he held even in later years (*Metaphysics* 987a).

But contrary to Heraclitus, and especially in opposition to relativistic Sophists such as Protagoras and Gorgias, who considered man the measure of things and belief in the divine mere human convention, Plato affirmed true knowledge of a reality beyond time and change: not the uncertain flux of becoming but the stable ground of being that truly is, *to ontōs on*, 'the really real.' Anaxagoras' doctrine that the mind or intelligence (*nous*) pervading the world 'is infinite and self-ruling, and is mixed with no thing, but is alone by itself' (DK 12), faulty though it already seemed to Socrates, contributed one element to Plato's conception of the cosmos as 'a living creature truly endowed with soul and intelligence by the providence of God' (*Timaeus* 30b-c): a conception that would have a long legacy in Stoic, Neoplatonic, and Christian thought. Still further, Plato and his followers, seeking an eternal structure of the fluid phenomenal world, developed mathematical concepts to the point that much that has been considered Pythagoreanism might better, as Aristotle recognized, be called Platonism. In Parmenides and the Eleatics Plato admired their rigorous logic while seeking to avert the impasse of denying all multiplicity and change. And out of Socrates' search for definitions of essential qualities he developed, Aristotle says (*Metaphysics* 987b), his theory of changeless Forms constituting the ultimate reality (even beyond that of mathematics) in which the mutable appearances of our temporal world somehow participate and which are accessible to the human intellect.

In contrast to both Heraclitus and the Sophists, then, Plato assumes, in Copleston's summation, that 'knowledge is attainable, and that knowledge must be (i) infallible and (ii) of the *real*' (1962, p. 173). In Plato's epistemology, especially as set forth in *Republic* VI (209d-211e), increasingly less partial degrees of knowledge are attainable through ascent from mere opinion (*dóxa*) formed in response to external images of the visible world – the illusions dismissed by Parmenides and refuted in Plato's *Theaetetus* – to knowledge (*epistēmē*) of the intelligible world accessible through dialectic to disciplined reason. Here is the foundation and prototype of all Western rationalism. Important parallels remain with earlier modes of knowing such as those that Cornford and Dodds associated, rightly or wrongly, with shamanism. Above all, images of the sensible world, which is intrinsically part of the divine cosmos, though often illusory, are *not* dismissed as mere delusions (as by Parmenides) or evils (as by later Gnostics), for 'true opinion' can exist. Rather, these images may be stages toward transcendent geometrical and philosophical knowledge, which the philosopher of Plato's ideal republic, like Socrates (and his hypothetical shamanistic forebears) endeavors, through active involvement in the civic sphere, to share with others to the extent that their capacities permit.

Still more reminiscent of the shamanistic quest are other aspects of Plato's restless search that eventuate in no absolute knowledge, but in myth. The prominence of myths throughout his dialogues testifies to their importance; the opinions they embody suggest a possible truth not finally ascertainable, perhaps, by reason – and certainly not expressible in words, especially written words, of which Plato, for all his consummate verbal artistry, resembled Socrates in depreciating. Poetic inspiration may not, as Socrates ironically shows in the *Ion*, be truly knowledge, since the poet or rhapsode cannot explain what he is doing; but so rhapsodic is his own account that it would long inspire poets and thinkers who thought themselves Platonists, ignoring his caveat:

> the poet is a light and winged and holy thing, and there is no invention in him until he has been inspired and is out of his senses, and the mind is no longer in him: when he has not attained to this state, he is powerless and is unable to utter his oracles (*Ion* 534B).

Through *érōs*, or love, Diotima tells Socrates in the *Symposium*, the soul may ascend from the beauty of this world to the *vision* of absolute and changeless beauty. Inspiration through the divine madness of poetry and love is also Socrates' theme in the *Phaedrus*, where the chariot of the soul may ascend from earth to heaven drawn by memory of its beauty, which sight of earth's beauties has aroused. In the parable of the cave in *Republic* VII, apperception of the Forms is portrayed as a vision of light. Such central concepts as the immortality and transmigration of the soul, the nature of the afterlife, the recollection of earlier lives, and the creation and geometric structure of the cosmos, all of which lie beyond certain knowledge, are expressed through the vision of Er the Pamphylian with which the *Republic* concludes; the description of the underworld in the *Phaedo* of which a man of reason may believe (114D) that 'something of the kind is true'; the 'glorious truth' said in the *Meno* (81A-B) to have been spoken by priests and priestesses and inspired poets such as Pindar; and the 'probable myth' of the Demiurge in the *Timaeus*. As Marjorie Grene remarks (1974, p. 26), there is 'an ambiguity here which is essential to Plato's thought':

> The flash of fire that brings knowledge of the real [a phrase from Plato's Seventh Letter] is more than, not less than, rational. By a sudden step, a turning of the mind, it brings men (the few men capable of it) face to face with the really real, the eternal, itself by itself (ibid.).

For Aristotle, 'the world itself, and our minds within it, are so ordered,' Grene writes (op. cit., p. 36), 'that the certainty of knowledge is attainable within this perceptible cosmos itself,' not in a separate realm of immutable Forms; Aristotle's extensive writings on logic examine ways by which knowledge is not so much attained as corroborated and demonstrated. Certainly the visionary element in this third great 'rationalist' of our tradition is far less prominent than in Plato. Yet like many shamanistic cosmologies, Aristotle's sharply differentiates this lower world from the incorruptible heavens, composed not of the four sublunary elements but of a 'fifth element,' the fiery aether. Though the heavenly bodies are 'excellent beyond compare and divine' (*Parts of Animals* 644b), the heaven 'in which we believe the divine to reside' is explicitly called (*On the Heavens* 278b) a 'natural body.' Thus both the perishable and imperishable are natural substances, and both – in different degrees – are living and divine: the true relation between them (as between body and soul, and between all matter and its perfecting form) is of potential to actual (*On the Heavens* 311a).

Between sublunary and superlunary worlds there is no insuperable breach. Our own, in its endless fascination – no philosopher has been a keener observer of nature than Aristotle, whose biological writings make up far the largest part of his corpus – is a dynamically connected and fluid world of complex interdependencies. He maintained

> that fire, air, water and earth are transformable one into another, and that each is potentially latent in the others (*Meteorologica* 339a-b).

Man is a composite, the microcosm whose upper and lower parts correspond to those of the universe (*History of Animals* 494a), and who combines the nutritive soul of plants and sentient soul of animals with a rational soul whose matter is the divine *pneúma* analogous to the ethereal element of the stars (*Generation of Animals* 736b): a view not wholly remote from the tribal shaman's. The poet, especially in public performances of dramatic poetry, can communicate the universal through a *mímêsis* that is no mere imitation, but actualization of the potential by giving form to unformed matter (*Poetics* 1451b). But the greatest human fulfillment is the life of contemplative vision:

> we must not follow those who advise us, being men, to think of human things, and, being mortal, of mortal things, but must, so far as we can, make ourselves immortal, and strain every nerve to live in accordance with the best thing in us (*Nicomachean Ethics* 1177b).

Second only to Plato, Aristotle influenced Plotinus and subsequent Neoplatonists (and through them, early Christian and Muslim thinkers) for whom not only the human soul but all of the natural world contemplatively yearned for ecstatic reunion with the primal One from which multiplicity had derived.

Out of the pre-Socratics (notably Heraclitus), Plato, and Aristotle, the Stoics evolved a cosmology that incorporated many visionary dimensions, though reducing the ecstasy of Plato's lover, already much muted in Aristotle's contemplation, to the apathy of the Stoic sage. The Stoics developed a complex epistemology rooted – like that of the materialistic Epicureans, whose spokesman Lucretius is among the passionate visionary poets of literature – in sense experience, transformed by various degrees of mental assent into knowledge. At least since Zeno's successor Cleanthes in the third century B.C., however, the religious dimension of Stoicism furthered its wide appeal, to which its assimilation of astrology as an expression of the universal sympathy of earth and heaven immensely contributed. The *Astronomica* of the Roman Stoic poet Manilius in the first century A.D. is a hymn to the 'great work' of astrology, by whose means the human soul is reunited with the heavens from which it came:

> Who can doubt, then, that man is linked with heaven? ...
> Who could know heaven save by heaven's gift
> and find god, save by being part divine?
> Who, by his narrow intellect, could compass
> this vaulted infinite, the dancing stars,
> the flaming roof of heaven, the everlasting
> combat of planets with the constellations,
> if Nature had not given sacred vision
> to kindred minds directed toward herself
> through this great work, or if from heaven nothing
> called us to heaven's sacred fellowship? (II.105, 115-9, 121-5, 127)[3]

Such views, common in some measure to Platonic and Aristotelian, Stoic and Neoplatonic thought, were absorbed by patristic Christianity and remained influential through the Middle Ages and Renaissance. They were fully compatible with visionary revelations of both the Hebrew scriptures – as in Jacob's vision of 'a ladder set up on earth, and the top of it reached to heaven' (Genesis 28:12); Moses' of Yahweh's messenger 'in a flame of fire out of the midst of a bush' (Exodus 3:2); Elisha's of Elijah ascending in 'a chariot of fire, and horses of fire, ... up by a whirlwind into heaven' (II Kings 2:11); Isaiah's of Yahweh surrounded by seraphim crying 'Holy, holy, holy, is the LORD of hosts' (Isaiah 6:3); and visions of other prophets and the psalmist – and of the New Testament, notably in Christ's transfiguration (Matthew 17:1-9); the Pentecostal descent on the apostles of 'cloven tongues like as of fire' (Acts 2:2-3); Paul's vision of a blinding 'light from heaven' on the road to Damascus (Acts 9:3-8), and his account of a man 'caught up to the third heaven' (II Corinthians 12:1-6); and the apocalypse of St. John the divine. The need to reconcile reason and revelation – revelation both through scriptural authority and through personal visions of orthodox saints, not only deluded heretics – was a central concern of Christian, Muslim, and Jewish philosophy in the Middle Ages, both in the Platonism of the twelfth-century 'School of Chartres' and in the highly intellectual Scholasticism that followed translation of

Aristotle from Arabic and Greek. All these thinkers, like their ancient predecessors, affirmed a belief in the possibility of transcending the sensible world through ascent of the mind or soul to a cognate divine realm not catastrophically sundered from it, as in Gnostic and Manichaean dualisms (revived in the Middle Ages by Albigensians and others of the 'pure') between evil matter and supernal spirit, but in communion with it.

The visionary bent of Western thought was intensified in the Renaissance by the Platonic Academy of Florence. Marsilio Ficino translated not only Plato but Plotinus and other Neoplatonists, the Gnostic *Corpus Hermeticum*, and the mystical 'Orphic Hymns'; in his *Platonic Theology* he strove – as later Christian humanists, artists, and poets such as Erasmus, Michelangelo, and Spenser, also did – to accommodate Platonism to Christianity. A strong tradition of occult magic and esoteric mysticism, fueled by kabbalistic, Neoplatonic, and hermetic lore, accompanies Renaissance humanism in Pico della Mirandola, Giordano Bruno, and others. Nor were such concepts alien to the Scientific Revolution of the sixteenth and seventeenth centuries. Copernicus, who thought of himself as following the Pythagorean-Platonic tradition, pictured the sun as 'the Lamp, the Mind, the Ruler of the Universe' and 'the Visible God' of Hermes Trismegistus (*De Revolutionibus* I.10). Kepler imagined he had discovered the geometrical solids of Plato's *Timaeus* inscribed in the orbits of the planets. Gilbert, in *De Magnete*, not only deemed the lodestone a living thing, as Thales had done two thousand years before, but invoked Hermes, Zoroaster, and Orpheus to support his belief

> that the whole universe is animated, and that all the globes, all the stars, and also the noble earth have been governed since the beginning by their own appointed souls (op. cit., V.xii).

And Newton, often excoriated for mechanization of the cosmos, not only advanced a theory of universal gravitation for which he could offer no explanation ('I frame no hypotheses'), and whose seemingly mystical 'attraction at a distance' many scientists scorned, but continued throughout his life to seek in alchemical studies and biblical prophecies the visionary truth that even the deep mysteries of mathematics were insufficient to assure (see Cajori 1962, p. 547).

From Descartes to Kant

Only in Descartes' version of the Western 'ideal of impersonal and explicit knowledge' is a divinely living cosmos reduced to mechanistic determinism, and visionary knowledge of it wholly eclipsed by analytical deduction: yet paradoxically this 'objective' epistemology opens toward an abyss of subjective uncertainty. Cartesian knowledge is built up by methodical inquiry, after initial doubt, through ideas as clear and distinct as those of mathematics. But all these – including certainty that God exists because a distinct idea of his perfection could derive only from a perfect source – are dependent on the unshakable initial experience

> *I think, therefore I am*, is the first and most certain of all that occurs to one who philosophises in an orderly way (*Principles* I.vii).

Only thought, and nothing beyond the self, is the ground of existence:

> I am not more than a thing which thinks, that is to say a mind or a soul, or an understanding, or a reason ... (*Meditations* II).

All is either mind or matter (extension), which is ruled by strictly mechanical laws: not only the inanimate cosmos of intermeshing vortices but animals are mere machines. Mind can know itself, and attain partial knowledge of other objects, but can never transcend the self which is the source of its knowing. This assertion that others' existence can be known only by analogy with the self makes Descartes' *cogito*, in Grene's view (1974, p. 86), 'one of the great falsehoods of philosophy.'

For over a thousand years, Gilson remarks (1936, p. 38), Christian writers had held, as Bossuet did, that 'From the knowledge of self we rise to the knowledge of God'; the Cartesian program of establishing both a method of certain knowledge and certainty of ignorance by any other method, Grene observes,

> was only a transformation of the Thomistic claim to secure 'truths of faith' for revelation, safe from the depredations of philosophical scepticism (op. cit., p. 95).

But his impact – not only on those who considered themselves his followers – was immense. There is 'in all philosophy derived from Descartes,' Russell declares,

> a tendency to subjectivism, and to regarding matter as something only knowable, if at all, by inference from what is known of mind. These two tendencies exist both in Continental idealism and in British empiricism – in the former triumphantly, in the latter regretfully (1945, p. 564).

From the 'individualistic and subjective character' of Cartesian epistemology developed (op. cit., pp. 493-4) the extreme subjectivity of the romantics, which Russell considers 'a form of madness.' And 'since God was for Descartes the bridge from the world of himself and his ideas to anything outside that world,' and 'the proofs of God are invalid,' Bernard Williams contends,

221

Descartes's own transcendental religious metaphysics has had a legacy which – when not merely hopeless solipsism – has consisted of phenomenalism and idealism, which Descartes would have regarded, rightly, as failing to offer knowledge of a real world (1978, p. 210).

Any reality transcending self evanesces, along with God, into nothing, 'until in the heel of the hunt,' as Grene (1974, p. 95) says of Locke's later emphasis on the mind's limits, 'there was neither nature left to know nor mind to know it.'

The connection between Cartesian rationalism and British empiricism, often portrayed as opposites, is close, and might almost be thought of as causal. For the *cogito*, whatever may follow from it, is not a thought but an experience: in later empiricism, Roger Scruton remarks (1981, p. 38), Descartes' first-person paradigm of certainty is 'developed to its full.' Locke in his *Essay Concerning Human Understanding* rejected innate ideas, which Descartes had already whittled down to a bare residue of self-consciousness, and developed Bacon's axiom (*Novum Organum* 19) that 'the true way' of discovering truth is to 'begin from the senses and particulars,' since the mind's 'white paper' can only be 'furnished' by experience and observation of both 'external sensible objects' and 'the internal operations of our minds' (II.i.2). By careful distinctions between simple and complex ideas, primary and secondary qualities, he concluded that

> Wherever we perceive the agreement or disagreement of our *ideas*, there is certain knowledge; and wherever we are sure those *ideas* agree with the reality of things, there is certain real knowledge (op. cit., IV.iv.18).

He thus appeared to have saved the rationalistic tradition from the quasi-Gnostic dualism and near-solipsistic subjectivity of Descartes' mentalism. Like Descartes (and previous Christian thinkers) he also carefully preserved the prerogatives of revelation, or 'natural reason enlarged' (IV.xix.4), by subjecting it to 'the clear and evident sentence of reason' (IV.xviii.6) and distinguishing it from the ungrounded fancies of religious enthusiasts claiming access to 'inner light.' No less than Descartes, Locke could affirm (IV.xix.13) that 'Reason must be our last judge and guide in everything.'

But far from establishing the attenuated rationalist tradition on securely empirical foundations, Locke's commonsensical way of knowing the world soon proved as insubstantially based as Descartes' disembodied self-reflection. Berkeley undercut his crucial distinction of primary from secondary qualities.[4] Despite Berkeley's insistence (*Treatise* 40) that there are no 'principles more opposite to scepticism than those we have laid down,' his arguments, Hume devastatingly contended (*Enquiry* XII.i note), 'form the best lessons of scepticism, which are to be found either among the ancient or modern philosophers.' In Hume, the Western rationalist ideal of totally objective knowledge would appear to have met its nemesis.

What is fascinating about Kant's salvage operation in the *Critique of Pure Reason, Prolegomena to Any Future Metaphysics*, and elsewhere is how equivocal it appeared at the time, and remains. All knowledge, for Kant, begins with experience, and Plato's flight from the sensible world was thus misguided; but not all knowledge derives from fallible experience alone, for some judgments – 'synthetic a priori judgments,' notably those of mathematics – permit a certainty more than merely formal. (Such judgments have been vigorously contested: 'The proof that all pure mathematics, including Geometry, is nothing but formal logic,' Russell writes [1917, p. 91], 'is a fatal blow to the Kantian philosophy'). But what such knowledge is knowledge *of* is difficult to discern in a 'transcendental' philosophy that appears to bar all transcendence, since the mysterious noumenon, or thing in itself, is veiled behind impenetrable layers of phenomena. Kant (1949) remarks that,

> we only know nature as the sum-total of phenomena, i.e., as the sum total of images or representations in our mind ... The intellect does not derive its laws (a priori) from nature but prescribes them to nature (op. cit., §36).

Whatever he meant by this, or by characterizing himself as both 'transcendental idealist' and 'empirical realist,' to his immediate successors, Kant's endeavor to reconstitute objective knowledge of the real through painstaking critical circumscription of its limits 'had not so much laid the foundations of a true objectivity,' Scruton observes (1981, p. 161), 'as explored the reaches of subjectivity' – in this respect resembling the unintended effect of Berkeley's or even Descartes'. Such 'doubt as to the nature and scope of Kant's enterprise' (op. cit., p. 160) is owing to more than the contortions of Kant's famously difficult style. Strawson remarks,

> The fact that within the framework of the theory of transcendental idealism a form of reconciliation is possible between the thesis that we are aware of bodies in space as objects distinct from our perceptions and the thesis that bodies in space have no existence apart from our perceptions has no power to restore to the theory of transcendental idealism the coherence and intelligibility it has been shown to lack ... [for Kant has] ... no refuge but incoherence from the question how the connexion is to be made, in the way of identity, between the natural being, the man, with a mental history of thoughts, perceptions, and feelings and the supersensible being, with no history at all (1966, pp. 260, 249).

Transcendental idealism provides no means of transcendence, no way to bridge the gap between the inescapably self-conscious Cartesian mind and a timeless truth somewhere beyond it: between the moral law within and the starry heavens above. Whatever religion is possible within the bounds of reason alone will assuredly not be 'shamanistic.'

'Near and Hard to Grasp': Visionary Poetry in a Post-Kantian Age

Yet the visionary impulse had continued strong if not unabated in the centuries between Descartes and Kant: the centuries of Pascal, to whom certitude came not from experimental science or mathematics, at which he excelled, but from fiery vision of the God of Abraham, Isaac, and Jacob, 'not of the philosophers and scientists' (Pascal 1961, p. 71); of Milton, voyaging like a tribal shaman through worlds both below and above; of Vico, entranced by the savage sublimity of Homeric epic from a bygone heroic age; of Rousseau, marveling with Saint-Preux in *La nouvelle Héloïse* (I.xxiii) at the grandeur of the Alps where, 'as we approach the aethereal regions, the soul imbibes something of their eternal purity,' or soaring 'on the wings of imagination,' set free from earthly cares, to converse with heavenly spirits on the île de Saint-Pierre (*Reveries*, Walk 5). Above all, it found expression in German poets of the age of Goethe, and in the Romantics and their English and French successors: Blake, Wordsworth, and Coleridge, Keats and Shelley, Nerval and Hugo, Baudelaire, Mallarmé, and Rimbaud – poets who gave impassioned expression also to the human need for communion with nature. The yearning for visionary transcendence through flight to other worlds is as compelling in these poets as in their predecessors from Manilius to Dante and Milton. But now the vision is overshadowed by uncertainty as to its nature or its reality, for exalted aspirations toward an undefinable infinite repeatedly collapse into doubt, or into the bottomless abyss of the self, whenever ecstatic longing gives way to despair (cf. Torrance 1987). Keats's questions at the end of 'Ode to a Nightingale' are paradigmatic:

> Was it a vision, or a waking dream?
> Fled is that music: – Do I wake or sleep?

The indispensable yet intangible noumenon lingers tantalizingly near, like a lover on a Grecian urn, 'For ever warm and still to be enjoyed,' almost in one's very arms, but always just out of reach.

For no poet was the anguish of visionary yearning more acute than for Friedrich Hölderlin. A splendid sunset may arouse intense desire to ascend among crimson clouds and dissolve in light and air, but no sooner is this momentary magic dispersed than

> dunkel wird's und einsam
> Unter dem Himmel, wie immer bin ich.[5]

Like the young hero of *Hyperion*, the poet of 'Der Archipelagus,' having looked into the infinite void and felt his isolation from a world alien to his spiritual longings, seeks communion with the divine not in faraway cultures but in the visionary splendor of ancient Greece that continues to speak to him from

224

deep within his own culture: 'Aber droben das Licht, es spricht noch heute zu Menschen.'[6] But when the gods live in another world cut off from ours, he laments in 'Brot und Wein,' he knows of no purpose the poet can serve. In this dilemma the poet, seeking renewal through oneness with the natural world and festive celebration with his countrymen, turns not to the desiccated reason of Descartes or Kant, which leads only deeper into the self, but to the holy madness and mental wandering once compatible with the logos of Heraclitus or Plato, and to figures like Dionysus and Christ who combine the powers of earth and heaven, bread and wine, and act as guardian spirits to guide this modern shaman on his journey into the heavens or over the rivers of Germany back to ancestral Greece and the Caucasus.

The opening lines of 'Patmos' seem a commentary on the perils and hopes of transcendent vision in the Kantian age:

> Nah ist
> Und schwer zu fassen der Gott.
> Wo aber Gefahr ist, wächst
> Das Rettende auch.
> Im Finstern wohnen
> Die Adler, und furchtlos gehn
> Die Söhne der Alpen über den Abgrund weg
> Auf leichtgebaueten Brücken....
> So gib unschuldig Wasser,
> O Fittige gib uns, treuesten Sinns
> Hinüberzugehn und wiederzukehren.[7]

No poet was more intensely aware, as shadows of apartness and madness overspread him, that the very language of the tribe essential to the prophet's function was imperiled; as he hauntingly wrote in the second version of 'Mnemosyne,'

> Ein Zeichen sind wir, deutungslos,
> Schmerzlos sind wir und haben fast
> Die Sprache in der Fremde verloren.[8]

Yet, as he writes in 'Wie wenn am Feiertage,' he devoted himself as few others have done to the shamanistic vocation of mediating 'zwischen Himmel und Erd und unter den Völkern,'[9] Semele's house had been struck by lightning when she wished to see Zeus, this poem continues, and she had given birth to the thunderstorm's fruit, holy Bacchus:

> Und daher trinken himmlisches Feuer jetzt
> Die Erdensöhne ohne Gefahr.
> Doch uns gebührt es, unter Gottes Gewittern,
> Ihr Dichter! mit enblößtem Haupte zu stehen,

Des Vaters Strahl, ihn selbst, mit eigner Hand
Zu fassen und dem Volk ins Lied
Gehüllt die himmlische Gabe zu reichen.[10]

Such was the visionary call which this shaman-poet knew was embedded at the very heart of Western culture, descending from Homer and Empedocles, Euripides and Plato, down to his own dark and troubled time.

That impulse finds expression in poems evoking both distant lands (Coleridge's 'Kubla Khan') and ancient Greece (Part II of Goethe's *Faust*, the choruses of Shelley's *Hellas*, or the sonnets of Nerval's *Les Chimères*, where the mysteries of Orpheus, Dionysus, and Artemis merge with those of Horus and Osiris, Christ and the Tarot). Baudelaire above all was tormented by yearning for the pure air of the 'azure' sky and the marvelous clouds floating over its vast surface. But this paradise, like others of a post-Kantian age no longer assured of contact with an inaccessible and possibly nonexistent divine, continually receded into vague distances or plunged into the emptiness of a self made all the vaster by their lack. He is a *homo duplex* seeking communion, like seers and shamans of yore, with the transcendent beyond and communication of it to fellow outcasts from his acquisitive bourgeois society; he searches incessantly for an infinity beyond him that he finds nowhere but in the cosmic inner emptiness that he calls the abyss. And despite sporadic longings for vaguely imagined places farther than China or India it is to Greece that this disillusioned poet of the modern metropolis returns in one of his masterpieces, 'Le Cygne,' which combines reminiscence of Hector's widow Andromache, in sorrowful exile (as Virgil depicts her) by a 'false Simoïs' pathetically evoking fallen Troy, with memory of a swan the poet once saw in the bustling market of a Paris now changed beyond recognition. Escaping from its cage, the bird was bathing its wings in the dust and craning its neck upward 'Vers le ciel ironique et cruellement bleu,'[11] as if addressing reproaches to an absent God.

The 'transcendence' sought through such a vision – as through many others from Baudelaire's age to our own, above all in Proust, and in psychoanalytical theory – is transcendence of present time and personal self through *memory*, both individual and collective, by which the poet is united with others out of place in their time: widowed queen, urban negress, orphaned child, marooned sailor, and whoever has lost what will never again be found. For only in such expansion of the self-enclosed personal consciousness, and in solidarity with those who share its aloneness, can be found an escape from the bottomless abyss that neither ironically blue skies, the languors of sensuality, nor the 'false paradises' of drugs can offer – an escape otherwise imaginable only somewhere 'out of the world,' with no assurance of any other beyond it, except in death. In 'Le Voyage,' the poet relinquishes the failed Eldorados, chimerical lands, and envisioned Americas that have made the abyss more bitter, to sail highheartedly toward the one reality indisputably beyond. Toward this emancipation, at least, plunging 'Au fond de l'Inconnu pour trouver du *nouveau*,'[12] this shaman-poet of modernity can lead fellow voyagers whose hearts, like his, are filled with light as they sail together from present ennui to seek whatever awaits, crying only 'En avant!'

The 'visionary gleam' of poets such as Wordsworth and Baudelaire was central also to the French Symbolists of the late nineteenth century; but vision, however intense, was now constricted by absence of any transcendent object possibly adequate to it: those precariously built bridges over the abyss had led nowhere. Mallarmé, haunted like Baudelaire by the azure sky, ambivalently aspired to the absolute purity of a swan frozen in ice, and having found through desolate encounter with the void that the true object of transcendent vision is Nothingness, aspired to the silence that Rimbaud, renouncing poetry with adolescence, achieved in death. To twentieth-century inheritors of this Symbolist tradition such as Rilke in the *Duino Elegies* and Valéry in the 'Cimetière marin,' transcendence comes not from a Platonic or Christian – or 'shamanistic' – world beyond our own, but in the return from nothingness, or death, to heightened awareness of the present world. The isolated self can be transcended only by passionate adhesion to life in the world to which it inseparably belongs.

Many Western poets of the last few centuries have resembled the popular image of the tribal shaman not only in their quest for visionary transcendence but also in the intensity of their communion with vegetable and animal life. From Burns's mouse to Blake's tiger, Wordsworth's daffodil to Keats's nightingale and Shelley's skylark, Hopkins's dappled things 'counter, original, spare, strange,' to Hardy's darkling thrush and Lawrence's Bavarian gentians, and from Baudelaire's transcendentally homeless swan to Rilke's restlessly caged panther and Valéry's mediating palm tree, these poets have felt a close kinship with the nonhuman denizens of the world around them. Here again they have draw on a long Western heritage. For though Church doctors since St. Augustine denied animals a soul, and Descartes declared them mere machines, a strong counter-tradition of oneness between the human and natural worlds, and of admiration for the animal kingdom, has run through Western culture. This is, for example, evidenced by Pythagorean and Platonic metempsychosis and ancient theories of correspondence between microcosm and macrocosm; by St. Francis's preaching to the birds and conversion of the wolf; by Plutarch's 'Gryllus,' in which a companion of Odysseus transformed by Circe to a swine refuses to reassume human form; by Montaigne's affirmation of animals' mental capacities in the 'Apology for Raymond Sebond'; by Hume's assertion (*Treatise* I.iii.16, *Enquiry* IX) of fundamental identity between human and animal reason; and by Darwin's theory of evolution through natural selection. We need go no farther than our children's stories to be reminded how close a bond has existed between human and animal beings in our culture.

'Instinctive Reason' and Things that Must Be Put into Words: Recent Western Poetry and Thought

Charles Sanders Peirce, now widely recognized as the greatest American philosopher, insisted that an adequate theory of knowledge required not only inductive and deductive reasoning, on which Western epistemology had rested from Bacon and Descartes (if not from Aristotle) to Kant, but also the formulation of hypotheses, or 'spontaneous conjectures of instinctive reason,' which he called Abduction or Retroduction (1958, p. 371). In this definitive mental operation man is akin to other animals that 'rise far above the general level of their intelligence in those performances that are their proper function ...; and what is man's proper function if it be not to embody general ideas in art-creations, in utilities, and above all in theoretical cognition?' His conviction (op. cit., p. 372) 'that man's mind must have been attuned to the truth of things in order to discover what he has discovered' links him not with Descartes or Kant – he scorned 'the palpable falsity of that mechanical philosophy of the universe which dominates the modern world,' and repudiated Kant's proposition 'that there are certain impassable bounds to human knowledge' (op. cit., pp. 348-9) – but with an older Western rationalism descending from Plato and Aristotle. This insistence on correspondence between ideas and their objects allies him with both the Scholastic Realism of Duns Scotus and modern science, in which he was deeply versed, against the relativistic nominalists of his day.

> When we gaze upon the multifariousness of nature we are looking straight into the face of a living spontaneity. A day's ramble in the country ought to bring that home to us (op. cit., p. 348).

It is remarkable how many recent philosophers even of schools designated pragmatist, rationalist, logical empiricist, etc., have allowed for extra-rational sources of knowledge. William James, who was fascinated by psychical research, surmised

> that whatever it may be on its *farther* side, the 'more' with which in religious experience we feel ourselves connected is on its *hither* side the subconscious continuation of our conscious life (James 1902, p. 502).

Russell (1957, pp. 11-2) affirms 'an element of wisdom to be learned from the mystical way of feeling, which does not seem to be attainable by any other manner' and which 'is the inspirer of whatever is best in Man.' And Wittgenstein, ending the *Tractatus*, writes:

6.41   The sense of the world must lie outside the world ...
6.522   There are, indeed, things that cannot be put into words. They

make themselves manifest. They are what is mystical.

7   What we cannot speak about we must pass over in silence

(1961, pp. 145, 151).

The stereotype of a Western philosophical tradition solely ruled by a reductive logic inimical to visionary insight is almost as false for its latest as for its earliest manifestations. 'Shamans,' to be sure, Peirce and James, Russell and Wittgenstein, were most emphatically not: but they have left the door open for sources of knowledge not solely confined to the analytically rational.

From such sources the poets of modernity, some of whom have identified with tribal shamans as their predecessors did with pagan seers or Hebrew prophets, continue to speak of what they cannot pass over in silence. The language of shamanistic performance in Siberia, Central Asia, the American Arctic, and elsewhere was a public language in an oral tradition, as Snyder and Rothenberg have emphasized in claiming a shamanistic antecedent for the American poetry fathered by Walt Whitman. In setting out to 'utter the word Democratic, the word En-Masse' ('One's-Self I Sing'), and to 'sound my barbaric yawp over the roofs of the world' ('Song of Myself' 52), Whitman was substituting for the 'constipating, repressing, in-door, and artificial influence' of most contemporary poetry 'that freeing, dilating, joyous one, with which uncramp'd Nature works' (note to 'Poetry To-day in America'). His is a 'kosmical' poetry – 'I am mad with devouring ecstasy to make joyous hymns for the whole earth' ('Excelsior') – that proclaims a vibrantly living universe indistinguishable from the self that contains its multitudes: not so much transcendently visionary (for there is no transcending such a cosmic self) as devouringly immanent.

> Divine am I inside and out, and I make holy whatever I touch or am
> touch'd from ('Song of Myself' 24).

Identifying (like Baudelaire) with 'the enslaved, the overthrown, the hurt, the opprest of the whole earth' ('The Mystic Trumpeter' 7), Whitman rhapsodically celebrates communion with the animal world, from the dalliance of eagles to the noiseless patient spider – while celebrating also the 'great cathedral' of a 'sacred industry' fairer than Greek or Roman temples. In his demotic American English he found 'the medium that shall well nigh express the inexpressible' ('Democratic Vistas'), and made himself, if not quite a shaman-prophet to the industrious multitudes, the founder of a continually open, innovative, experimental, and vital poetic tradition.

In all this, Whitman is extending oral and public kinds of poetry embedded in Western tradition since its beginnings in Homeric epic and Biblical prophecy, to say nothing of rhapsodic recitations, dithyrambic and theatrical performances, philosophical disputations, and civic oratory. This is apparent in his exhortation,

Come Muse migrate from Greece and Ionia, ...
For know a better, fresher, busier sphere, a wide, untried domain awaits,
demands you ('Song of the Exposition' 2).

But the language of shamanistic narratives (like that of many spirit mediums, who may even speak foreign tongues) has been characterized not only by communal speech but by difficult, even obscure expression heightened by the thumps, screams, and animal noises that attended it. For Whitman (1950, p. 448), 'The art of art, the glory of expression ... is simplicity.' But shamanistic language is typically not plain and direct but elaborately sacred, and its very strangeness, by evoking another world, is crucial to its communal effect of drawing its audience beyond its normal state toward one in which dissonances are transcended.

Here, too, there are many parallels in the Western religious tradition (as in others): in the Delphic oracle or the Mystery cults, pentecostal speaking in tongues, or the Latin mass. Thus the efforts of visionary poets such as Hölderlin and Nerval, Mallarmé and Rimbaud, to give prophetic or Orphic voice to their encounter with a nearly ineffable beyond both complement and enrich, rather than merely contradict, the democratic enterprise of poets from Whitman to Rothenberg and Snyder. For it is neither one nor the other of these dimensions, the communal or the esoteric, that is most characteristic of 'shamanistic' performances – or of oracular pronouncements, prophetic proclamations, and many other sacred observances – but their visionary union, such as we find also in Pindar and Aeschylus, Dante and Milton, Goethe and Blake. 'Man is the dream of a shadow,' Pindar declares (Pythian 8), but when the godgiven splendor comes upon him he shines with a radiant light and life is like honey; the end of both the *Commedia* as a whole and of the *Paradiso* in particular, Dante (1973, pp. 101-2) writes to Can Grande, 'is to remove those living in this life from the state of misery and to lead them to the state of happiness.' These are transcendently visionary goals par excellence, goals of which the tribal shaman is now popularly seen as the supreme embodiment. Not merely by the publicly prophetic pursuit nor by the esoterically priestly, not by the yawp of Whitman nor the hermeticism of Mallarmé, but only through their fusion in that which is communally sacred and binds together by raising above, can such transcendence be most fully encompassed. Only thus can the poet again aspire – as did poets of ages long ago when earth and sky were not antagonists and reason was not hostile to vision – to give (as Mallarmé wrote in 'Le tombeau d'Edgar Poe') 'a purer sense to the words of the tribe' (un sens plus pur aux mots de la tribu), and by doing so to become 'such as into himself at last eternity changes him' (Tel qu'en Lui-même enfin l'éternité le change).

Though tribal shamanism and Western poetry and thought have often been opposed to each other by simplistic distortion of each, the affinities between these very different phenomena are thus far greater than this

230

opposition suggests.

Notes

1. Joffe (1997) of the *Süddeutsche Zeitung* of Munich suggests that the worldwide domination of American culture is taking place not only because of global distribution networks but because

    America has the world's most open culture, and therefore the world is most open to it.... The trend is toward individualization, nonhierarchical cooperation and breathless innovation. Creativity rather than order rules (op. cit., p. 6).

    It is instructive to observe how often the innovativeness that pervades American culture is denied by those who most exemplify it yet insistently ascribe it to cultures far more tradition-bound than their own.
2. Translations of the pre-Socratics are my own (Torrance 1998). Fragments identified as 'DK' are from section B under each thinker in Diels and Kranz (1954). Translations of Plato are by Jowett (1892). Those of Aristotle are from the Oxford translations as reprinted in McKeon (1941), and from the Loeb Classical Library, Cambridge.
3. The translation of Manilius is my own (Torrance 1998).
4. Berkeley conceived his monism (which denied to matter any independence of soul or spiritual substance, and any reality apart from perception grounded in the mind of God) as realist: 'Whatever we see, feel, hear, or anywise conceive or understand remains as secure as ever, and is as real as ever. There is a *rerum natura*' (*Treatise* 34). But its implications for those who followed were idealist, subjective, and relativist.
5. 'It grows dark, and lonely am I beneath the sky, as always' ('Abendphantasie,' trans. R.T.).
6. 'But above us the light speaks to men even today' (trans. R.T.).
7. 'Near is the god, and hard to grasp. But where there is danger, the saving power also grows. In darkness dwell the eagles, and fearless over the abyss walk the sons of the Alps on precariously built bridges.... Give us innocent water, then, give us wings, with most faithful mind to cross over and to return' (trans. R.T.).
8. 'A sign are we, uninterpretable; painless are we, and have almost lost speech in our estrangement' (trans. R.T.).
9. 'Between heaven and earth and among the peoples' (trans. R.T.).
10. 'And hence the sons of Earth drink heavenly fire now without danger. Yet it befits us, you poets! to stand bareheaded under God's thunderstorms, to grasp with our own hands the Father's ray itself, and to present the people with the heavenly gift, wrapped in song.' (trans. R.T.).
11. 'Toward the ironic and cruelly blue sky (trans. R.T.).
12. 'To the depths of the Unknown to discover something *new*' (trans. R.T.).

231

Bibliography

Bacon, Francis (1955), 'Novum Organum,' trans. James Spedding, in *Selected Writings*, Hugh G. Dick (ed.), The Modern Library: New York.

Baudelaire, Charles (1994) *Les Fleurs du Mal*, Antoine Adam (ed.), Garnier Frères: Paris.

Berkeley, George (1994), 'A Treatise Concerning the Principles of Human Knowledge,' in Edwin A. Burtt (ed.), *The English Philosophers from Bacon to Mill*, pp. 532-605, The Modern Library: New York.

Cajori, Florian (1962), *Sir Isaac Newton's Mathematical Principles of Natural Philosophy and His System of the World*, Vol. 2: The System of the World, trans Andrew Motte, University of California Press: Berkeley.

Copleston, Frederick (1962), *A History of Philosophy, Vol. I: Greece and Rome*, Part I, Doubleday: Garden City.

Cornford, Francis M. (1952), *Principium Sapientiae: The Origins of Greek Philosophical Thought*, Cambridge University Press: Cambridge.

Dante Alighieri (1973), 'The Letter to Can Grande,' in *Literary Criticism of Dante Alighieri*, pp. 95-111, trans. Robert S. Haller (ed.), University of Nebraska Press: Lincoln.

Descartes, René (1931), 'Meditations on First Philosophy,' pp. 131-99, and 'The Principles of Philosophy,' pp. 201-302, in Elizabeth S. Haldane and George R. T. Ross (eds and trans), *The Philosophical Works of Descates*, Vol. I, Dover Publications: New York.

Diels, Hermann and Kranz, Walther, eds (1954), *Die Fragmente der Vorsokratiker*, Weidmannsche Verlagsbuchhandlung: Berlin.

Diogenes Laërtius (1925), *Lives of the Eminent Philosophers*, Vol. II, trans. Robert D. Hicks, Loeb Classical Library 185, Harvard University Press: Cambridge.

Dodds, Eric R. (1951), *The Greeks and the Irrational*, University of California Press: Berkeley.

Gilbert, William (1900), *On the Magnet*, trans. Silvanus P. Thompson et al., Chiswick Press: London.

Gilson, Etienne (1936), *The Spirit of Mediaeval Philosophy*, trans. Alfred H. C. Downes, Charles Scribner's Sons: New York.

Grene, Marjorie (1974), *The Knower and the Known*, University of California Press: Berkeley.

Herodotus (1972), *The Histories*, trans. Aubrey de Sélincourt, Penguin Books: Harmondsworth.

Hölderlin, Friedrich (1969), *Werke und Briefe*, Friedrich Beißner and Jochen Schmidt (eds), Insel Verlag: Frankfurt am Main.

Hume, David (1888), *A Treatise of Human Nature*, Lewis A. Selby-Bigge (ed.), The Clarendon Press: Oxford.

— (1994), 'An Enquiry Concerning Human Understanding,' in Edwin A. Burtt (ed.), *The English Philosophers from Bacon to Mill*, pp. 611-721, The Modern

Library: New York.

James, William (1902), *The Varieties of Religious Experience*, The Modern Library: New York.

Joffe, Josef (1997), 'America the Inescapable: Relentless Adaptation, Innovation,' *Sacramento Bee*, Vol. 281, Sunday 6 July, Forum, pp. 1, 6.

Jowett, Benjamin trans. (1892), *The Dialogues of Plato*, Clarendon Press: Oxford.

Kant, Immanuel (1949), 'Prolegomena to Every Future Metaphysic that May Be Presented as Science,' in Carl J. Friedrich (ed.), *The Philosophy of Kant*, pp. 40-115, The Modern Library: New York.

Keats, John (1978), *The Poems of John Keats*, Jack Stillinger (ed.), Harvard University Press: Cambridge.

Locke, John (1965), *An Essay Concerning Human Understanding*, John W. Yolton (ed.), Everyman's Library: London.

Mallarmé, Stéphane (1945), *Poésies*, Éditions Gallimard: Paris.

McKeon, Richard, ed. (1941), *The Basic Works of Aristotle*, Random House: New York.

Nerval, Gérard de (1958), *Oeuvres*, Vol. 1, Henry Lemaitre (ed.), Garnier Frères: Paris.

Pascal, Blaise (1961), *Pensées*, Charles-Marc des Granges (ed.), Garnier Frères: Paris.

Peirce, Charles Sanders (1958), 'Science and Immortality,' in Philip P. Wiener (ed.), *Values in a Universe of Chance: Selected Writings of Charles S. Peirce*, pp. 345-79, Stanford University Press: Stanford.

Pindar (1947) *Pindari Carmina*, Cecil M. Bowra (ed.), Oxford University Press: Oxford.

Rothenberg, Jerome (1981), *Pre-Faces & Other Writings*, New Directions: New York.

— ed. (1972), *Shaking the Pumpkins: Traditional Poetry of the Indian North Americas*, Doubleday: Garden City.

— ed. (1968), *Technicians of the Sacred: A Range of Poetics from Africa, America, Asia, and Oceania*, Doubleday: New York.

Rothenberg, Jerome and Rothenberg, Diane eds (1983), *Symposium of the Whole: A Range of Discourse Toward an Ethnopoetics*, University of California Press: Berkeley.

Rousseau, Jean-Jacques (1977), *Les Rêveries du Promeneur Solitaire*, Univers des Lettres Bordas: Paris.

— (1960), *Julie, ou La Nouvelle Heloïse*, René Pomeau (ed.), Garnier Frères: Paris.

Russell, Bertrand (1957), *Mysticism and Logic*, Doubleday: Garden City.

— (1945), *A History of Western Philosophy*, Simon & Schuster: New York.

Scruton, Roger (1981), *From Descartes to Wittgenstein: A Short History of Modern Philosophy*, Routledge & Kegan Paul: London.

Snell, Bruno (1953), *The Discovery of the Mind: The Greek Origins of European Thought*, trans. Thomas G. Rosenmeyer, Basil Blackwell: Oxford.

Snyder, Gary (1995), *A Place in Space: Ethics, Aesthetics, and Watersheds*, Counterpoint: Washington.

— (1990), *The Practice of the Wild*, North Point Press: San Francisco.

— (1980), *The Real Work: Interviews & Talks 1964-1979*, Wm. Scott McLean (ed.), New Directions: New York.

— (1979), *He Who Hunted Birds in His Father's Village: The Dimensions of a Haida Myth*, Grey Fox Press: Bolinas.

— (1974), *Turtle Island*, New Directions: New York.

— (1969), *Earth House Hold: Technical Notes & Queries To Fellow Dharma Revolutionaries*, New Directions: New York.

Snyder, Gary; Welch, Lew; and Whalen, Philip (1977), *On Bread and Poetry*. Grey Fox Press: Bolinas.

Strawson, Peter F. (1966), *The Bounds of Sense: An Essay on Kant's Critique of Pure Reason*, Methuen: London.

Torrance, Robert M. ed. (1998), *Encompassing Nature: A Sourcebook*, Counterpoint: Washington.

— (1994), *The Spiritual Quest: Transcendence in Myth, Religion, and Science*, University of California Press: Berkeley.

— (1991), 'Gary Snyder and the Western Poetic Tradition,' in Jon Halper (ed.), *Gary Snyder: Dimensions of a Life*, Sierra Club Books: San Francisco.

— (1987), *Ideal and Spleen: The Crisis of Transcendent Vision in Romantic, Symbolist, and Modern Poetry*, Garland: New York.

Whitman, Walt (1950), *Leaves of Grass and Selected Prose*, John A. Kouwenhoven (ed.), The Modern Library: New York.

Williams, Bernard (1978), *Descartes: The Project of Pure Enquiry*, Penguin: Harmondsworth.

Wittgenstein, Ludwig (1961), *Tractatus Logico-Philosophicus*, trans. David F. Pears & Brian McGuinness, Routledge & Kegan Paul: London.

Yates, Frances A. (1964), *Giordano Bruno and the Hermetic Tradition*, University of Chicago Press: Chicago.

Index

P.

P.17 – personal – collective metaphor

★ P.18 – Knowing as a consequence of relationships discerned by the Self.

P.44 – 4 attributes of Kge System

P.80 – Pre Conquest setting

p.105 - 4 problems of cross cultural observation

p.127 - Shamani acquisition of Kge

p.211   Plato, Aristotle Descate - Kge